Mrs. Gaske

Elizabeth Cleghorn Gaskell

(Editor: Mrs. Ellis H. Chadwick)

Alpha Editions

This edition published in 2023

ISBN : 9789357957601

Design and Setting By
Alpha Editions
www.alphaedis.com
Email - info@alphaedis.com

Contents

Introduction

I

AMONG women writers of the nineteenth century, none deserve more grateful remembrance than Mrs. Gaskell. Though it is forty-six years since she passed away, her stories are still eagerly read, and there is a growing interest in her life, as was shown by the almost universal appreciation last year when her centenary was celebrated. To the lovers of Mrs. Gaskell's works, age has not settled on them, the lavender may lie between their pages, but it is still sweet, and there are many successful novelists of our own time whose works are far less read and more out of date than hers. Succeeding generations have kept her memory green, and the continued reprints of her novels prove their worth, not only for the period in which they were written, but for all time.

Such a busy, benevolent and beautiful life, though homely and uneventful, could not be suppressed altogether, for her devotees the world over claim her as one of their favourite authors, and as such they eagerly ask to know something of the woman who has charmed and cheered them by her kindly humour, and inspired and ennobled them by her sympathetic treatment of the social wrongs created by our industrial system.

Mrs. Gaskell is surely coming to the fuller recognition which she so justly deserves, although as a writer in the fifties and early sixties she took her place as a worthy contemporary of Charlotte Brontë and Charles Dickens, and had a most successful career. She who was always so generous in her appreciation of others, cannot escape the willing homage of her admirers.

Last August, when visiting a house where Mrs. Gaskell was often a very welcome guest, I was privileged to read a letter in which she mentioned her friend Florence Nightingale, for whom she expressed her great admiration. Shortly afterwards I learnt that at that very hour Florence Nightingale had passed away. That letter seemed to bring Mrs. Gaskell nearer, though she had preceded her friend by nearly half a century. Working on very different lines, those two noble women both heard a cry of distress and felt compelled to do something to alleviate it. Of the distinguished women of the nineteenth century few have deserved better of their country than the author of *Mary Barton* and the heroine of the Crimean War.

There are not many who personally remember Mrs. Gaskell, but I have been privileged to meet several, and they all think of her with gratitude, not only as a successful novelist, but also as a most gentle lady, a model mother, a devoted wife, and an excellent home manager and withal a staunch and true friend. Her sympathies were ever with the poor and needy, and she was a valuable acquisition to any cause which could secure her services.

Her first great novel, *Mary Barton*, written under the influence of strong emotion at the darkest time of her life, when she had lost her only son, not only proved her genius as a writer, but it revealed her intense sympathy for those who suffered injustice around her in Manchester.

Though modest and retiring almost to a fault, she had the courage of her convictions, and her pitiful story thrilled throughout the land, bearing its supreme message for tolerance and assistance to those who could not help themselves.

It was a bold step to criticise the doings of her neighbours, but how well she did it in *Mary Barton*! and when that novel was judged to be all on the side of the poor and against their employers, she struck the balance admirably in *North and South*, by giving both sides of the question.

It must be remembered that *Mary Barton* was written more than sixty years ago, when there was little organised help for the poor and oppressed, either by the Churches or the State. It was her clarion note which did much to arouse the rich and show them their rightful duty towards the poor.

Mrs. Gaskell was not afraid to write a story with a purpose. She practised what she preached, and with her husband, the faithful minister of Cross Street Chapel, she did her best to alleviate the awful poverty which she daily saw around her. This pioneer work which Mr. and Mrs. Gaskell did so quietly and unostentatiously bore fruit in later days, and Manchester holds their names in grateful remembrance.

Endowed with quick intuition, well-balanced judgment and sound common sense, she found no difficulty in depicting the actual life of the poverty-stricken operatives of Lancashire. Her first novel, in some ways her best because of the intense feeling which breathes through it, placed her at one bound in the ranks of the best writers of the day, a position which she retained for the remaining years of her life, producing novels which are noted for their pure and sweet homeliness and their tender touch. She never aspired to sensationalism, but was content to give us "everyday stories," as she was wont to call them, and for that reason she appeals to the young as well as the old and to all classes of society.

George Sand once remarked to Lord Houghton, "Mrs. Gaskell has done what neither I nor any other female writers in France can accomplish, she has written novels which excite the deepest interest in men of the world, and yet which every girl will be the better for reading."

Mary Barton, with its pathetic message, *Cranford*, that matchless prose idyll, and the fascinating *Life of Charlotte Brontë* are her best known works, but there are no less than six other novels: *Ruth*, *North and South*, *My Lady Ludlow*, *Sylvia's Lovers*, *Cousin Phillis*, and *Wives and Daughters*—her best and longest novel—all of which deserve to be much better known. In addition, she wrote about forty articles and short stories, principally for *Household Words* and *All the Year Round*, under the genial editorship of Charles Dickens. All these go to prove that Mrs. Gaskell was not limited to one type of writing, and that she was equally at home in dealing with so many and such varied subjects.

Unlike Charlotte Brontë, who, great artist as she was, had a very narrow range, Mrs. Gaskell culled from many sources, and her canvas was often very crowded, though her beautiful sketches of life are almost unrivalled for fulness and variety. "No one ever came near her in the gift of telling a story," said one who knew her before she became a writer.

Mrs. Gaskell had a great aversion to criticism, and whilst very indifferent to praise, she was acutely sensitive to blame, and for these reasons she wished her works to be her only memorial, and that, apart from the writer, they should be judged on their merits alone.

All that has been revealed of Mrs. Gaskell's life proves how naturally her own personality shone through her stories. "She is what her works show her to have been—a good, wise woman," wrote Frederick Greenwood in his eulogium in the *Cornhill Magazine* after her death.

The fact that many of her stories have been translated into several other languages gives them a very wide and general popularity.

II

Elizabeth Cleghorn Stevenson, to give Mrs. Gaskell's maiden name, first saw the light on September 29th, 1810, in Chelsea, within sight of the Thames, which she describes as a great solace to her in later days, when she was "very, very unhappy." The house in which she was born was in picturesque Lindsey Row, nearly opposite the old wooden Battersea Bridge beloved of artists and just at the bend of the river. The view from the house, which is now known as 93 Cheyne Walk, is still very fine.

Thirteen months almost to the day after Elizabeth Stevenson's birth, her mother died at 3 Beaufort Row, Chelsea, at the age of forty, and was buried on October 30, 1811. After the mother's death, the baby was taken care of by a neighbouring shopkeeper's wife, until Mr. Stevenson could make arrangements for his little daughter to be taken to Mrs. Lumb—the beautiful Aunt Hannah—who lived on the heathside at Knutsford. Within a few weeks of the mother's death, a friend of the Hollands, Mrs. Whittington, consented to take the baby back with her to Knutsford.

This statement concerning Mrs. Stevenson's death and the age when Mrs. Gaskell was left motherless, which is now made public for the first time, is confirmed by Mrs. Gaskell herself, who, writing to Mary Howitt on August 18, 1838, says: "Though a Londoner by birth, I was early motherless, and taken when only a year old to my dear, adopted native town Knutsford."

The long journey by stage-coach from Chelsea to Knutsford is said to have suggested "Babby's" journey from London to Manchester in *Mary Barton*. Now that we know that Elizabeth Stevenson was a little over a year old, and not one month old as has been stated by every previous writer on the subject, it is easy to understand that Mrs. Gaskell had for her prototype of "Babby" a baby of about a year old. It has always puzzled me as a mother, how a baby as young as "Babby" is represented to be in *Mary Barton* could have survived after being fed on "pobbies," and it is quite certain that a crust of bread, provided for the child according to the story, could not have been suitable for so young a baby.

Henceforth Knutsford—"My dear, adopted native town"—as Mrs. Gaskell affectionately termed it, became her home, until her marriage. The bringing of this baby to the little Cheshire town has led to the immortalising of the place as Cranford, for had Elizabeth Stevenson never lived there, the Knutsford of the Early Victorian period would probably have been buried in oblivion long ago, and whilst many have enjoyed the solace and charm of the place, it needed an artist "with something of an angel's touch" to reveal the beauty of the little country town and its quaint, kindly society of old maids.

Mrs. Lumb's house at Knutsford, where Elizabeth Stevenson grew to be a singularly beautiful girl, is still standing at the corner of the heath, over which the future novelist used to ramble and day-dream. In this neighbourhood she was surrounded by her mother's people. At Church House was her uncle, Dr. Holland, "who had his round of thirty miles and lived at Cranford." He was the father of the well-known Sir Henry Holland, physician to Queen Victoria. He delighted to take his niece with him on his country drives, just as Dr. Gibson of Hollingford, in *Wives and Daughters*, drove round the district with Molly Gibson.

Elizabeth Stevenson was fortunate in her parentage. Her father, William Stevenson, a remarkable and gifted man, was the son of Captain Stevenson of Berwick-on-Tweed. Formerly the name was spelt Stevensen, which betrayed its Scandinavian origin. Mrs. Gaskell was always fond of travel, and when about to start on a journey, she would remark, "The blood of the Vikings is stirring in my veins."

If heredity is to count for anything, Elizabeth Stevenson derived much of her literary talent from her father, who, according to the Annual Register for 1830, "was a man remarkable for the stores of knowledge which he possessed and for the simplicity and modesty by which his rare attainments were concealed." Mrs. Gaskell was very proud of her father's memory, as well she might be. One who knew him wrote, "No man had so few personal enemies and so many sincere, steady friends. He was kind and benevolent, and had little of the pride of authorship." These words might be written with all sincerity as equally applicable to his famous daughter.

William Stevenson played many parts. After his education was finished at the Daventry Academy, he became a tutor at Bruges, afterwards going to Manchester as Classical lecturer at the Academy and preacher at the Dob Lane Unitarian Chapel, Failsworth. Later he was a farmer in East Lothian, and then he moved to Edinburgh, where he became editor of the *Edinburgh Review* and a contributor to many magazines, besides writing a *Life of Caxton*. In 1807 he came to London as secretary to Lord Lauderdale, and eventually settled as Keeper of the Records at the Treasury Office, which position he held until his death in 1829. Mrs. Gaskell's mother was Elizabeth Holland, fourth daughter of Samuel Holland of the Sandlebridge Estate, near Knutsford. He also owned an estate known as Dogholes, near Great Warford.

Grandfather Holland was a very lovable man, and doubtless he contributed something to the beautiful character of the farmer preacher, Mr. Holman, in *Cousin Phillis*, and in a less degree to Thomas Holbrook, Miss Matty's faithful lover. The ancestral home at Sandlebridge is beautifully and accurately described as Hope Farm in *Cousin Phillis*, and as Woodley in *Cranford*. The history of several members of the distinguished Holland family was such that it could not escape wandering into the novels of such a genius as Mrs. Gaskell, though she never meant to put real people in her stories. If Leslie Stephen's definition of a novel is correct, "transfigured experience, not necessarily the author's own experience, but near enough to his everyday life to be within the range of his sympathy," then Mrs. Gaskell's novels bear the test well.

Little is known of the paternal grandmother, but her grandmother Holland is described as "A woman of extraordinary energy and will and rather the opposite of her husband, who, though firm, was far quieter and disposed to treat his servants with more leniency than his wife, who was exceedingly particular with them." Sir Henry Holland, in his *Recollections*, says that his grandfather, Samuel Holland, was the most practical optimist he ever knew, and although he farmed his own land, he could never be got to complain of "the distemperature of the seasons," and one of Samuel Holland's own sons states that his father's life had been "particularly smooth."

Elizabeth Stevenson stayed in Knutsford until she was thirteen, the only variation being an occasional visit to her father at Chelsea. Knutsford, with its curious old customs, must have made a very vivid impression on her mind, since afterwards she was able to portray the little country town in no less than six of her stories depicting English village life in the early part of the nineteenth century. These quaint stories are perfect little miniatures set in the beautiful scenery which abounds in that part of Cheshire, and they give us glimpses of the novelist at her best.

How few could have found in bygone Knutsford, with its prim old maids, a few aristocratic families, and the necessary doctor and lawyer, so much excellent material with which to weave stories that have charmed succeeding generations in many lands. It was Mrs. Gaskell's clear intuition which saw so much more than meets the eye of the ordinary mortal and supplied her with an unlimited and inexhaustible store, from which she could charm either by voice or pen. One who knew her before she was recognised as a gifted writer said of her, "She was a born story-teller," and we can well believe it.

When nearly fourteen Elizabeth Stevenson was sent to an excellent boarding-school at Stratford-on-Avon, kept by the Misses Byerley, who were related to the Hollands, as well as to her stepmother. There she stayed for two years, including holidays. The school was once known as "The Old House of St. Mary," and for a little while Shakespeare lived there. To be educated in a house in which Shakespeare once dwelt was a good augury for the future novelist.

Elizabeth's schooldays were very happy. Writing to Mary Howitt in 1838, she says, "I am unwilling to leave even in thought the haunts of such happy days as my schooldays were."

A book, presented to one of her schoolfellows, dated June 15th, 1824, lies before me, with Elizabeth Stevenson's signature. She was noted for her kindness to her school friends, and, like Charlotte Brontë, when at Roe Head it was said of her that she could often be found surrounded by a group of eager listeners, and even as a schoolgirl she had, like her dear Miss Matty, a leaning to ghost stories.

Her first separate literary effort was a letter describing an afternoon spent at Clopton Hall, Stratford-on-Avon, in company with her school friends, which she sent to William Howitt, who readily accepted it for insertion in his "Visits to Remarkable Places." It was written more than ten years after she left school, but it proves how observant as a girl she was, and how her love of research led her to explore the old house, rather than wander in the park which surrounds the hall.

Two years ago I was allowed by the courtesy of the owner to wander through Clopton Hall, which was once the Manor House. It has been partly rebuilt, but the recess parlour, in which the merry schoolgirls had tea, is still there with its beautiful painted windows, and the priest's room, in which our future novelist crept on her hands and knees, is to be seen with its barred windows and texts painted on the walls, and on the old oak staircase are oil paintings of Charlotte and Margaret Clopton, which Mrs. Gaskell mentions. Lovers of Mrs. Gaskell's works should not fail to read her graphic account of "A Visit to Clopton Hall."

About the year 1827 Elizabeth Stevenson returned to her good Aunt Lumb at Knutsford, but shortly afterwards her only brother, a naval lieutenant, left his ship when in port at Calcutta and was never heard of again. He it was, doubtless, who suggested "Poor Peter" in *Cranford* and "Dear Frederick" in *North and South*, though both these characters were allowed to return to their homes again. It is said that the posting of the letter to "Poor Peter" in India is founded on actual fact.

The disappearance of her brother was followed by her father's serious illness, which took her to Chelsea, where she devotedly nursed him until his death in 1829. Afterwards we find her leaving her stepmother and half-brother William and her half-sister Catherine, and returning once more to Knutsford, where she did not remain long, as at this time she paid a long visit to Newcastle-on-Tyne, to the home of the Rev. William Turner, so beautifully described in her second novel, *Ruth*, in "A Dissenting Minister's Household." In the quiet atmosphere of this religious home, she found her prototype for Thurstan Benson. Thurstan, as she explains, was an old family name, and it is still retained in the family. There was a Thurstan Holland of Denton, in the early part of the fifteenth century, who was one of her ancestors.

From Newcastle-on-Tyne Elizabeth Stevenson went to spend the last winter of her maidenhood in Edinburgh. There her remarkable beauty attracted painters and sculptors, and fortunately she was persuaded to sit to David Dunbar, a former pupil of Chantrey. He sculptured the beautiful marble bust of the fair debutante, which, enclosed in a glass case, is one of the most cherished possessions in her old home at Manchester. About this time she also had an exquisite miniature painted, the pose of which reminds us of the description of *Ruth* by Bellingham: "Such a superb turn of the head, she might be a Percy or a Howard."

In August, 1832, before she had attained her twenty-second birthday, Elizabeth Cleghorn Stevenson was married to the Rev. William Gaskell, M.A., minister of Cross Street Unitarian Chapel, Manchester. The ceremony was performed in the old Parish Church of Knutsford, as Dissenters were not allowed to be married in their own chapels in those days. The Hollands and the Gaskells were already connected by marriage, Mr. Gaskell's sister having married Charles Holland, a cousin of Elizabeth Stevenson.

In one of her letters, Mrs. Gaskell tells us that the streets of Knutsford were sanded in accordance with the custom at weddings, and that there were general rejoicings. The honeymoon was spent in North Wales, in the neighbourhood of Festiniog, where Mr. Charles Holland had extensive slate quarries.

The marriage was an ideal one. The young wife at once threw herself into her husband's work, helping in the Sunday School and visiting the sick and needy. Her beauty and winning personality endeared her to the members of her husband's congregation, which was said to be the most intellectual and wealthy in Manchester in those days, more than thirty private carriages often being found waiting after the conclusion of the morning service. *Mary Barton* gives the readers the other side of the society in which Mrs. Gaskell moved, and where she became "a very angel of light" in the poverty-stricken districts of Ancoats and Hulme.

Their home was always a centre of light and learning first for ten years at 14 Dover Street, afterwards at 121 Upper Rumford Street, and finally, from 1849, the present family residence in Plymouth Grove, which has always been noted for its sunny hospitality and genial intellectual atmosphere. Lord Houghton said of this home that such was its beneficent influence in the great cotton city, "It made Manchester a possible centre for literary people." Mr. and Mrs. Gaskell gathered around them a warm circle of friends, who joined in trying to ameliorate the impoverished districts of that part of Lancashire. When the Chartist riots had reduced many of the cotton operatives to starvation, Mrs. Gaskell's home was a rendezvous from which she distributed through her windows in the early morning loaves and other necessities.

Thomas Wright, a working-man of Manchester, who gave up all his spare time in visiting the prisons and helping the fallen, found good friends in the Gaskells. Mrs. Gaskell has written an appreciative note about him in *Mary Barton*. Mr. G. F. Watts painted "The Good Samaritan" in 1850, and presented it to the city of Manchester as a tribute of admiration to the noble philanthropy of Thomas Wright. Mrs. Gaskell was instrumental in getting Mr. Watts to paint the beautiful water-colour portrait of Thomas Wright, which now hangs in the National Portrait Gallery.

The Rev. Travers Madge was another who worked with the Gaskells, giving up his salary as a minister and devoting his life to the poor. The Misses Winkworth were also willing helpers, as also was John Bamford, whose poem, "God help the poor," found a place in *Mary Barton*. In addition to the practical help which the Gaskells gave, they both cherished a wish to wield the pen in the interests of the poor, and in 1837 they jointly published in *Blackwood's Magazine* a poem, marked No. 1, *Sketches among the Poor*. It is really a poetical rendering of the homely life of "Old Alice," who figures so pathetically in *Mary Barton*. No other poem succeeded this, though it is well known that Mrs. Gaskell frequently expressed herself in verse, and Mr. Gaskell wrote a number of beautiful hymns, some of which are still to be found in various collections. He also translated hymns from the German, and was an expert in writing in the Lancashire dialect. In addition to his other duties, he was for a time a lecturer in English Literature and Logic at Owens College, now known as the Victoria University, Manchester.

The quiet life in Knutsford and Stratford-on-Avon inspired Mrs. Gaskell with those beautiful thoughts of the country which she has so well expressed in her pastoral stories, but it was the busy city of Manchester that roused her latent talent and winged her pen in writing of "the silent sorrows of the poor."

The death of her only boy from scarlet fever in September, 1842, at Festiniog, where she had gone for a holiday, was succeeded by a lingering illness, and it was whilst lying on her couch that she found the necessary time to write her first novel. It has been said that *Mary Barton* contained too many death-bed scenes, but it is well to remember that it was from a death-bed that Mrs. Gaskell drew the inspiration which enabled her to depict in such realistic colours common scenes in the lives of the poor. The complaint that *Mary Barton* and *Lizzie Leigh* were much too sad—"stories with a sob in them"— probably prompted Mrs. Gaskell to prove that she could write in a humorous vein, hence her delightful sketches of *Cranford Society*. *Mary Barton* hadattracted to her many literary friends, amongst the most enthusiastic being Charles Dickens, at whose request she became a regular contributor to *Household Words*, which he had just started. When Mrs. Gaskell sent him her first short paper entitled *Our Society in Cranford*, which included chapters one and two, she meant it for a complete sketch, but Dickens asked for more and still more, and so the history of the Cranfordian Society was chronicled bit by bit and afterwards compiled to form the book which is certainly the most popular of all Mrs. Gaskell's works. "If my name is ever immortalised, it will be through *Cranford*, for so many people have mentioned it to me," said Mrs. Gaskell, and she has proved a true prophet. Wherever the English tongue is spoken, *Cranford* is treasured, for its quiet, sunny humour is irresistible, and it has become a classic, which stands alone for its delightful winsomeness and tender pathos.

With splendid fidelity Mrs. Gaskell kept to her inimitable style, and the sketches are, as compared with those of Dickens and Thackeray, like carefully finished water-colour paintings beside the strong, bold canvas of a Rubens or a Vandyke. Instead of uproarious mirth *Cranford* provokes the kindly smile, which seldom broadens into a loud laugh, but it always leaves the reader the better for its kindly influence. *Cranford* gives the best reflection of Mrs.

Gaskell's beautiful character. She loved to tell stories of bygone days and to whet the appetite for amusing tales, which, while perfectly true to life, bordered on the ridiculous and dealt gently with the foibles and weaknesses of some phases of society. Of these stories she had a goodly store, which with gentle satire she could tell in her own sweet way. She was fond of making a pun or asking a riddle, which would at once arrest the attention, and, like Miss Galindo in *My Lady Ludlow*, she believed—"When everything goes wrong, one would give up breathing if one could not lighten one's heart by a joke."

In 1850, a short time before Mrs. Gaskell commenced *Cranford*, she met her great contemporary, Charlotte Brontë, at Briery Close, Windermere.

Sixty years afterwards, almost to the day, I was invited by the kind courtesy of the owner to visit this interesting house on the shores of Lake Windermere. The cosy drawing-room in which those two novelists met and their respective bedrooms, next to each other, from which there is a magnificent view of the lake and the hills beyond, are still held sacred to the associations of that August holiday in 1850, when the shy, elusive Charlotte Brontë first met her future biographer.

One of the party who met the two novelists during that visit once told me of the marked difference in these two women. Charlotte Brontë, in her black silk dress, sat on the couch nervous and shy, "looking as if she would be glad if the floor would open and swallow her, whilst Mrs. Gaskell, bright and vivacious, looked quite at home and equal to anything." The two great novelists became attached to each other, and Charlotte Brontë visited Mrs. Gaskell's home in Manchester on three separate occasions, and in return Mrs. Gaskell once spent a week in the old vicarage at Haworth. This friendship bore fruit in years to come, when Mrs. Gaskell was asked by old Patrick Brontë to write his daughter's life, to which she willingly consented and at which she worked heartily and sometimes even passionately with so difficult a task.

This admirable biography has become a classic, and is a fitting memorial to the author of *Jane Eyre* both as a tribute of affection from one novelist to another, and a faithful record of a noble life. "I did so try to tell the truth," wrote the biographer, and we know how well she succeeded, though on the publication of the third edition she found herself in a veritable "hornet's nest," and the worry and trouble from one source and another caused a temporary distaste for writing. After a time, however, the desire for wielding the pen came back to her, and she wrote *My Lady Ludlow* and *Round the Sofa Stories*, which undoubtedly owe something to her Stratford-on-Avon days in 1824-27 and her life in Edinburgh in 1829-31.

After a holiday in the Isle of Man in 1856, Mrs. Gaskell took a new departure and decided to write a maritime story. A visit to Whitby in 1858 resulted in the truly pathetic tale of *Sylvia's Lovers*, which has the quaint fisher town of Whitby for its background. Descriptions of the old seaport are beautifully and accurately rendered, and a visit to Whitby is not complete unless *Sylvia's Lovers* has been read within sight and sound of the sea around that rugged coast. The farms and homesteads mentioned can be localised, and they answer minutely to the descriptions given. Haytersbank Farm, Sylvia's old home, Moss Brow, where the Corneys lived, old Foster's shop in the Market-place, are all still there.

Mrs. Gaskell confessed to having taken greater pains with *Sylvia's Lovers* than with any other of her novels, and this historical story is one of her best and marks a second stage in her work. It is a story founded on fact in the cruel press-gang days, and Mrs. Gaskell has been wonderfully successful in her delineation of the characters. She does not try to make them perfect, but describes them with their flaws, and there is no exaggeration but just the unvarnished conversation natural to the people of the period with which the story deals. The descriptive parts are most perfectly rendered, and it was a high tribute to Mrs. Gaskell's faithful word-painting when Du Maurier was led to use actual sketches of Whitby to help him in illustrating *Sylvia's Lovers* before he knew that Monkshaven and Whitby were one and the same place. Some of the scenes are exquisitely drawn, and Mrs. Gaskell rose to her highest in word portraiture in *Sylvia's Lovers*. The sailor's funeral in the old God's Acre around the ancient Parish Church is a masterpiece. The New Year's Party at Moss Brow and Philip Hepburn going out into the darkness on that memorable night show a wonderful insight into human nature. The last scene, where Philip and Sylvia meet only to part again when it is too late, is a pathetic picture that few could have painted with such soul-stirring emotion.

Cousin Phillis is a prose idyll, which for beauty of language and wealth of original incidents is unique—"A gem without a flaw"—and one of the most perfect stories of old-world romance, fitted in the rich setting of her grandfather Holland's picturesque farm at Sandlebridge, near Knutsford. It is a story to be read over and over again. The heroine, Phillis Holman, is one of the most perfectly sketched characters in any English novel, and yet there is nothing overdrawn, all is simple, quiet, and dignified, and withal so real and faithful to life. Though not as well-known as *Cranford, Cousin Phillis* richly deserves to hang side by side with it as a miniature of great beauty, in soft subdued colours. The story is surrounded by the atmosphere of the practical, religious home-life of the godly family at Hope Farm, which surely owes something to Mrs. Gaskell's own kinsfolk.

This story was quickly succeeded by what, alas, became Mrs. Gaskell's last and notably her best work, *Wives and Daughters*. She calls it an everyday story, and yet it grips the reader from the beginning to the end. The heroine is a typical well-bred English girl, who endears herself to her readers by her natural simplicity and common sense. The story is of Knutsford once more, and it takes us to the well-wooded parks and lordly mansions on the outskirts of the village. Those who knew the Knutsford of the fifties were wont to say how true to life it was. The characters are drawn with a master hand. Molly Gibson and Cynthia Kirkpatrick are a splendid study in contrasts, and Mrs. Gaskell's powers were never more fully taxed, nor does she ever succeed so well, except perhaps when she draws Cynthia's mother, the stepmother of Molly and the second Mrs. Gibson.

The book is nearly related to *Cranford*, for this story of *Wives and Daughters* is of the near kinsfolk of the Cranford dames. Though the novelist touches lightly the foibles and failings of Mrs. Gibson, she shows her clear insight and reads character with shrewdness, albeit so kindly.

Mrs. Gibson and Cynthia Kirkpatrick are worthy of Thackeray himself, and possibly owe something to his influence. Both characters are difficult to delineate, and in the hands of a less capable writer we should have despised and disliked them, but with the kindly benevolent spirit which shines through all Mrs. Gaskell's works, we are driven to make allowances and pity their shallowness whilst smiling at the worldly wisdom displayed. How different would they have been revealed by George Eliot, and with what merciless scorn would Charlotte Brontë have treated them. "Molly Gibson is the best heroine you have had yet," wrote Madame Mohl. She is certainly a cousin to Margaret Hale in *North and South* and a sister to Phillis Holman in *Cousin Phillis*. This type of English girlhood suited Mrs. Gaskell's pen. Her heroines are generally better drawn than her heroes, which may be accounted for to some extent by the fact that she viewed everything from a woman's standpoint, and that during the whole of her literary life she had the companionship of her own devoted daughters, well educated, happy, and like their mother, always anxious to do the right. Molly Gibson's character has always been associated with Mrs. Gaskell's own girlhood, but quite recently I received a letter from the grandson of one of Mrs. Gaskell's school friends at Stratford-on-Avon, and he tells me that he was always given to understand that his grandmother was the prototype of Molly Gibson. Truly Mrs. Gaskell's characters in many of her stories fit many originals, hence her determination to class them as "everyday stories," though, as a matter of fact, they are probably not drawn from any one individual.

Mrs. Gaskell has suffered more than most writers from being accused of putting real people into her stories, but though imagination is a great quality, it is not more essential than the power to recognise and handle the simple facts of life; for while there are many who can create a character, few can faithfully delineate it, and the same is true of locality.

Before the concluding chapter of *Wives and Daughters* was finished the pen dropped from the novelist's hand, just when she was at the zenith of her power as a writer. This novel was written as a serial for the *Cornhill Magazine* when Mr. Frederick Greenwood was editor. The latter part was written at Pontresina during the summer of 1865, when Mrs. Gaskell was travelling with her son-in-law, Mr. Charles Compton, Q.C., and her three daughters. She returned to Manchester in June, and was far from well. During the whole of her literary life she had been longing for a *pied-à-terre* in the country, where she could get the necessary quiet for her work. The North of England was too cold in the winter, though in the summer she found a delightful spot on Morecambe Bay—a little old-world village which is known by the euphonious name of Silverdale. There for a part of many summers she went with her daughters and her faithful nurse to a farm which is accurately described in *Ruth*. Silverdale lives as Abermouth in that noble story.

The country home which Mrs. Gaskell chose was known as The Lawn, Holybourne, near Alton, in Hampshire. She purchased it with the two thousand pounds which she received for *Wives and Daughters*, and she kept the secret from her husband, meaning to present it to him when it was altered and renovated to her own artistic taste. But alas! before it was completed she suddenly passed away on Sunday afternoon, November 14th, 1865. She had been feeling really better, and on that very Sunday attended service at the quaint old church at Holybourne in company with her daughters, when, during tea, without a moment's warning her head lowered and she was gone. Writing of this sad time, one of her daughters wrote: "Mama's last days had been full of loving thought and tender help for others. She was so sweet and dear and noble beyond words."

Wives and Daughters was all but finished. She was waiting for some special information with regard to one of the characters, Roger Hamley, who, along with his brother Osborne, made an admirable pair to match Molly Gibson and Cynthia Kirkpatrick, before she concluded the story. The very last words that Mrs. Gaskell wrote are: "And now cover me up close, and let me go to sleep and dream about my dear Cynthia and my new shawl." One who loved Mrs. Gaskell dearly said it would not be inappropriate to alter the words *Cynthia* to husband and *new shawl* to new house, for during her stay at Holybourne her thoughts were often with her husband, the busy Unitarian minister in Manchester, and she was looking forward "with the glee of a child" to giving him a country home in the South of England, to which she hoped he would retire with her, though she looked forward to many years of usefulness both for herself and her husband.

The brief stay at Holybourne, with its tragic ending, was a sad memory for the husband and daughters. The house is still in the possession of the family. The intended gift which the mother bought so cheerfully has been kept as a last token of love, though the family never resided there after Mrs. Gaskell's death.

Mr. Frederick Greenwood added a tenderly written eulogium at the end of *Wives and Daughters* which has been published along with the novel, and it formed a beautiful and fitting close to the story. "What promised to be the crowning work of a life is a memorial of death. A few days longer and it would have been a triumphal column, crowned with a capital of festal leaves and flowers, now it is another sort of column—one of those sad white pillars which stand broken in the churchyard."

Wives and Daughters was issued in book form in 1866 by Messrs. Smith, Elder and Co., and was extremely popular, partly because of the tragic death of the author, but more so for the beauty of the story. To those who know the little Cheshire town of Knutsford, it is interesting to locate the Cumnor Tower and the Park gates through which Molly Gibson drove when attending her first garden party from Church House, formerly her uncle Holland's home, now known by the picture postcards as Molly Gibson's House. The home of the Hamleys is to be identified with one of the old halls in the district, but the charm of the story is its naturalness and the characters are so well balanced. When putting down the book one involuntarily says, as Mrs. Gaskell wrote of Charlotte Brontë, "If she had but lived." This novel displays her as a writer grown to maturity, and as one who had advanced from simple, didactic, domestic stories for the Parish Magazine, to novels which charm a very much wider circle and are acceptable to all classes of society.

Mrs. Gaskell is buried in her beloved Knutsford, in the old Unitarian burial ground around the church, where a simple granite cross marks the resting-place. On her grave is often to be found a wreath or bouquet as a tribute of grateful homage from one of her many admirers. Her writing was done in the spirit of true helpfulness, and it is impossible to read her stories without feeling the better for their perusal. She brought a well-trained mind to her work, and whatever she did was done conscientiously. Her life was not an eventful one, but it was crowded with good deeds.

The revival of the Gaskell cult is helping to familiarise the present generation with her beautiful stories of the mid-Victorian period. It is noticeable that although she spent many of her holidays on the Continent, France, Germany, and Italy being her favourite holiday resorts, all her novels tell of English life, for she was careful never to get out of her depths. She wrote of what she had experienced and of what she saw in the daily life of those around her. Future generations will read Mrs. Gaskell's novels and feel that she was a keen observer of humanity, and she had not only the desire but the capacity to comprehend it.

The outstanding qualities of her novels are individuality, truthfulness, and purity. The power of entering into the feelings of her characters is almost unique, as *Mary Barton, Ruth, Sylvia's Lovers* and *Wives and Daughters* prove abundantly. Those of a past generation could best testify to the truthfulness of her stories. They were real word-pictures beautifully conceived and true to life, and there was an absence of exaggeration—one of Mrs. Gaskell's pet aversions.

The purity of her writing is proverbial. There is no author who has excelled her in that quality, and her novels are all free from dross and censoriousness. Hers was a spirit that made for the morning and heralded a purer day, and the immortality of her name rests on the Pauline injunction, "Whatsoever things are honest, whatsoever things are just, whatsoever things are pure, whatsoever things are lovely, whatsoever things are of good report, if there be any virtue and if there be any praise, think on these things."

ESTHER ALICE CHADWICK.

WEST BRAE, ENFIELD, MIDDLESEX,
August 25th, 1911.

Calendar of Principal Events in Mrs. Gaskell's Life

1810.   Elizabeth Cleghorn Stevenson, born at 12 Lindsey Row, Chelsea, September 29th.

1811.   Removed to 3 Beaufort Row, Chelsea, June, 1811.

Mother died, October, 1811, at 3 Beaufort Row.

1812.   Elizabeth taken to Knutsford when fourteen months old.

1824.   Sent to school at Stratford-on-Avon.

1827.   Her only brother, John Stevenson, disappeared at Calcutta.

1829.   Father died at 3 Beaufort Row, Chelsea.

Visited her relatives at Newcastle-on-Tyne.

1830.   Visited Edinburgh.

1831.   Marble bust sculptured by Dunbar.

1832.   Married the Rev. William Gaskell, M.A., August 30th.

1832-42.   Resided at 14 Dover Street, Manchester.

1837.   Mrs. Lumb died at Knutsford, May 1st.

1842-49.   Resided at 121 Upper Rumford Street, Manchester.

1844.   Only son died at Festiniog, September, 1844.

1849-65.   Resided at 84 Plymouth Grove, Manchester.

1848.   First novel, *Mary Barton*, published.

First met Charles Dickens.

1850.   Mr. Gaskell's mother, Margaret Gaskell, died in January.

1850.   First met Charlotte Brontë, August, 1850.

Published *The Moorland Cottage*.

1853.   Second novel, *Ruth*, published.

Cranford published.

1854.   Visited Paris and met Madame Mohl.

1855.   *North and South* published.

           Lizzie Leigh and Other Tales published.

1857.   *Life of Charlotte Brontë* published.

           Edited *Mabel Vaughan* and wrote preface.

1859.   *Round the Sofa Stories* published.

           My Lady Ludlow and Other Tales published.

1862.   Preface to *Garibaldi at Cabrera* by Colonel Vecchj.

           Inaugurated Sewing schools for poor in Manchester.

1863.   *Sylvia's Lovers* published.

           Mrs. Gaskell's daughter, Florence Elizabeth, married to Mr. Charles Compton, Q.C., on September 8th.

           Visited Rome and stayed with W. W. Story.

1865.   *Cousin Phillis* published.

           Wives and Daughters published in "Cornhill Magazine."

           Mrs. Gaskell died at Holybourne, Hants, November 12th.

           Buried, November 16th, in the Unitarian Chapel Burial Ground, Knutsford.

I
Poetry

Poetry was not Mrs. Gaskell's *forte*, but her poetical instinct revealed itself especially in her prose idylls—*Cranford* and *Cousin Phillis*.

Almost all her articles and sketches were written for *Household Words* and *All the Year Round*, though Mrs. Gaskell's fame rests on her novels. Charles Dickens eagerly secured Mrs. Gaskell as a regular contributor to his magazine, and her versatility was shown by the many different subjects which she discussed with so much ability.

Poetry

Sketches Among the Poor

Blackwood's Magazine, January, 1837

No. I

This poem was written by Mrs. Gaskell in collaboration with her husband, and is her first published work. Writing to Mary Howitt in 1838, she says: "We once thought of *trying* to write sketches among the poor, *rather* in the manner of Crabbe (now don't think this presumptuous), but in a more seeing-beauty spirit; and one—the only one—was published in *Blackwood*, January, 1837. But I suppose we spoke our plan near a dog rose, for it never went any further." The poem is interesting, as it foreshadows Mrs. Gaskell's sympathetic insight into the lives of the poor, and is a worthy prelude to her first novel, for the character of "Mary" is based on the same original as "Old Alice" in *Mary Barton*.

IN childhood's days, I do remember me

Of one dark house behind an old elm tree,

By gloomy streets surrounded, where the flower

Brought from the fresher air, scarce for an hour

Retained its fragrant scent; yet men lived there,

Yea, and in happiness; the mind doth clear

In most dense airs its own bright atmosphere.

But in the house of which I spake there dwelt

One by whom all the weight of smoke was felt.

She had o'erstepped the bound 'twixt youth and age

A single, not a lonely, woman, sage

And thoughtful ever, yet most truly kind:

Without the natural ties, she sought to bind

Hearts unto hers, with gentle, useful love,

Prompt at each change in sympathy to move.

And so she gained the affection, which she prized

From every living thing, howe'er despised—

A call upon her tenderness whene'er

The friends around her had a grief to share;

And, if in joy the kind one they forgot,

She still rejoiced, and more was wanted not.

Said I not truly, she was not alone,

Though none at evening shared her clean hearthstone?

To some she might prosaic seem, but me

She always charmed with daily poesy.

Felt in her every action, never heard,

E'en as the mate of some sweet singing-bird,

That mute and still broods on her treasure-nest,

Her heart's fond hope hid deep within her breast.

In all her quiet duties, one dear thought

Kept ever true and constant sway, not brought

Before the world, but garnered all the more

For being to herself a secret store.

Whene'er she heard of country homes, a smile

Came brightening o'er her serious face the while;
She knew not that it came, yet in her heart
A hope leaped up, of which that smile was part.
She thought the time might come, e'er yet the bowl
Were broken at the fountain, when her soul

Might listen to its yearnings, unreproved
By thought of failure to the cause she loved;
When she might leave the close and noisy street,
And once again her childhood's home might greet.
It was a pleasant place, that early home!
The brook went singing by, leaving its foam
Among the flags and blue forget-me-not;
And in a nook, above that shelter'd spot,
For ages stood a gnarlèd hawthorn-tree;
And if you pass'd in spring-time, you might see
The knotted trunk all coronal'd with flowers,
That every breeze shook down in fragrant showers;
The earnest bees in odorous cells did lie,
Hymning their thanks with murmuring melody;
The evening sun shone brightly on the green,
And seem'd to linger on the lonely scene.
And, if to others Mary's early nest
Show'd poor and homely, to her loving breast
A charm lay hidden in the very stains
Which time and weather left; the old dim panes,
The grey rough moss, the house-leek, you might see
Were chronicled in childhood's memory;
And in her dreams she wander'd far and wide

Among the hills, her sister at her side—

That sister slept beneath a grassy tomb

Ere time had robbed her of her first sweet bloom.

O Sleep! thou bringest back our childhood's heart,

Ere yet the dew exhale, the hope depart;

Thou callest up the lost ones, sorrow'd o'er

Till sorrow's self hath lost her tearful power;

Thine is the fairy-land, where shadows dwell,

Evoked in dreams by some strange hidden spell.

But Day and Waking have their dreams, O Sleep,

When Hope and Memory their fond watches keep;

And such o'er Mary held supremest sway,

When kindly labours task'd her hands all day.

Employ'd her hands, her thoughts roam'd far and free,

Till sense call'd down to calm reality.

A few short weeks, and then, unbound the chains

Which held her to another's woes or pains,

Farewell to dusky streets and shrouded skies,

Her treasur'd home should bless her yearning eyes,

And fair as in the days of childish glee

Each grassy nook and wooded haunt should be.

Yet ever, as one sorrow pass'd away,

Another call'd the tender one to stay,

And, where so late she shared the bright glad mirth,

The phantom Grief sat cowering at the hearth.

So days and weeks pass'd on and grew to years,

Unwept by Mary, save for others' tears.

As a fond nurse, that from the mother's breast

Lulls the tired infant to its quiet rest,

First stills each sound, then lets the curtain fall

To cast a dim and sleepy light o'er all,

So age grew gently o'er each wearied sense

A deepening shade to smooth the parting hence.

Each cherish'd accent, each familiar tone

Fell from her daily music, one by one;

Still her attentive looks could rightly guess

What moving lips by sound could not express,

O'er each loved face next came a filmy veil,

And shine and shadow from her sight did fail.

And, last of all, the solemn change they saw

Depriving Death of half its regal awe;

The mind sank down to childishness, and they,

Relying on her counsel day by day

(As some lone wanderer, from his home afar,

Takes for his guide some fix'd and well-known star,

Till clouds come wafting o'er its trembling light,

And leave him wilder'd in the pathless night),

Sought her changed face with strange uncertain gaze,

Still praying her to lead them through the maze.

 They pitied her lone fate, and deemed it sad;

Yet as in early childhood she was glad;

No sense had she of change, or loss of thought,

With those around her no communion sought;

Scarce knew she of her being. Fancy wild

Had placed her in her father's house a child;

It was her mother sang her to her rest;

The lark awoke her, springing from his nest;

The bees sang cheerily the live long day,

Lurking 'mid flowers wherever she did play;

The Sabbath bells rang as in years gone by,

Swelling and falling on the soft wind's sigh;

Her little sisters knelt with her in prayer,

And nightly did her father's blessing share;

So, wrapt in glad imaginings, her life

Stole on with all her sweet young memories rife.

I often think (if by this mortal light

We e'er can read another's lot aright),

That for her loving heart a blessing came,

Unseen by many, clouded by a name;

And all the outward fading from the world

Was like the flower at night, when it has furled

Its golden leaves, and lapped them round its heart,

To nestle closer in its sweetest part.

Yes! angel voices called her childhood back,

Blotting out life with its dim sorrowy track;

Her secret wish was ever known in heaven,

And so in mystery was the answer given.

In sadness many mourned her latter years,

But blessing shone behind that mist of tears,

And, as the child she deemed herself, she lies

In gentle slumber, till the dead shall rise.

Articles and Sketches
Clopton Hall

From W. Howitt's *Visits to Remarkable Places*, 1840

This account of a visit to Clopton House, written in 1838, is Mrs. Gaskell's first separate contribution to literature. It took the form of a letter addressed to William Howitt, after reading his *Visits to Remarkable Places*, and was included in his *Visit to Stratford-on-Avon*, published in 1840. The Mr. and Mrs. W— mentioned here are Mr. and Mrs. Wyatt. The oil-painting of Charlotte Clopton "with paly gold hair" now hangs on the staircase of Clopton House.

I WONDER if you know Clopton Hall, about a mile from Stratford-on-Avon. Will you allow me to tell you of a very happy day I once spent there? I was at school in the neighbourhood, and one of my schoolfellows was the daughter of a Mr. W—, who then lived at Clopton. Mrs. W— asked a party of the girls to go and spend a long afternoon, and we set off one beautiful autumn day, full of delight and wonder respecting the place we were going to see. We passed through desolate half-cultivated fields, till we came within sight of the house—a large, heavy, compact, square brick building, of that deep, dead red almost approaching to purple. In front was a large formal court, with the massy pillars surmounted with two grim monsters; but the walls of the court were broken down, and the grass grew as rank and wild within the enclosure as in the raised avenue walk down which we had come. The flowers were tangled with nettles, and it was only as we approached the house that we saw the single yellow rose and the Austrian briar trained into something like order round the deep-set diamond-paned windows. We trooped into the hall, with its tesselated marble floor, hung round with strange portraits of people who had been in their graves two hundred years at least; yet the colours were so fresh, and in some instances they were so life-like, that looking merely at the faces, I almost fancied the originals might be sitting in the parlour beyond. More completely to carry us back, as it were, to the days of the civil wars, there was a sort of military map hung up, well finished with pen and ink, shewing the stations of the respective armies, and with old-fashioned writing beneath, the names of the principal towns, setting forth the strength of the garrison, etc. In this hall we were met by our kind hostess, and told we might ramble where we liked, in the house or out of the house, taking care to be in the 'recessed parlour' by tea-time. I preferred to wander up the wide shelving oak staircase, with its massy balustrade all crumbling and worm-eaten. The family then residing at the hall did not occupy one-half—no, not one-third of the rooms; and the old-fashioned furniture was undisturbed in the greater part of them. In one of the bed-rooms (said to be haunted), and which, with its close pent-up atmosphere and the long shadows of evening creeping on, gave me an 'eerie' feeling, hung a portrait so singularly beautiful! a sweet-looking girl, with paly gold hair combed back from her forehead and falling in wavy ringlets on her neck, and with eyes that 'looked like violets filled with dew,' for there was the glittering of unshed tears before their deep dark blue—and that was the likeness of

Charlotte Clopton, about whom there was so fearful a legend told at Stratford church. In the time of some epidemic, the sweating-sickness or the plague, this young girl had sickened, and to all appearance died. She was buried with fearful haste in the vaults of Clopton chapel, attached to Stratford church, but the sickness was not stayed. In a few days another of the Cloptons died, and him they bore to the ancestral vault; but as they descended the gloomy stairs, they saw by the torchlight, Charlotte Clopton in her grave-clothes leaning against the wall; and when they looked nearer, she was indeed dead, but not before, in the agonies of despair and hunger, she had bitten a piece from her white, round shoulder! Of course, she had *walked* ever since. This was 'Charlotte's chamber,' and beyond Charlotte's chamber was a state-chamber carpeted with the dust of many years, and darkened by the creepers which had covered up the windows, and even forced themselves in luxuriant daring through the broken panes. Beyond, again, there was an old Catholic chapel, with a chaplain's room, which had been walled up and forgotten till within the last few years. I went in on my hands and knees, for the entrance was very low. I recollect little in the chapel; but in the chaplain's room were old, and I should think rare, editions of many books, mostly folios. A large yellow-paper copy of Dryden's '*All for Love, or the World Well Lost,*' date 1686, caught my eye, and is the only one I particularly remember. Every here and there, as I wandered, I came upon a fresh branch of a staircase, and so numerous were the crooked, half-lighted passages, that I wondered if I could find my way back again. There was a curious carved old chest in one of these passages, and with girlish curiosity I tried to open it; but the lid was too heavy, till I persuaded one of my companions to help me, and when it was opened, what do you think we saw?—BONES!—but whether human, whether the remains of the lost bride, we did not stay to see, but ran off in partly feigned and partly real terror.

The last of these deserted rooms that I remember, the last, the most deserted, and the saddest was the Nursery—a nursery without children, without singing voices, without merry chiming footsteps! A nursery hung round with its once inhabitants, bold, gallant boys, and fair, arch-looking girls, and one or two nurses with round, fat babies in their arms. Who were they all? What was their lot in life? Sunshine, or storm? or had they been 'loved by the gods, and died young?' The very echoes knew not. Behind the house, in a hollow now wild, damp, and overgrown with elder-bushes, was a well called Margaret's Well, for there had a maiden of the house of that name drowned herself.

I tried to obtain any information I could as to the family of Clopton of Clopton. They had been decaying ever since the civil wars; had for a generation or two been unable to live in the old house of their fathers, but had toiled in London, or abroad, for a livelihood; and the last of the old family, a bachelor, eccentric, miserly, old, and of most filthy habits, if report said true, had died at Clopton Hall but a few months before, a sort of boarder in Mr. W—'s family. He was buried in the gorgeous chapel of the Cloptons in Stratford Church, where you see the banners waving, and the armour hung over one or two splendid monuments. Mr. W— had been the old man's solicitor, and completely in his confidence, and to him he left the estate, encumbered and in bad condition. A year or two afterwards, the heir-at-law, a very distant relation living in Ireland, claimed and obtained the estate, on the plea of undue influence, if not of forgery, on Mr. W—'s part; and the last I heard of our kind entertainers on that day was that they were outlawed, and living at Brussels.

A Greek Wedding

From "Modern Greek Songs," *Household Words*, 1854

Mrs. Gaskell was a keen student of popular customs and traditions, and several of her articles prove how observant and delightfully inquisitive she always was, where an opportunity of investigating any tradition or custom presented itself.

NOW let us hear about the marriage-songs. Life seems like an opera amongst the modern Greeks; all emotions, all events, require the relief of singing. But a marriage is a singing time among human beings as well as birds. Among the Greeks the youth of both sexes are kept apart, and do not meet excepting on the occasion of some public feast, when the young Greek makes choice of his bride, and asks her parents for their consent. If they give it, all is arranged for the betrothal; but the young people are not allowed to see each other again until that event. There are parts of Greece where the young man is allowed to declare his passion himself to the object of it. Not in words, however, does he breathe his tender suit. He tries to meet with her in some path, or other place in which he may throw her an apple or a flower. If the former missile be chosen, one can only hope that the young lady is apt at catching, as a blow from a moderately hard apple is rather too violent a token of love. After this apple or flower throwing, his only chance of meeting with his love is at the fountain; to which all Greek maidens go to draw water, as Rebekah went, of old, to the well.

The ceremony of betrothal is very simple. On an appointed evening, the relations of the lovers meet together in the presence of a priest, either at the house of the father of the future husband, or at that of the parents of the bride elect. After the marriage contract is signed, two young girls bring in the affianced maiden—who is covered all over with a veil—and present her to her lover, who takes her by the hand, and leads her up to the priest. They exchange rings before him, and he gives them his blessing. The bride then retires; but all the rest of the company remain, and spend the day in merry-making and drinking the health of the young couple. The interval between the betrothal and the marriage may be but a few hours; it may be months and it may be years; but, whatever the length of time, the lovers must never meet again until the wedding day comes. Three or four days before that time, the father or mother of the bride send round their notes of invitation; each of which is accompanied by the present of a bottle of wine. The answers come in with even more substantial accompaniments. Those who have great pleasure in accepting, send a present with their reply; the most frequent is a ram or lamb dressed up with ribands and flowers; but the poorest send their quarter of mutton as their contribution to the wedding-feast.

The eve of the marriage, or rather during the night, the friends on each side go to deck out the bride and groom for the approaching ceremony. The bridegroom is shaved by his paranymph or groom's man, in a very grave and dignified manner, in the presence of all the young ladies invited. Fancy the attitude of the bridegroom, anxious and motionless under the hands of his unpractised barber, his nose held lightly up between a finger and thumb, while a crowd of young girls look gravely on at the graceful operation! The bride is decked, for her part, by her young companions; who dress her in white, and cover her all over with a long veil made of the finest stuff. Early the next morning the young man and all his friends come forth, like a bridegroom out of his chamber, to seek the bride, and carry her off from her father's house. Then she, in songs as ancient as the ruins of the old temples that lie around her, sings her sorrowful farewell to the father who has cared for her and protected her hitherto; to the mother who has borne her and cherished her; to the companions of her maidenhood; to her early home; to the fountain whence she daily fetched water; to the trees which shaded her childish play; and every now and then she gives way to natural tears; then, according to immemorial usage, the paranymph turns to the glad yet sympathetic procession and says in a sentence which has become proverbial on such occasions—"Let her alone! she weeps!" To which she must make answer, "Lead me away, but let me weep!" After the *cortège* has borne the bride to the house of her husband, the whole party adjourn to church, where the religious ceremony is performed. Then they return to the dwelling of the bridegroom, where they all sit down and feast; except the bride, who remains veiled, standing alone, until the middle of the banquet, when the paranymph draws near, unlooses the veil, which falls down, and she stands blushing, exposed to the eyes of all the guests. The next day is given up to the performance of dances peculiar to a wedding. The third day the relations and friends meet all together, and lead the bride to the fountain, from the waters of which she fills a new earthen vessel; and into which she throws various provisions. They afterwards dance in circles round the fountain.

Tenir un Salon

From "Company Manners," *Household Words*, 1854

This article gives an insight into the remark which has often been made, "if anybody in Manchester knew how *tenir un salon* it was certainly Mrs. Gaskell"; she studied and practised the art of entertaining to perfection.

MADAME DE SABLÉ had all the requisites which enabled her *tenir un salon* with honour to herself and pleasure to her friends.

Apart from this crowning accomplishment, the good French lady seems to have been commonplace enough. She was well-born, well-bred, and the company she kept must have made her tolerably intelligent. She was married to a dull husband, and doubtless had her small flirtations after she early became a widow; M. Cousin hints at them, but they were never scandalous or prominently before the public. Past middle life, she took to the process of "making her salvation," and inclined to the Port-Royalists. She was given to liking dainty things to eat, in spite of her Jansenism. She had a female friend that she quarrelled with, off and on, during her life. And (to wind up something like Lady O'Looney, of famous memory) she knew how *tenir un salon*. M. Cousin tells us that she was remarkable in no one thing or quality, and attributes to that single, simple fact the success of her life.

Now, since I have read these memoirs of Madame de Sablé, I have thought much and deeply thereupon. At first, I was inclined to laugh at the extreme importance which was attached to this art of "receiving company"—no, that translation will not do!—"holding a drawing-room" is even worse, because that implies the state and reserve of royalty;—shall we call it the art of "Sabléing"? But when I thought of my experience in English society—of the evenings dreaded before they came, and sighed over in recollection, because they were so ineffably dull—I saw that, to Sablé well, did require, as M. Cousin implied, the union of many excellent qualities and not-to-be-disputed little graces. I asked some French people if they could give me the recipe, for it seemed most likely to be traditional, if not still extant in their nation. I offer to you their ideas, fragmentary though they be, and then I will tell you some of my own; at last, perhaps, with the addition of yours, oh most worthy readers! we may discover the lost art of Sabléing.

Said the French lady: "A woman to be successful in Sabléing must be past youth, yet not past the power of attracting. She must do this by her sweet and gracious manners, and quick, ready tact in perceiving those who have not had their share of attention, or leading the conversation away from any subject which may give pain to any one present." "Those rules hold good in England," said I. My friend went on: "She should never be prominent in anything; she should keep silence as long as anyone else will talk; but, when conversation flags, she should throw herself into the breach with the same spirit with which I notice that the young ladies of the house, where a ball is given, stand quietly by till the dancers are tired, and then spring into the arena, to carry on the spirit and the music till the others are ready to begin again."

"But," said the French gentleman, "even at this time, when subjects for conversation are wanted, she should rather suggest than enlarge—ask questions rather than give her own opinions."

"To be sure," said the lady. "Madame Récamier, whose salons were the most perfect of this century, always withheld her opinions on books, or men, or measures, until all around her had given theirs; then she, as it were, collected and harmonised them, saying a kind thing here, and a gentle thing there, and speaking ever with her own quiet sense, till people the most oppressed learnt to understand each other's point of view, which it is a great thing for opponents to do."

"Then the number of the people whom you receive is another consideration. I should say not less than twelve or more than twenty," continued the gentleman. "The evenings should be appointed—say weekly—fortnightly at the beginning of January, which is our season. Fix an early hour for opening the room. People are caught then in their freshness, before they become exhausted by other parties."

The lady spoke: "For my part, I prefer catching my friends after they have left the grander balls or receptions. One hears then the remarks, the wit, the reason, and the satire which they had been storing up during the evening of imposed silence or of ceremonious speaking."

"A little good-humoured satire is a very agreeable sauce," replied the gentleman, "but it must be good-humoured, and the listeners must be good-humoured; above all, the conversation must be general, and not the chat, chat, chat up in a corner, by which the English so often distinguish themselves. You do not go into society to exchange secrets with your intimate friends; you go to render yourselves agreeable to everyone present, and to help all to pass a happy evening."

"Strangers should not be admitted," said the lady, taking up the strain. "They would not start fair with the others; they would be ignorant of the allusions that refer to conversations on the previous evenings; they would not understand the—what shall I call it—slang? I mean those expressions having relation to past occurrences, or bygone witticisms common to all those who are in the habit of meeting."

"Madame de Duras and Madame Récamier never made advances to any stranger. Their *salons* were the best that Paris has known in this generation. All who wished to be admitted had to wait and prove their fitness by being agreeable elsewhere: to earn their diploma, as it were, among the circle of these ladies' acquaintances; and, at last, it was a high favour to be received by them."

"They missed the society of many celebrities by adhering so strictly to this unspoken rule," said the gentleman.

"Bah!" said the lady. "Celebrities! what has one to do with them in society? As celebrities, they are simply bores. Because a man has discovered a planet, it does not follow that he can converse agreeably, even on his own subjects; often people are drained dry by one action or expression of their lives— drained dry for all the purposes of a 'salon.' The writer of books, for instance, cannot afford to talk twenty pages for nothing, so he is either profoundly silent, or else he gives you the mere rinsings of his mind. I am speaking now of him as a mere celebrity, and justifying the wisdom of the ladies we were speaking of, in not seeking after such people; indeed, in being rather shy of them. Some of their friends were the most celebrated people of their day, but they were received in their old capacity of agreeable men; a higher character, by far. Then," said she, turning to me, "I believe that you English spoil the perfection of conversation by having your rooms brilliantly lighted for an evening, the charm of which depends on what one hears, as for an evening when youth and beauty are to display themselves among flowers and festoons, and every kind of pretty ornament. I would never have a room affect people as being dark on their first entrance into it; but there is a kind of moonlight as compared to sunlight, in which people talk more freely and naturally; where shy people will enter upon a conversation without a dread of every change of colour or involuntary movement being seen—just as we are always more confidential over a fire than anywhere else—as women talk most openly in the dimly-lighted bedroom at curling-time."

"Away with your shy people," said the gentleman. "Persons who are self-conscious, thinking of an involuntary redness or paleness, an unbecoming movement of the countenance, more than the subject of which they are talking, should not go into society at all. But, because women are so much more liable to this nervous weakness than men, the preponderance of people in a salon should always be on the side of the men."

I do not think I gained more hints as to the lost art from my French friends. Let us see if my own experience in England can furnish any more ideas.

First, let us take the preparations to be made before our house, our room, or our lodgings can be made to receive society. Of course, I am not meaning the preparations needed for dancing or musical evenings. I am taking those parties which have pleasant conversation and happy social intercourse for their affirmed intention. They may be dinners, suppers, tea—I don't care what they are called, provided their end is defined. If your friends have not dined, and it suits you to give them a dinner, in the name of Lucullus, let them dine; but take care that there shall be something besides the mere food and wine to make their fattening agreeable at the time and pleasant to remember, otherwise you had better pack up for each his portions of the dainty dish, and send it separately, in hot-water trays, so that he can eat comfortably behind a door, like Sancho Panza, and have done with it. And yet I don't see why we should be like ascetics; I fancy there is a grace of preparation, a sort of festive trumpet call, that is right and proper to distinguish the day on which we receive our friends from common days, unmarked by such white stones. The thought and care we take for them to set before them of our best, may imply some self-denial on our less fortunate days. I have been in houses where all, from the scullion-maid upward, worked double tides gladly, because "Master's friends" were coming; and every thing must be nice, and good, and all the rooms must look bright, and clean, and pretty. And, as "a merry heart goes all the way," preparations made in this welcoming, hospitable spirit, never seem to tire anyone half so much as where servants instinctively feel that it has been said in the parlour, "We must have so-and-so," or "Oh, dear! we have never had the so-and-so's." Yes, I like a little pomp, and luxury, and stateliness, to mark our happy days of receiving friends as a festival; but I do not think I would throw my power of procuring luxuries solely into the eating and drinking line.

My friends would probably be surprised (some wear caps, and some wigs) if I provided them with garlands of flowers, after the manner of the ancient Greeks; but, put flowers on the table (none of your shams, wax or otherwise; I prefer an honest wayside root of primroses, in a common vase of white ware, to the grandest bunch of stiff rustling artificial rarities in a silver épergne). A flower or two by the side of each person's plate would not be out of the way, as to expense, and would be a very agreeable, pretty piece of mute welcome. Cooks and scullion-maids, acting in the sympathetic spirit I have described, would do their very best, from boiling the potatoes well, to sending in all the dishes in the best possible order. I think I would have every imaginary dinner sent up on the "original" Mr. Walker's plan; each dish separately, hot and hot. I have an idea that, when I go to live in Utopia (not before next Christmas), I will have a kind of hot-water sideboard, such as I think I have seen in great houses, and that nothing shall appear on the table but what is pleasant to the eye. However simple the food, I would do it and my friends (and may I not add the Giver?) the respect of presenting it at table as well-cooked, as eatable, as wholesome as my poor means allowed; and to this end rather than to a variety of dishes, would I direct my care. We have no associations with beef and mutton; geese may remind us of the Capitol, and peacocks of Juno; a pigeon-pie, of the simplicity of Venus' doves, but who thinks of the leafy covert which has been her home in life, when he sees a roasted hare? Now, flowers as an ornament do lead our thoughts away from their present beauty and fragrance. I am almost sure Madame de Sablé had flowers in her salon; and, as she was fond of dainties herself, I can fancy her smooth benevolence of character, taking delight in some personal preparations made in the morning for the anticipated friends of the evening. I can fancy her stewing sweetbreads in a silver saucepan, or dressing salad with her delicate, plump, white hands—not that I ever saw a silver saucepan. I was formerly ignorant enough to think that they were only used in the Sleeping Beauty's kitchen, or in the preparations for the marriage of Ricquet-with-the-Tuft; but I have been assured that there are such things, and that they impart a most delicate flavour, or no flavour to the victuals cooked therein; so I assert again, Madame de Sablé cooked sweetbreads for her friends in a silver saucepan; but never to fatigue herself with those previous labours. She knew the true taste of her friends too well; they cared for her, firstly, as an element in their agreeable evening—the silver saucepan in which they were all to meet; the oil in which their several ingredients were to be softened of what was harsh or discordant—very secondary would be their interest in her sweetbreads.

"Of sweetbreads they'll get mony an ane,

  Of Sablé ne'er anither."

On Furnishing, Conversation, and Games

From "Company Manners," *Household Words*, 1854

I HEARD, or read, lately, that we make a great mistake in furnishing our reception-rooms with all the light and delicate colours, the profusion of ornament, and flecked and spotted chintzes, if we wish to show off the human face and figure; that our ancestors and the great painters knew better, with their somewhat sombre and heavy-tinted backgrounds, relieving, or throwing out into full relief, the rounded figure and the delicate peach-like complexion.

I fancy Madame de Sablé's salon was furnished with deep warm soberness of tone; lighted up by flowers, and happy animated people, in a brilliancy of dress which would be lost nowadays against our satin walls and flower-bestrewn carpets, and gilding, gilding everywhere. Then, somehow, conversation must have flowed naturally into sense or nonsense, as the case might be. People must have gone to her house well prepared for either lot. It might be that wit would come uppermost, sparkling, crackling, leaping, calling out echoes all around; or the same people might talk with all their might and wisdom, on some grave and important subject of the day, in that manner which we have got into the way of calling "earnest," but which term has struck me as being slightly flavoured by cant, ever since I heard of an "earnest uncle." At any rate, whether grave or gay, people did not go up to Madame de Sablé's salons with a set purpose of being either the one or the other. They were carried away by the subject of the conversation, by the humour of the moment. I have visited a good deal among a set of people who piqued themselves on being rational. We have talked what they called sense, but what I call platitudes, till I have longed, like Southey, in the "Doctor," to come out with some interminable nonsensical word (Aballibogibouganorribo was his, I think) as a relief for my despair at not being able to think of anything more that was sensible. It would have done me good to have said it, and I could have started afresh on the rational tack. But I never did. I sank into inane silence, which I hope was taken for wisdom. One of this set paid a relation of mine a profound compliment, for so she meant it to be: "Oh, Miss F.; you are so trite!" But as it is not in everyone's power to be rational, and "trite," at all times and in all places, discharging our sense at a given place, like water from a fireman's hose; and as some of us are cisterns rather than fountains, and may have our stores exhausted, why is it not more general to call in other aids to conversation, in order to enable us to pass an agreeable evening?

But I will come back to this presently. Only let me say that there is but one thing more tiresome than an evening when everybody tries to be profound and sensible, and that is an evening when everybody tries to be witty. I have a disagreeable sense of effort and unnaturalness at both times; but the everlasting attempt, even when it succeeds, to be clever and amusing is the worst of the two. People try to say brilliant rather than true things; they not only catch eager hold of the superficial and ridiculous in other persons and in events generally, but, from constantly looking out for subjects for jokes, and "mots," and satire, they become possessed of a kind of sore susceptibility themselves, and are afraid of their own working selves, and dare not give way to any expression of feeling, or any noble indignation or enthusiasm. This kind of wearying wit is far different from humour, which wells up and forces its way out irrepressibly, and calls forth smiles and laughter, but not very far apart from tears. Depend upon it, some of Madame de Sablé's friends had been moved in a most abundant and genial measure. They knew how to narrate, too. Very simple, say you? I say, no! I believe the art of telling a story is born with some people, and these have it to perfection; but all might acquire some expertness in it, and ought to do so, before launching out into the muddled, complex, hesitating, broken, disjointed, poor, bald, accounts of events which have neither unity, nor colour, nor life, nor end in them, that one sometimes hears.

But as to the rational parties that are in truth so irrational, when all talk up to an assumed character instead of showing themselves what they really are, and so extending each other's knowledge of the infinite and beautiful capacities of human nature—whenever I see the grave sedate faces, with their good but anxious expression, I remember how I was once, long ago, at a party like this; everyone had brought out his or her wisdom, and aired it for the good of the company; one or two had, from a sense of duty, and without any special living interest in the matter, improved us by telling us of some new scientific discovery, the details of which were all and each of them wrong, as I learnt afterwards; if they had been right, we should not have been any the wiser—and just at the pitch when any more useful information might have brought on congestion of the brain, a stranger to the town—a beautiful, audacious, but most feminine romp—proposed a game, and such a game, for us wise men of Gotham! But she (now long still and quiet after her bright life, so full of pretty pranks) was a creature whom all who looked on loved; and with grave, hesitating astonishment we knelt round a circular table at her word of command. She made one of the circle, and producing a feather out of some sofa pillow, she told us she should blow it up into the air, and whichever of us it floated near, must puff away to keep it from falling on the table. I suspect we all looked like Keeley in the "Camp at Chobham," and were surprised at our own obedience to this ridiculous, senseless mandate, given with a graceful imperiousness, as if it were too royal to be disputed. We knelt on, puffing away with the utmost intentness, looking like a set of elderly—

"Fools!" No, my dear sir. I was going to say elderly cherubim. But making fools of ourselves was better than making owls, as we had been doing.

On Books

From "Company Manners," *Household Words*, 1854

I HAVE said nothing of books. Yet I am sure that, if Madame de Sablé lived now, they would be seen in her salon as part of its natural indispensable furniture; not brought out, and strewed here and there when "company was coming," but as habitual presences in her room, wanting which, she would want a sense of warmth and comfort and companionship. Putting out books as a sort of preparation for an evening, as a means for making it pass agreeably, is running a great risk. In the first place, books are by such people, and on such occasions, chosen more for their outside than their inside. And in the next, they are the "mere material with which wisdom (or wit) builds"; and if persons don't know how to use the material, they will suggest nothing. I imagine Madame de Sablé would have the volumes she herself was reading, or those which, being new, contained any matter of present interest, left about, as they would naturally be. I could also fancy that her guests would not feel bound to talk continually, whether they had anything to say or not, but that there might be pauses of not unpleasant silence—a quiet darkness out of which they might be certain that the little stars would glimmer soon. I can believe that in such pauses of repose, some one might open a book, and catch on a suggestive sentence, might dash off again into a full flow of conversation. But I cannot fancy any grand preparations for what was to be said among people, each of whom brought the best dish in bringing himself; and whose own store of living, individual thought and feeling, and mother-wit, would be indefinitely better than any cut-and-dry determination to devote the evening to mutual improvement. If people are really good and wise, their goodness and their wisdom flow out unconsciously, and benefit like sunlight. So, books for reference, books for impromptu suggestion, but never books to serve for texts to a lecture. Engravings fall under something like the same rules. To some they say everything; to ignorant and unprepared minds, nothing. I remember noticing this in watching how people looked at a very valuable portfolio belonging to an acquaintance of mine, which contained engraved and authentic portraits of almost every possible person; from king and kaiser down to notorious beggars and criminals; including all the celebrated men, women, and actors, whose likenesses could be obtained. To some, this portfolio gave food for observation, meditation, and conversation. It brought before them every kind of human tragedy—every variety of scenery and costume and grouping in the background, thronged with figures called up by their imagination. Others took them up and laid them down, simply saying, "This is a pretty face!" "Oh, what a pair of eyebrows!" "Look at this queer dress!"

Yet, after all, having something to take up and to look at is a relief, and of use to persons who, without being self-conscious, are nervous from not being accustomed to society, O Cassandra! Remember when you, with your rich gold coins of thought, with your noble power of choice expression, were set down, and were thankful to be set down, to look at some paltry engravings, just because people did not know how to get at your ore, and you did not care a button whether they did or not, and were rather bored by their attempts, the end of which you never found out. While I, with my rattling tinselly rubbish, was thought "agreeable and an acquisition!" You would have been valued at Madame de Sablé's, where the sympathetic and intellectual stream of conversation would have borne you and your golden fragments away with it by its soft, resistless, gentle force.

French Receptions

From "French Life," *Fraser's Magazine*, 1864

Mrs. Gaskell spent many happy days in France, often staying in Paris with the eccentric but faithful Madame Mohl. When on holiday there in 1862 she kept a diary which supplied her with the material for the three bright, chatty papers, which appeared anonymously in *Fraser's Magazine* in April, May, and June, 1864.

OUR conversation drifted along to the old French custom of receiving in bed. It was so highly correct, that the newly-made wife of the Duc de St. Simon went to bed, after the early dinner of those days, in order to receive her wedding-visits. The Duchesse de Maine, of the same date, used to have a bed in the ball-room at Sceaux, and to lie (or half-sit) there, watching the dancers. I asked if there was not some difference in dress between the day- and the night-occupation of the bed. But Madame A— seemed to think there was very little. The custom was put an end to by the Revolution; but one or two great ladies preserved the habit until their death. Madame A— had often seen Madame de Villette receiving in bed; she always wore white gloves, which Madame A— imagined was the only difference between the toilet of day and night. Madame de Villette was the adopted daughter of Voltaire, and, as such, all the daring innovators upon the ancient modes of thought and behaviour came to see her, and pay her their respects. She was also the widow of the Marquis de Villette, and as such she received the homage of the ladies and gentlemen of the *ancien régime*.

Altogether her weekly receptions must have been very amusing, from Madame A—'s account. The old Marquise lay in bed; around her sat the company, and, as the climax of the visit, she would desire her *femme de chambre* to hand round the heart of Voltaire, which he had bequeathed to her, and which she preserved in a little golden case. Then she would begin and tell anecdotes about the great man; great to her, and with some justice. For he had been travelling in the South of France, and had stopped to pass the night in a friend's house, where he was very much struck by the deep sadness on the face of a girl of seventeen, one of his friend's daughters; and, on inquiring the cause, he found out that, in order to increase the portion of the others, this young woman was to be sent into a convent—a destination which she extremely disliked. Voltaire saved her from it by adopting her, and promising to give her a dot sufficient to insure her a respectable marriage. She had lived with him for some time at Ferney before she became Marquise de Villette. (You will remember the connexion existing between her husband's family and Madame de Maintenon, as well as with Bolingbroke's second wife.)

Madame de Villette must have been an exceedingly *inconséquente* person, to judge from Madame A—'s very amusing description of her conversation.

Her sentences generally began with an assertion which was disproved by what followed. Such as, "It was wonderful with what ease Voltaire uttered witty impromptus. He would shut himself up in his library all the morning, and in the evening he would gracefully lead the conversation to the point he desired, and then bring out the verse or the epigram he had composed for the occasion, in the most unpremeditated and easy manner!" Or, "He was the most modest of men. When a stranger arrived at Ferney, his first care was to take him round the village, and to show him all the improvements he had made, the good he had done, the church he had built. And he was never easy until he had given the new-comer the opportunity of hearing his most recent compositions." Then she would show an old grandfather's high-backed, leather arm-chair in which she said he wrote his *Henriade*, forgetting that he was at that time quite a young man.

Madame A— said that Madame de Villette's receptions were worth attending, because they conveyed an idea of the ways of society before the Revolution.

February 16th, 1863.—Again in Paris! and, as I remember a young English girl saying with great delight, "we need never be an evening at home!" But her visions were of balls; our possibilities are the very pleasant one of being allowed to go in on certain evenings of the week to the houses of different friends, sure to find them at home ready to welcome any who may come in. Thus, on Mondays, Madame de Circourt receives; Tuesdays, Madame —; Wednesdays, Madame de M—; Thursdays, Monsieur G—; and so on. There is no preparation of entertainment; a few more lights, perhaps a Baba, or cake savouring strongly of rum, and a little more tea is provided. Every one is welcome, and no one is expected. The visitors may come dressed just as they would be at home; or in full toilette, on their way to balls and other gaieties. They go without any formal farewell; whence, I suppose, our expression "French leave."

Of course the agreeableness of these informal receptions depends on many varying circumstances, and I doubt if they would answer in England. A certain talent is required in the hostess; and this talent is not kindness of heart, or courtesy, or wit, or cleverness, but that wonderful union of all these qualities, with a dash of intuition besides, which we call tact. Madame Récamier had it in perfection. Her wit or cleverness was of the passive or receptive order; she appreciated much, and originated little. But she had the sixth sense, which taught her when to speak, and when to be silent. She drew out other people's powers by her judicious interest in what they said; she came in with sweet words before the shadow of a coming discord was perceived. It could not have been all art; it certainly was not all nature. As I have said, invitations are not given for these evenings. Madame receives on

Tuesdays. Any one may go. But there are temptations for special persons which can be skilfully thrown out. You may say in the hearing of one whom you wish to attract, "I expect M. Guizot will be with us on Tuesday; he is just come back to Paris"—and the bait is pretty sure to take; and of course you can vary your fly with your fish. Yet, in spite of all experience and all chances, some houses are invariably dull. The people who would be dreary at home, go to be dreary there. The gay, bright spirits are always elsewhere; or perhaps come in, make their bows to the hostess, glance round the room, and quietly vanish. I cannot make out why this is; but so it is.

But a delightful reception, which will never take place again—a more than charming hostess, whose virtues, which were the real source of her charms, have ere this "been planted in our Lord's garden"—awaited us to-night. In this one case I must be allowed to chronicle a name—that of Madame de Circourt—so well known, so fondly loved, and so deeply respected. Of her accomplished husband, still among us, I will for that reason say nothing, excepting that it was, to all appearances, the most happy and congenial marriage I have ever seen. Madame de Circourt was a Russian by birth, and possessed that gift for languages which is almost a national possession. This was the immediate means of her obtaining the strong regard and steady friendship of so many distinguished men and women of different countries. You will find her mentioned as a dear and valued friend in several memoirs of the great men of the time. I have heard an observant Englishman, well qualified to speak, say she was the cleverest woman he ever knew. And I have also heard one, who is a saint for goodness, speak of Madame de Circourt's piety and benevolence and tender kindness, as unequalled among any woman she had ever known. I think it is Dekker who speaks of our Saviour as "the first true gentleman that ever lived." We may choose to be shocked at the freedom of expression used by the old dramatist; but is it not true? Is not Christianity the very core of the heart of all gracious courtesy? I am sure it was so with Madame de Circourt. There never was a house where the weak and dull and humble got such kind and unobtrusive attention, or felt so happy and at home. There never was a place that I heard of, where learning and genius and worth were more truly appreciated, and felt more sure of being understood. I have said that I will not speak of the living; but of course every one must perceive that this state could not have existed without the realisation of the old epitaph—

They were so one, it never could be said

Which of them ruled, and which of them obeyed.

There was between them but this one dispute,

'Twas which the other's will should execute.

In the prime of life, in the midst of her healthy relish for all social and intellectual pleasures, Madame de Circourt met with a terrible accident; her dress caught fire, she was fearfully burnt, lingered long and long on a sick-bed, and only arose from it with nerves and constitution shattered for life. Such a trial was enough, both mentally and physically, to cause that form of egotism which too often takes possession of chronic invalids, and which depresses not only their spirits, but the spirits of all who come near them. Madame de Circourt was none of these folks. Her sweet smile was perhaps a shade less bright; but it was quite as ready. She could not go about to serve those who needed her; but, unable to move without much assistance, she sat at her writing-table, thinking and working for others still. She could never again seek out the shy or the slow or the awkward; but, with a pretty, beckoning movement of her hand, she could draw them near her, and make them happy with her gentle sensible words. She would no more be seen in gay, brilliant society; but she had a very active sympathy with the young and the joyful who mingled in it; could plan their dresses for them; would take pains to obtain a supply of pleasant partners at a ball to which a young foreigner was going; and only two or three days before her unexpected death—for she had suffered patiently for so long that no one knew how near the end was—she took much pains to give a great pleasure to a young girl of whom she knew very little, but who, I trust, will never forget her.

Description of Duncombe

From "Mr. Harrison's Confessions," *The Ladies' Companion*, 1851

This is Mrs. Gaskell's first attempt at portraying the bygone life of the little country town of Knutsford, which she has idealised in her stories under six different names, and immortalised as *Cranford*. The beautiful description of the old Cheshire town is true of Knutsford to-day, for fortunately "the hand of the builder" has not yet been allowed to spoil its quaint picturesque beauty.

I WAS too lazy to do much that evening, and sat in the little bow-window which projected over Jocelyn's shop, looking up and down the street. Duncombe calls itself a town, but I should call it a village. Really, looking from Jocelyn's, it is a very picturesque place. The houses are anything but regular; they may be mean in their details; but altogether they look well; they have not that flat unrelieved front, which many towns of far more pretensions present. Here and there a bow-window—every now and then a gable, cutting up against the sky—occasionally a projecting upper story— throws good effect of light and shadow along the street; and they have a queer fashion of their own of colouring the whitewash of some of the houses with a sort of pink blotting-paper tinge, more like the stone of which Mayence is built than anything else. It may be very bad taste, but to my mind it gives a rich warmth to the colouring. Then, here and there a dwelling house has a court in front, with a grass-plot on each side of the flagged walk, and a large tree or two—limes or horse-chestnuts—which send their great projecting upper branches over into the street, making round dry places of shelter on the pavement in the times of summer showers.

A Race for Life Across the Quicksands in Morecambe Bay

From "The Sexton's Hero," *Howitt's Journal*, 1847

The complete story was reprinted together with *Christmas Storms and Sunshine* in a little booklet and presented by Mrs. Gaskell as a contribution to a fête held in Macclesfield for the benefit of the Public Baths and Wash-houses in 1850. A copy of the booklet was sold for two guineas a few years ago. A railway bridge now spans this treacherous part of Morecambe bay.

WELL! we borrowed a shandry, and harnessed my old grey mare, as I used in th' cart, and set off as grand as King George across the sands about three o'clock, for you see it were high-water about twelve, and we'd to go and come back same tide, as Letty could not leave her baby for long. It were a merry afternoon were that; last time I ever saw Letty laugh heartily; and, for that matter, last time I ever laughed downright hearty myself. The latest crossing-time fell about nine o'clock, and we were late at starting. Clocks were wrong; and we'd a piece of work chasing a pig father had given Letty to take home; we bagged him at last, and he screeched and screeched in the back part o' th' shandry, and we laughed and they laughed; and in the midst of all the merriment the sun set, and that sobered us a bit, for then we knew what time it was. I whipped the old mare, but she was a deal beener than she was in the morning, and would neither go quick up nor down the brows, and they've not a few 'twixt Kellet and the shore. On the sands it were worse. They were very heavy, for the fresh had come down after the rains we'd had. Lord! how I did whip the poor mare, to make the most of the red light as yet lasted. You, maybe, don't know the sands, gentlemen! From Bolton side, where we started from, it is better than six mile to Cart Lane, and two channels to cross, let alone holes and quicksands. At the second channel from us the guide waits, all during crossing-time from sunrise to sunset; but for the three hours on each side high-water he's not there, in course. He stays after sunset if he's forespoken, not else. So now you know where we were that awful night. For we'd crossed the first channel about two mile, and it were growing darker and darker above and around us, all but one red line of light above the hills, when we came to a hollow (for all the sands look so flat, there's many a hollow in them where you lose all sight of the shore). We were longer than we should ha' been in crossing the hollow, the sand was so quick; and when we came up again, there, against the blackness, was the white line of the rushing tide coming up the bay! It looked not a mile from us; and when the wind blows up the bay it comes swifter than a galloping horse. "Lord help us!" said I; and then I were sorry I'd spoken, to frighten Letty; but the words were crushed out of my heart by the terror. I felt her shiver up by my side and clutch my coat. And as if the pig (as had screeched himself hoarse some time ago) had found out the danger we were all in, he took to squealing again, enough to bewilder any man. I cursed him between my teeth for his noise; and yet it was God's answer to my prayer, blind sinner as I was. Ay! you may smile, sir, but God can work through many a scornful thing, if need be.

By this time the mare was all in a lather, and trembling and panting, as if in mortal fright; for, though we were on the last bank afore the second channel, the water was gathering up her legs; and she so tired out! When we came close to the channel she stood still, and not all my flogging could get her to stir; she fairly groaned aloud, and shook in a terrible quaking way. Till now Letty had not spoken; only held my coat tightly. I heard her say something, and bent down my head.

"I think, John—I think—I shall never see baby again!"

And then she sent up such a cry—so loud, and shrill, and pitiful! It fairly maddened me. I pulled out my knife to spur on the old mare, that it might end one way or the other, for the water was stealing sullenly up to the very axle-tree, let alone the white waves that knew no mercy in their steady advance. That one quarter of an hour, sir, seemed as long as all my life since. Thoughts and fancies, and dreams and memory ran into each other. The mist, the heavy mist, that was like a ghastly curtain, shutting us in for death, seemed to bring with it the scents of the flowers that grew around our own threshold; it might be, for it was falling on them like blessed dew, though to us it was a shroud. Letty told me after that she heard her baby crying for her, above the gurgling of the rising waters, as plain as ever she heard anything; but the sea-birds were skirling, and the pig shrieking; I never caught it; it was miles away, at any rate.

Just as I'd gotten my knife out, another sound was close upon us, blending with the gurgle of the near waters, and the roar of the distant (not so distant though); we could hardly see, but we thought we saw something black against the deep lead colour of wave, and mist, and sky. It neared and neared: with slow, steady motion, it came across the channel right to where we were.

Oh, God! it was Gilbert Dawson on his strong bay horse.

Few words did we speak, and little time had we to say them in. I had no knowledge at that moment of past or future—only of one present thought—how to save Letty, and, if I could, myself. I only remembered afterwards that Gilbert said he had been guided by an animal's shriek of terror; I only heard when all was over, that he had been uneasy about our return, because of the depth of fresh, and had borrowed a pillion, and saddled his horse early in the evening, and ridden down to Cart Lane to watch for us. If all had gone well, we should ne'er have heard of it. As it was, Old Jonas told it, the tears down-dropping from his withered cheeks.

We fastened his horse to the shandry. We lifted Letty to the pillion. The waters rose every instant with sullen sound. They were all but in the shandry. Letty clung to the pillion handles, but drooped her head as if she had yet no hope of life. Swifter than thought (and yet he might have had time for thought and for temptation, sir—if he had ridden off with Letty, he would have been saved, not me) Gilbert was in the shandry by my side.

"Quick!" said he, clear and firm. "You must ride before her, and keep her up. The horse can swim. By God's mercy I will follow. I can cut the traces, and if the mare is not hampered with the shandry, she'll carry me safely through. At any rate, you are a husband and a father. No one cares for me."

Do not hate me, gentlemen. I often wish that night was a dream. It has haunted my sleep ever since like a dream, and yet it was no dream. I took his place on the saddle, and put Letty's arms around me, and felt her head rest on my shoulder. I trust in God I spoke some word of thanks; but I can't remember. I only recollect Letty raising her head, and calling out—

"God bless you, Gilbert Dawson, for saving my baby from being an orphan this night." And then she fell against me, as if unconscious.

I took Letty home to her baby, over whom she wept the livelong night. I rode back to the shore about Cart Lane; and to and fro, with weary march, did I pace along the brink of the waters, now and then shouting out into the silence a vain cry for Gilbert. The waters went back and left no trace. Two days afterwards he was washed ashore near Flukeborough. The shandry and poor old mare were found half-buried in a heap of sand by Arnside Knot. As far as we could guess, he had dropped his knife while trying to cut the traces, and so had lost all chance of life. Any rate, the knife was found in a cleft of the shaft.

Advice to a Young Doctor

From "Mr. Harrison's Confessions," *The Ladies' Companion*, 1851

THE next morning Mr. Morgan came before I had finished breakfast. He was the most dapper little man I ever met. I see the affection with which people cling to the style of dress that was in vogue when they were beaux and belles, and received the most admiration. They are unwilling to believe that their youth and beauty are gone, and think that the prevailing mode is unbecoming. Mr. Morgan will inveigh by the hour together against frock-coats, for instance, and whiskers. He keeps his chin close shaven, wears a black dress-coat, and dark grey pantaloons; and in his morning round to his town patients, he invariably wears the brightest and blackest of Hessian boots, with dangling silk tassels on each side. When he goes home, about ten o'clock, to prepare for his ride to see his country patients, he puts on the most dandy top-boots I ever saw, which he gets from some wonderful bootmaker a hundred miles off. His appearance is what one calls "jemmy"; there is no other word that will do for it. He was evidently a little discomfited when he saw me in my breakfast costume, with the habits which I brought with me from the fellows at Guy's; my feet against the fire-place, my chair balanced on its hind-legs (a habit of sitting which I afterwards discovered he particularly abhorred); slippers on my feet (which, also, he considered a most ungentlemanly piece of untidiness "out of a bedroom"); in short, from what I afterwards learned, every prejudice he had was outraged by my appearance on this first visit of his. I put my book down, and sprang up to receive him. He stood, hat and cane in hand.

"I came to inquire if it would be convenient for you to accompany me on my morning's round, and to be introduced to a few of our friends." I quite detected the little tone of coldness, induced by his disappointment at my appearance, though he never imagined that it was in any way perceptible. "I will be ready directly, sir," said I, and bolted into my bedroom, only too happy to escape his scrutinising eye.

When I returned, I was made aware, by sundry indescribable little coughs and hesitating noises, that my dress did not satisfy him. I stood ready, hat and gloves in hand; but still he did not offer to set off on our round. I grew very red and hot. At length he said:

"Excuse me, my dear young friend, but may I ask if you have no other coat besides that—'cut-away,' I believe you call them? We are rather sticklers for propriety, I believe, in Duncombe; and much depends on a first impression. Let it be professional, my dear sir. Black is the garb of our profession. Forgive my speaking so plainly; but I consider myself *in loco parentis*."

He was so kind, so bland, and, in truth, so friendly that I felt it would be most childish to take offence; but I had a little resentment in my heart at this way of being treated. However, I mumbled, "Oh, certainly, sir, if you wish it," and returned once more to change my coat—my poor cut-away.

"Those coats, sir, give a man rather too much of a sporting appearance, not quite befitting the learned profession; more as if you came down here to hunt than to be the Galen or Hippocrates of the neighbourhood." He smiled graciously, so I smothered a sigh; for, to tell you the truth, I had rather anticipated—and, in fact, had boasted at Guy's of—the runs I hoped to have with the hounds; for Duncombe was in a famous hunting district. But all these ideas were quite dispersed when Mr. Morgan led me to the inn-yard, where there was a horse-dealer on his way to a neighbouring fair, and "strongly advised me"—which in our relative circumstances was equivalent to an injunction—to purchase a little, useful, fast-trotting, brown cob, instead of a fine showy horse, "who would take any fence I put him to," as the horse-dealer assured me. Mr. Morgan was evidently pleased when I bowed to his decision, and gave up all hopes of an occasional hunt.

"My dear young friend, there are one or two hints I should like to give you about your manner. The great Sir Everard Home used to say, 'A general practitioner should either have a very good manner, or a very bad one.' Now, in the latter case, he must be possessed of talents and acquirements sufficient to ensure his being sought after, whatever his manner might be. But the rudeness will give notoriety to these qualifications. Abernethy is a case in point. I rather, myself, question the taste of bad manners. I, therefore, have studied to acquire an attentive, anxious politeness, which combines ease and grace with a tender regard and interest. I am not aware whether I have succeeded (few men do) in coming up to my ideal; but I recommend you to strive after this manner, peculiarly befitting our profession. Identify yourself with your patients, my dear sir. You have sympathy in your good heart, I am sure, to really feel pain when listening to their account of their sufferings, and it soothes them to see the expression of this feeling in your manner. It is, in fact, sir, manners that make the man in our profession. I don't set myself up as an example—far from it; but—— This is Mr. Huttons, our vicar; one of the servants is indisposed, and I shall be glad of the opportunity of introducing you. We can resume our conversation at another time."

I had not been aware that we had been holding a conversation, in which, I believe, the assistance of two persons is required.

The Choice of Odours

From "My Lady Ludlow," *Household Words*, 1858

THE room was full of scent, partly from the flowers outside, and partly from the great jars of pot-pourri inside. The choice of odours was what my lady piqued herself upon, saying nothing showed birth like a keen susceptibility of smell. We never named musk in her presence, her antipathy to it was so well understood through the household; her opinion on the subject was believed to be, that no scent derived from an animal could ever be of a sufficiently pure nature to give pleasure to any person of good family, where, of course, the delicate perception of the senses had been cultivated for generations. She would instance the way in which sportsmen preserve the breed of dogs who have shown keen scent; and how such gifts descend for generations amongst animals, who cannot be supposed to have anything of ancestral pride, or hereditary fancies about them. Musk, then, was never mentioned at Hanbury Court. No more were bergamot or southernwood, although vegetable in their nature. She considered these two latter as betraying a vulgar taste in the person who chose to gather or wear them. She was sorry to notice sprigs of them in the button-hole of any young man in whom she took an interest, either because he was engaged to a servant of hers or otherwise, as he came out of church on a Sunday afternoon. She was afraid that he liked coarse pleasures; and I am not sure if she did not think that his preference for these coarse sweetnesses did not imply a probability that he would take to drinking. But she distinguished between vulgar and common. Violets, pinks, and sweetbriar were common enough; roses and mignonette, for those who had gardens, honeysuckle for those who walked along the bowery lanes; but wearing them betrayed no vulgarity of taste; the queen upon her throne might be glad to smell at a nosegay of the flowers. A beaupot (as we call it) of pinks and roses freshly gathered was placed every morning that they were in bloom on my lady's own particular table. For lasting vegetable odours she preferred lavender and sweet-woodruff to any extract whatever. Lavender reminded her of old customs, she said, and of homely cottage-gardens, and many a cottager made his offering to her of a bundle of lavender. Sweet-woodruff, again, grew in wild, woodland places, where the soil was fine and the air delicate; the poor children used to go and gather it for her up in the woods on the higher lands; and for this service she always rewarded them with bright new pennies, of which my lord, her son, used to send her down a bagful fresh from the Mint in London every February.

Attar of roses, again, she disliked. She said it reminded her of the city and of merchants' wives, over-rich, over-heavy in its perfume. And lilies of the valley somehow fell under the same condemnation. They were most graceful and elegant to look at (my lady was quite candid about this), flower, leaf, and colour—everything was refined about them but the smell. That was too strong. But the great hereditary faculty on which my lady piqued herself, and with reason, for I never met with any person who possessed it, was the power she had of perceiving the delicious odour arising from a bed of strawberries in the late autumn, when the leaves were all fading and dying. *Bacon's Essays* was one of the few books that lay about in my lady's room; and, if you took it up and opened it carelessly, it was sure to fall apart at his "Essay on Gardens." "Listen," her ladyship would say, "to what that great philosopher and statesman says. 'Next to that'—he is speaking of violets, my dear—'is the musk-rose—of which you will remember the great bush at the corner of the south wall just by the Blue Drawing-room windows; that is the old musk-rose, Shakespeare's musk-rose, which is dying out through the kingdom now. But to return to my Lord Bacon: 'Then the strawberry leaves, dying with a most cordial excellent smell.' Now the Hanburys can always smell this excellent cordial odour, and very delicious and refreshing it is. You see, in Lord Bacon's time there had not been so many intermarriages between the court and the city as there have been since the needy days of his Majesty Charles the Second; and altogether, in the time of Queen Elizabeth, the great old families of England were a distinct race, just as a cart-horse is one creature and very useful in its place, and Childers or Eclipse is another creature, though both are of the same species. So the old families have gifts and powers of a different and higher class to what the other orders have. My dear, remember that you try if you can smell the scent of dying strawberry leaves in this next autumn. You have some of Ursula Hanbury's blood in you, and that gives you a chance."

But when October came, I sniffed and sniffed, and all to no purpose; and my lady—who had watched the little experiment rather anxiously—had to give me up as a hybrid. I was mortified, I confess, and thought that it was in some ostentation of her own powers that she ordered the gardener to plant a border of strawberries on that side of the terrace that lay under her windows.

St. Valentine's Day

From "Libbie Marsh's Three Eras," *Howitt's Journal*, 1847

It is noticeable that all Mrs. Gaskell's earlier stories are tales of life in and around Manchester. In 1848 they were re-published under the title *Life in Manchester*, by Cotton Mather Mills, Esq., the *nom de guerre* under which Mrs. Gaskell tried to hide her identity.

HER idea was this; her mother came from the east of England, where, as perhaps you know, they have the pretty custom of sending presents on St. Valentine's Day, with the donor's name unknown, and, of course, the mystery constitutes half the enjoyment. The fourteenth of February was Libbie's birthday too, and many a year, in the happy days of old, had her mother delighted to surprise her with some little gift, of which she more than half guessed the giver, although each Valentine's Day the manner of its arrival was varied. Since then the fourteenth of February had been the dreariest of all the year because the most haunted by memory of departed happiness. But now, this year, if she could not have the old gladness of heart herself, she would try and brighten the life of another. She would save, and she would screw, but she would buy a canary and a cage for that poor little laddie opposite, who wore out his monotonous life with so few pleasures and so much pain.

I doubt I may not tell you here of the anxieties and the fears, of the hopes and the self-sacrifices—all, perhaps, small in the tangible effect as the widow's mite, yet not the less marked by the viewless angels who go about continually among us—which varied Libbie's life before she accomplished her purpose. It is enough to say it was accomplished. The very day before the fourteenth she found time to go with her half-guinea to a barber's who lived near Albemarle Street, and who was famous for his stock of singing-birds. There are enthusiasts about all sorts of things, both good and bad, and many of the weavers in Manchester know and care more about birds than anyone would easily credit. Stubborn, silent, reserved men on many things, you have only to touch on the subject of birds to light up their faces with brightness. They will tell you who won the prizes at the last canary show, where the prize birds may be seen, and give you all the details of those funny but pretty and interesting mimicries of great people's cattle shows. Among these amateurs, Emanuel Morris, the barber, was an oracle.

He took Libbie into his little back room, used for private shaving of modest men, who did not care to be exhibited in the front shop decked out in the full glories of lather; and which was hung round with birds in rude wicker cages, with the exception of those who had won prizes, and were consequently honoured with gilt-wire prisons. The longer and thinner the body of the bird was, the more admiration it received, as far as external beauty went; and when, in addition to this, the colour was deep and clear, and its notes strong and varied, the more did Emanuel dwell upon its perfections. But these were all prize birds; and, on inquiry, Libbie heard, with some little sinking at heart, that their price ran from one to two guineas.

"I'm not over-particular as to shape and colour," said she. "I should like a good singer, that's all!"

She dropped a little in Emanuel's estimation. However, he showed her his good singers, but all were above Libbie's means.

"After all, I don't think I care so much about the singing very loud; it's but a noise after all, and sometimes noise fidgets folks."

"They must be nesh folks as is put out with the singing o' birds," replied Emanuel, rather affronted.

"It's for one who is poorly," said Libbie deprecatingly.

"Well," said he, as if considering the matter, "folk that are cranky often take more to them as shows 'em love than to them as is clever and gifted. Happen yo'd rather have this'n," opening a cage door and calling to a dull-coloured bird, sitting moped up in a corner. "Here—Jupiter, Jupiter!"

The bird smoothed its feathers in an instant, and, uttering a little note of delight, flew to Emanuel, putting his beak to his lips, as if kissing him, and then, perching on his head, it began a gurgling warble of pleasure, not by any means so varied or so clear as the song of the others, but which pleased Libbie more; for she was always one to find out she liked the gooseberries that were accessible, better than the grapes that were beyond her reach. The price, too, was just right, so she gladly took possession of the cage, and hid it under her cloak, preparatory to carrying it home. Emanuel meanwhile was giving her directions as to its food, with all the minuteness of one loving his subject.

"Will it soon get to know anyone?" asked she.

"Give him two days only, and you and he'll be as thick as him and me are now. You've only to open his door and call him, and he'll follow you round the room; but he'll first kiss you, and then perch on your head. He only wants larning, which I have no time to give him, to do many another accomplishment."

"What's his name? I did not rightly catch it."

"Jupiter—it's not common; but the town's overrun with Bobbies and Dickies, and as my birds are thought a bit out o' the way, I like to have better names for 'em, so I just picked a few out o' my lad's school-books. It's just as ready, when you're used to it, to say Jupiter as Dicky."

"I could bring my tongue round to Peter better; would he answer to Peter?" asked Libbie, now on the point of departing.

"Happen he might, but I think he'd come readier to the three syllables."

On Valentine's Day, Jupiter's cage was decked round with ivy leaves, making quite a pretty wreath on the wicker-work; and to one of them was pinned a slip of paper, with these words, written in Libbie's best round hand:

"From your faithful Valentine. Please take notice his name is Peter, and he'll come if you call him, after a bit."

But little work did Libbie do that afternoon; she was so engaged in watching for the messenger who was to bear her present to her little Valentine, and run away as soon as he had delivered up the canary, and explained to whom it was sent.

At last he came; then there was a pause before the woman of the house was at liberty to take it upstairs. Then Libbie saw the little face flush up into a bright colour, the feeble hands tremble with delighted eagerness, the head bent down to try and make out the writing (beyond his power, poor lad, to read), the rapturous turning round of the cage in order to see the canary in every point of view, head, tail, wings, and feet; an intention in which Jupiter, in his uneasiness at being again among strangers, did not second, for he hopped round so as continually to present a full front to the boy. It was a source of never-wearying delight to the little fellow, till daylight closed in; he evidently forgot to wonder who had sent it him, in his gladness at his possession of such a treasure; and when the shadow of his mother darkened on the blind, and the bird had been exhibited, Libbie saw her do what, with all her tenderness, seemed rarely to have entered into her thoughts—she bent down and kissed her boy, in a mother's sympathy with the joy of her child.

The canary was placed for the night between the little bed and window; and when Libbie rose once, to take her accustomed peep, she saw the little arm put fondly round the cage, as if embracing his new treasure even in his sleep. How Jupiter slept this first night is quite another thing.

Whit-Monday in Dunham Park.

From "Libbie Marsh's Three Eras," *Howitt's Journal*, 1847

FOR years has Dunham Park been the favourite resort of the Manchester workpeople; for more years than I can tell; probably ever since "the Duke," by his canals, opened out the system of cheap travelling. Its scenery, too, which presents such a complete contrast to the whirl and turmoil of Manchester; so thoroughly woodland, with its ancestral trees (here and there lightning-blanched); its "verdurous walls"; its grassy walks leading far away into some glade, where you start at the rabbit rustling among the last year's fern, and where the wood-pigeon's call seems the only fitting and accordant sound. Depend upon it, this complete sylvan repose, this accessible quiet, this lapping the soul in green images of the country, forms the most complete contrast to a town's-person, and consequently has over such the greatest power of charm.

Presently Libbie found out she was very hungry. Now they were but provided with dinner, which was, of course, to be eaten as near twelve o'clock as might be; and Margaret Hall, in her prudence, asked a working-man near to tell her what o'clock it was.

"Nay," said he, "I'll ne'er look at clock or watch to-day. I'll not spoil my pleasure by finding out how fast it's going away. If thou'rt hungry, eat. I make my own dinner-hour, and I have eaten mine an hour ago."

So they had their veal pies, and then found out it was only half-past ten o'clock; by so many pleasureable events had that morning been marked. But such was their buoyancy of spirits, that they only enjoyed their mistake, and joined in the general laugh against the man who had eaten his dinner somewhere about nine. He laughed most heartily of all till, suddenly stopping, he said:

"I must not go on at this rate; laughing gives one such an appetite."

"Oh, if that's all," said a merry-looking man lying at full length, and brushing the fresh scent out of the grass, while two or three little children tumbled over him, and crept about him, as kittens or puppies frolic with their parents, "if that's all, we'll have a subscription of eatables for them improvident folk as have eaten their dinner for their breakfast. Here's a sausage pasty and a handful of nuts for my share. Bring round the hat, Bob, and see what the company will give."

Bob carried out the joke, much to little Franky's amusement; and no one was so churlish as to refuse, although the contributions varied from a peppermint drop up to a veal pie and a sausage pasty.

"It's a thriving trade," said Bob, as he emptied his hatful of provisions on the grass by Libbie's side. "Besides, it's tiptop, too, to live on the public. Hark! what is that?"

The laughter and the chat were suddenly hushed, and mothers took their little ones to listen—as, far away in the distance, now sinking and falling, now swelling and clear, came a ringing peal of children's voices, blended together in one of those psalm tunes which we are all of us so familiar with, and which bring to mind the old, old days, when we, as wondering children, were first led to worship "Our Father," by those beloved ones who have since gone to the more perfect worship. Holy was that distant choral praise, even to the most thoughtless; and when it, in fact, was ended, in the instant's pause, during which the ear awaits the repetition of the air, they caught the noontide hum and buzz of the myriads of insects who danced away their lives in the glorious day; they heard the swaying of the mighty woods in the soft but resistless breeze, and then again once more burst forth the merry jests and the shouts of childhood; and again the elder ones resumed their happy talk, as they lay or sat "under the greenwood tree." Fresh parties came dropping in; some laden with wild flowers—almost with branches of hawthorn, indeed; while one or two had made prizes of the earliest dog-roses, and had cast away campion, stitchwort, ragged robin, all to keep the lady of the hedges from being obscured or hidden by the community.

One after another drew near to Franky, and looked on with interest as he lay sorting the flowers given to him. Happy parents stood by, with their household bands around them, in health and comeliness, and felt the sad prophecy of those shrivelled limbs, those wasted fingers, those lamp-like eyes, with their bright, dark lustre. His mother was too eagerly watching his happiness to read the meaning of those grave looks, but Libbie saw them and understood them; and a chill shudder went through her, even on that day, as she thought on the future.

"Ay! I thought we should give you a start!"

A start they did give, with their terrible slap on Libbie's back, as she sat idly grouping flowers, and following out her sorrowful thoughts. It was the Dixons. Instead of keeping their holiday by lying in bed, they and their children had roused themselves, and had come by the omnibus to the nearest point. For an instant the meeting was an awkward one, on account of the feud between Margaret Hall and Mrs. Dixon, but there was no long resisting of kindly mother Nature's soothings, at that holiday time, and in that lonely tranquil spot; or if they could have been unheeded, the sight of Franky would have awed every angry feeling into rest, so changed was he since the Dixons had last seen him; and since he had been the Puck or Robin Goodfellow of the neighbourhood, whose marbles were always rolling under other people's feet, and whose top-strings were always hanging in nooses to catch the unwary. Yes, he, the feeble, mild, almost girlish-looking lad had once been a merry, happy rogue, and as such often cuffed by Mrs. Dixon, the very Mrs. Dixon who now stood gazing with the tears in her eyes. Could she, in sight of him, the changed, the fading, keep up a quarrel with his mother?

"How long hast thou been here?" asked Dixon.

"Welly on for all day," answered Libbie.

"Hast never been to see the deer, or the king and queen oaks? Lord! how stupid!"

His wife pinched his arm, to remind him of Franky's helpless condition, which, of course, tethered the otherwise willing feet. But Dixon had a remedy. He called Bob, and one or two others; and, each taking a corner of the strong plaid shawl, they slung Franky as in a hammock, and thus carried him merrily along, down the wood paths, over the smooth, grassy turf, while the glimmering shine and shadow fell on his upturned face. The women walked behind, talking, loitering along, always in sight of the hammock; now picking up some green treasure from the ground, now catching at the low-hanging branches of the horse-chestnut. The soul grew much on this day, and in these woods, and all unconsciously, as souls do grow. They followed Franky's hammock-bearers up a grassy knoll, on the top of which stood a group of pine trees, whose stems looked like dark red gold in the sunbeams. They had taken Franky there to show him Manchester, far away in the blue plain, against which the woodland foreground cut with a soft clear line. Far, far away in the distance, on that flat plain, you might see the motionless cloud of smoke hanging over a great town, and that was Manchester—ugly, smoky Manchester—dear, busy, earnest, noble-working Manchester; where their children had been born, and where, perhaps, some lay buried; where their homes were, and where God had cast their lives, and told them to work out their destiny.

"Hurrah! for oud smoke-jack!" cried Bob, putting Franky softly down on the grass, before he whirled his hat round, preparatory to a shout. "Hurrah! hurrah!" from all the men. "There's the rim of my hat lying like a quoit yonder," observed Bob quietly, as he replaced his brimless hat on his head with the gravity of a judge.

"Here's the Sunday-school children a-coming to sit on this shady side, and have their buns and milk. Hark! they're singing the infant-school grace."

They sat close at hand, so that Franky could hear the words they sang, in rings of children, making, in their gay summer prints, newly donned for that week, garlands of little faces, all happy and bright upon that green hill-side. One little "dot" of a girl came shyly behind Franky, whom she had long been watching, and threw her half-bun at his side, and then ran away and hid herself, in very shame at the boldness of her own sweet impulse. She kept peeping from her screen at Franky all the time; and he meanwhile was almost too pleased and happy to eat; the world was so beautiful, and men, women, and children all so tender and kind; so softened, in fact, by the beauty of this earth, so unconsciously touched by the spirit of love, which was the Creator of this lovely earth. But the day drew to an end; the heat declined; the birds once more began their warblings; the fresh scents again hung about plant, and tree, and grass, betokening the fragrant presence of the reviving dew, and—the boat time was near. As they trod the meadow path once more, they were joined by many a party they had encountered during the day, all abounding in happiness, all full of the day's adventures. Long-cherished quarrels had been forgotten, new friendships formed. Fresh tastes and higher delights had been imparted that day. We have all of us our look, now and then, called up by some noble or loving thought (our highest on earth), which will be our likeness in heaven. I can catch the glance on many a face, the glancing light of the cloud of glory from heaven, "which is our home." That look was present on many a hard-worked, wrinkled countenance, as they turned backwards to catch a longing, lingering look at Dunham woods, fast deepening into blackness of night, but whose memory was to haunt, in greenness and freshness, many a loom, and workshop, and factory, with images of peace and beauty.

That night, as Libbie lay awake, revolving the incidents of the day, she caught Franky's voice through the open windows. Instead of the frequent moan of pain, he was trying to recall the burden of one of the children's hymns:

"Here we suffer grief and pain,

Here we meet to part again;

In Heaven we part no more.

Oh! that will be joyful," etc.

She recalled his question, the whispered question, to her in the happiest part of the day. He asked Libbie: "Is Dunham like Heaven? The people here are as kind as angels, and I don't want Heaven to be more beautiful than this place. If you and mother would but die with me, I should like to die, and live always there!" She had checked him, for she feared he was impious; but now the young child's craving for some definite idea of the land to which his inner wisdom told him he was hastening, had nothing in it wrong, or even sorrowful, for—

"In Heaven we part no more."

II
Novels

Mary Barton, *Lizzie Leigh*, *Ruth*, and *North and South*, Mrs. Gaskell's earlier novels, were written with a purpose—"to defend the poor"—and in them she discusses some of the social problems of the day, which she tried to solve. Later she proved how well she could write in a humorous vein, as in *Cranford*, *Mr. Harrison's Confessions*, and *My Lady Ludlow*.

As a descriptive writer she excelled, notably in *Mary Barton*, *Ruth*, *Cousin Phillis*, and *Sylvia's Lovers*. She was always very observant, and many of her stories recall her talent for exquisite word painting.

Social Questions

Poor *versus* Rich

From *Mary Barton*, 1848

"THOU never could abide the gentlefolk," said Wilson, half amused at his friend's vehemence.

"And what good have they ever done me that I should like them?" asked Barton, the latent fire lighting up his eye; and bursting forth, he continued: "If I am sick, do they come and nurse me? If my child lies dying (as poor Tom lay, with his white wan lips quivering, for want of better food than I could give him), does the rich man bring the wine or broth that might save his life? If I am out of work for weeks in the bad times, and winter comes, with black frost, and keen east wind, and there is no coal for the grate, and no clothes for the bed, and the thin bones are seen through the ragged clothes, does the rich man share his plenty with me, as he ought to do, if his religion wasn't a humbug! When I lie on my death-bed, and Mary (bless her!) stands fretting, as I know she will fret," and here his voice faltered a little, "will a rich lady come and take her to her own home if need be, till she can look round and see what best to do? No, I tell you it's the poor, and the poor only, as does such things for the poor. Don't think to come over me with th' old tale, that the rich know nothing of the trials of the poor; I say, if they don't know, they ought to know. We're their slaves as long as we can work; we pile up their fortunes with the sweat of our brows, and yet we are to live as separate as if we were in two worlds; ay, as separate as Dives and Lazarus, with a great gulf between us; but I know who was best off then;" and he wound up his speech with a low chuckle that had no mirth in it.

At all times it is a bewildering thing to the poor weaver to see his employer removing from house to house, each one grander than the last, till he ends in building one more magnificent than all, or withdraws his money from the concern, or sells his mill, to buy an estate in the country, while all the time the weaver, who thinks he and his fellows are the real makers of this wealth, is struggling on for bread for his children, through the vicissitudes of lowered wages, short hours, fewer hands employed, etc. And when he knows trade is bad, and could understand (at least partially) that there are not buyers enough in the market to purchase the goods already made, and consequently that there is no demand for more; when he would bear and endure much without complaining, could he also see that his employers were bearing their share; he is, I say, bewildered and (to use his own words) "aggravated" to see that all goes on just as usual with the mill-owners. Large houses are still occupied, while spinners' and weavers' cottages stand empty, because the families that once filled them are obliged to live in rooms or cellars. Carriages still roll along the streets, concerts are still crowded by subscribers, the shops for expensive luxuries still find daily customers, while the workman loiters away his unemployed time in watching these things, and thinking of the pale, uncomplaining wife at home, and the wailing children asking in vain for enough of food—of the sinking health, of the dying life of those near and dear to him. The contrast is too great. Why should he alone suffer from bad times?

I know that this is not really the case; and I know what is the truth in such matters; but what I wish to impress is what the workman feels and thinks. True, that with child-like improvidence, good times will often dissipate his grumbling, and make him forget all prudence and foresight.

But there are earnest men among these people, men who have endured wrongs without complaining, but without ever forgetting or forgiving those whom (they believe) have caused all this woe.

Among these was John Barton. His parents had suffered; his mother had died from absolute want of the necessaries of life. He himself was a good, steady workman, and, as such, pretty certain of steady employment. But he spent all he got with the confidence (you may also call it improvidence) of one who was willing, and believed himself able, to supply all his wants by his own exertions. And when his master suddenly failed, and all hands in the mill were turned back, one Tuesday morning, with the news that Mr. Hunter had stopped, Barton had only a few shillings to rely on; but he had good heart of being employed at some other mill, and accordingly, before returning home, he spent some hours in going from factory to factory, asking for work. But at every mill was some sign of depression of trade! some were working short hours, some were turning off hands, and for weeks Barton was out of work, living on credit. It was during this time that his little son, the apple of his eye, the cynosure of all his strong power of love, fell ill of the scarlet fever. They dragged him through the crisis, but his life hung on a gossamer thread. Everything, the doctor said, depended on good nourishment, on generous living, to keep up the little fellow's strength, in the prostration in which the fever had left him. Mocking words! when the commonest food in the house would not furnish one little meal. Barton tried credit; but it was worn out at the little provision shops, which were now suffering in their turn. He thought it would be no sin to steal, and would have stolen; but he could not get the opportunity in the few days the child lingered. Hungry himself, almost to an animal pitch of ravenousness, but with the bodily pain swallowed up in anxiety for his little sinking lad, he stood at one of the shop windows where all edible luxuries are displayed; haunches of venison, Stilton cheeses, moulds of jelly—all appetising sights to the common passer-by. And out of this shop came Mrs. Hunter! She crossed to her carriage, followed by the shopman loaded with purchases for a party. The door was quickly slammed to, and she drove away; and Barton returned home with a bitter spirit of wrath in his heart, to see his only boy a corpse!

You can fancy, now, the hoards of vengeance in his heart against the employers. For there are never wanting those who, either in speech or in print, find it their interest to cherish such feelings in the working classes; who know how and when to rouse the dangerous power at their command; and who use their knowledge with unrelenting purpose to either party.

Working Men's Petition to Parliament, 1839

From *Mary Barton*, 1848

FOR three years past trade has been getting worse and worse, and the price of provisions higher and higher. This disparity between the amount of the earnings of the working classes and the price of their food, occasioned, in more cases than could well be imagined, disease and death. Whole families went through a gradual starvation. They only wanted a Dante to record their sufferings. And yet even his words would fall short of the awful truth; they could only present an outline of the tremendous facts of the destitution that surrounded thousands upon thousands in the terrible years of 1839, 1840, and 1841. Even philanthropists who had studied the subject were forced to own themselves perplexed in their endeavour to ascertain the real causes of the misery; the whole matter was of so complicated a nature that it became next to impossible to understand it thoroughly. It need excite no surprise, then, to learn that a bad feeling between working men and the upper classes became very strong in this season of privation. The indigence and sufferings of the operatives induced a suspicion in the minds of many of them that their legislators, their magistrates, their employers, and even the ministers of religion, were, in general, their oppressors and enemies; and were in league for their prostration and enthralment. The most deplorable and enduring evil that arose out of the period of commercial depression to which I refer, was this feeling of alienation between the different classes of society. It is so impossible to describe, or even faintly to picture, the state of distress which prevailed in the town at that time, that I will not attempt it; and yet I think again that surely, in a Christian land, it was not known even so feebly as words could tell it, or the more happy and fortunate would have thronged with their sympathy and their aid. In many instances the sufferers wept first and then they cursed. Their vindictive feelings exhibited themselves in rabid politics. And when I hear, as I have heard, of the sufferings and privations of the poor, of provision shops, where ha'porths of tea, sugar, butter, and even flour, were sold to accommodate the indigent—of parents sitting in their clothes by the fireside during the whole night for seven weeks together, in order that their only bed and bedding might be reserved for the use of their large family—of others sleeping upon the cold hearthstone for weeks in succession, without adequate means of providing themselves with food or fuel—and this in the depth of winter—of others being compelled to fast for days together, uncheered by any hope of better fortune, living, moreover, or rather starving, in a crowded garret, or damp cellar, and gradually sinking under the pressure of want and despair, into a premature grave; and when this has been confirmed by the evidence of their careworn looks, their excited feelings, and their desolate homes—can I wonder that many of them, in such times of misery and destitution, spoke and acted with ferocious precipitation?

An idea was now springing up among the operatives, that originated with the Chartists, but which came at last to be cherished as a darling child by many and many a one. They could not believe that Government knew of their misery: they rather chose to think it possible that men could voluntarily assume the office of legislators for a nation who were ignorant of its real state; as who should make domestic rules for the pretty behaviour of children without caring to know that those children had been kept for days without food. Besides, the starving multitudes had heard that the very existence of their distress had been denied in Parliament; and though they felt this strange and inexplicable, yet the idea that their misery had still to be revealed in all its depths, and that then some remedy would be found, soothed their aching hearts, and kept down their rising fury.

So a petition was framed, and signed by thousands in the bright spring days of 1839, imploring Parliament to hear witnesses who could testify to the unparalleled destitution of the manufacturing districts. Nottingham, Sheffield, Glasgow, Manchester, and many other towns were busy appointing delegates to convey this petition, who might speak, not merely of what they had seen, and had heard, but from what they had borne and suffered. Life-worn, gaunt, anxious, hunger-stamped men were those delegates.

One of them was John Barton. He would have been ashamed to own the flutter of spirits his appointment gave him. There was the childish delight of seeing London—that went a little way, and but a little way. There was the vain idea of speaking out his notions before so many grand folk—that went a little further; and last, there was the really pure gladness of heart arising from the idea that he was one of those chosen to be instruments in making known the distresses of the people, and consequently in procuring them some grand relief, by means of which they should never suffer want or care any more. He hoped largely, but vaguely, of the results of his expedition. An argosy of the precious hopes of many otherwise despairing creatures was that petition to be heard concerning their sufferings.

The night before the morning on which the Manchester delegates were to leave for London, Barton might be said to hold a levée, so many neighbours came dropping in. Job Legh had early established himself and his pipe by John Barton's fire, not saying much, but puffing away, and imagining himself of use in adjusting the smoothing-irons that hung before the fire, ready for Mary when she should want them. As for Mary, her employment was the same as that of Beau Tibbs' wife, "just washing her father's two shirts," in the pantry back-kitchen; for she was anxious about his appearance in London. (The coat had been redeemed, though the silk handkerchief was forfeited.) The door stood open, as usual, between the house-place and the back-kitchen, so she gave her greeting to their friends as they entered.

"So, John, yo're bound for London, are yo?" said one.

"Ay, I suppose, I mun go," answered John, yielding to necessity as it were.

"Well, there's many a thing I'd like yo to speak on to the Parliament people. Thou'lt not spare 'em, John, I hope. Tell 'em our minds; how we're thinking we'n been clemmed long enough, and we donnot see whatten good they'n been doing, if they can't give us what we're all crying for sin' the day we were born."

"Ay, ay! I'll tell 'em that, and much more to it, when it gets to my turn; but thou knows there's many will have their word afore me."

"Well, thou'll speak at last. Bless thee, lad, do ask 'em to make th' masters to break th' machines. There's never been good times sin' spinning-jennies came up."

"Machines is th' ruin of poor folk," chimed in several voices.

"For my part," said a shivering, half-clad man, who crept near the fire, as if ague-stricken, "I would like thee to tell 'em to pass th' Short-hours Bill. Flesh and blood gets wearied wi' so much work; why should factory hands work so much longer nor other trades? Just ask 'em that, Barton, will ye?"

Barton was saved the necessity of answering, by the entrance of Mrs. Davenport, the poor widow he had been so kind to; she looked half-fed, and eager, but was decently clad. In her hand she brought a little newspaper parcel, which she took to Mary, who opened it, and then called out, dangling a shirt-collar from her soapy fingers:

"See, father, what a dandy you'll be in London! Mrs. Davenport has brought you this; made new cut, all after the fashion. Thank you for thinking on him."

"Eh, Mary!" said Mrs. Davenport, in a low voice, "whatten's all I can do, to what he's done for me and mine? But, Mary, sure I can help ye, for you'll be busy wi' this journey."

"Just help me wring these out, and then I'll take 'em to the mangle."

So Mrs. Davenport became a listener to the conversation; and after awhile joined in.

"I'm sure, John Barton, if yo are taking messages to the Parliament folk, yo'll not object to telling 'em what a sore trial it is, this law o' theirs, keeping childer fra' factory work, whether they be weakly or strong. There's our Ben; why, porridge seems to go no way wi' him, he eats so much; and I han gotten no money to send him t' school, as I would like; and there he is, rampaging about the streets a' day, getting hungrier and hungrier, and picking up a' manner o' bad ways; and th' inspector won't let him in to work in th' factory, because he's not right age; though he's twice as strong as Sankey's little ritling of a lad, as works till he cries for his legs aching so, though he is right age, and better."

"I've one plan I wish to tell John Barton," said a pompous, careful-speaking man, "and I should like him for to lay it afore the Honourable House. My mother comed out o' Oxfordshire, and were under-laundry-maid in Sir Francis Dashwood's family; and when we were little ones, she'd tell us stories of their grandeur; and one thing she named were that Sir Francis wore two shirts a day. Now he were all as one as a Parliament man; and many on 'em, I han no doubt, are like extravagant. Just tell 'em, John, do, that they'd be doing the Lancashire weavers a great kindness, if they'd ha' their shirts a' made o' calico; 'twould make trade brisk, that would, wi' the power o' shirts they wear."

Job Legh now put in his word. Taking the pipe out of his mouth, and addressing the last speaker, he said:

"I'll tell ye what, Bill, and no offence, mind ye; there's but hundreds of them Parliament folk as wear so many shirts to their back; but there's thousands and thousands o' poor weavers as han only gotten one shirt i' the world; ay, and don't know where t' get another when that rag's done, though they're turning out miles o' calico every day; and many a mile o't is lying in warehouses, stopping up trade for want o' purchasers. Yo take my advice, John Barton, and ask Parliament to set trade free, so as workmen can earn a decent wage, and buy their two, ay and three, shirts a year; that would make weaving brisk."

He put his pipe in his mouth again, and redoubled his puffing, to make up for lost time.

"I'm afeard, neighbours," said John Barton, "I've not much chance o' telling 'em all yo say: what I think on, is just speaking out about the distress that they say is nought. When they hear o' children born on wet flags, without a rag t' cover 'em or a bit o' food for th' mother: when they hear of folk lying down to die i' th' streets, or hiding their want i' some hole o' a cellar till death come to set 'em free; and when they hear o' all this plague, pestilence, and famine, they'll surely do somewhat wiser for us than we can guess at now. Howe'er, I han no objection, if so be there's an opening, to speak up for what yo say; anyhow, I'll do my best, and yo see now, if better times don't come after Parliament knows all."

Meeting Between the Masters and their Employees

From *Mary Barton*, 1848

THE day arrived on which the masters were to have an interview with the deputation of the workpeople. The meeting was to take place in a public room at an hotel; and there, about eleven o'clock, the mill-owners who had received the foreign orders began to collect.

Of course, the first subject, however full their minds might be of another, was the weather. Having done their duty by all the showers and sunshine which had occurred during the past week, they fell to talking about the business which brought them together. There might be about twenty gentlemen in the room, including some, by courtesy, who were not immediately concerned in the settlement of the present question; but who, nevertheless, were sufficiently interested to attend. These were divided into little groups, who did not seem by any means unanimous. Some were for a slight concession, just a sugar-plum to quieten the naughty child, a sacrifice to peace and quietness. Some were steadily and vehemently opposed to the dangerous precedent of yielding one jot or one tittle to the outward force of a turn-out. It was teaching the workpeople how to become masters, said they.

Did they want the wildest thing hereafter, they would know that the way to obtain their wishes would be to strike work. Besides, one or two of those present had only just returned from the New Bailey, where one of the turn-outs had been tried for a cruel assault on a poor North-country weaver, who had attempted to work at the low price. They were indignant, and justly so, at the merciless manner in which the poor fellow had been treated; and their indignation at wrong took (as it often does) the extreme form of revenge. They felt as if, rather than yield to the body of men who were resorting to such cruel measures towards their fellow workmen, they, the masters, would sooner relinquish all the benefits to be derived from the fulfilment of the commission in order that the workmen might suffer keenly. They forgot that the strike was in this instance the consequence of want and need, suffered unjustly, as the endurers believed; for, however insane, and without ground of reason, such was their belief, and such was the cause of their violence. It is a great truth that you cannot extinguish violence by violence. You may put it down for a time; but while you are crowing over your imaginary success, see if it does not return with seven devils worse than its former self!

No one thought of treating the workmen as brethren and friends, and openly, clearly, as appealing to reasonable men, stating exactly and fully the circumstances which led the masters to think it was the wise policy of the time to make sacrifices themselves, and to hope for them from the operatives.

In going from group to group in the room, you caught such a medley of sentences as the following—

"Poor devils! they're near enough to starving, I'm afraid. Mrs. Aldred makes two cows' heads into soup every week, and people come many miles to fetch it; and if these times last, we must try and do more. But we must not be bullied into anything!"

"A rise of a shilling or so won't make much difference, and they will go away thinking they've gained their point."

"That's the very thing I object to. They'll think so, and whenever they've a point to gain, no matter how unreasonable, they'll strike work."

"It really injures them more than us."

"I don't see how our interests can be separated."

"The d—d brute had thrown vitriol on the poor fellow's ankles, and you know what a bad part that is to heal. He had to stand still with the pain, and that left him at the mercy of the cruel wretch, who beat him about the head till you'd hardly have known he was a man. They doubt if he'll live."

"If it were only for that, I'll stand out against them, even if it is the cause of my ruin."

"Ay, I for one won't yield one farthing to the cruel brutes; they're more like wild beasts than human beings."

(Well, who might have made them different?)

"I say, Carson, just go and tell Duncombe of this fresh instance of their abominable conduct. He's wavering, but I think this will decide him."

The door was now opened, and the waiter announced that the men were below, and asked if it were the pleasure of the gentlemen that they should be shown up.

They assented, and rapidly took their places round the official table; looking as like as they could to the Roman senators who awaited the irruption of Brennus and his Gauls.

Tramp, tramp, came the heavy clogged feet up the stairs; and in a minute five wild, earnest-looking men stood in the room. John Barton, from some mistake as to time, was not among them. Had they been larger-boned men you would have called them gaunt; as it was, they were little of stature, and their fustian clothes hung loosely upon their shrunk limbs. In choosing their delegates, too, the operatives had had more regard to their brains and power of speech, than to their wardrobes; they might have read the opinions of that worthy Professor Teufelsdröckh, in *Sartor Resartus*, to judge from the dilapidated coats and trousers which yet clothed men of parts and of power. It was long since many of them had known the luxury of a new article of dress; and air-gaps were to be seen in their garments. Some of the masters were rather affronted at such a ragged detachment coming between the wind and their nobility; but what cared they?

At the request of a gentleman hastily chosen to officiate as chairman, the leader of the delegates read, in a high-pitched, psalm-singing voice, a paper containing the operatives' statement of the case at issue, their complaints, and their demands, which last were not remarkable for moderation.

He was then desired to withdraw for a few minutes, with his fellow-delegates, to another room, while the masters considered what should be their definite answer.

When the men had left the room, a whispered, earnest consultation took place, everyone reurging his former arguments. The conceders carried the day, but only by a majority of one. The minority haughtily and audibly expressed their dissent from the measures to be adopted, even after the delegates re-entered the room; their words and looks did not pass unheeded by the quick-eyed operatives; their names were registered in bitter hearts.

The masters could not consent to the advance demanded by the workmen. They would agree to give one shilling per week more than they had previously offered. Were the delegates empowered to accept such offer?

They were empowered to accept or decline any offer made that day by the masters.

Then it might be as well for them to consult among themselves as to what should be their decision. They again withdrew.

It was not for long. They came back, and positively declined any compromise of their demands.

Then up sprang Mr. Henry Carson, the head and voice of the violent party among the masters, and addressing the chairman, even before the scowling operatives, he proposed some resolutions, which he, and those who agreed with him, had been concocting during this last absence of the deputation.

They were, first, withdrawing the proposal just made, and declaring all communication between the masters and that particular Trades Union at an end; secondly, declaring that no master would employ any workman in future, unless he signed a declaration that he did not belong to any Trades Union, and pledged himself not to assist or subscribe to any society having for its object interference with the master's powers; and, thirdly, that the masters should pledge themselves to protect and encourage all workmen willing to accept employment on those conditions, and at the rate of wages first offered. Considering that the men who now stood listening with lowering brows of defiance were all of them leading members of the Union, such resolutions were in themselves sufficiently provocative of animosity: but not content with simply stating them, Harry Carson went on to characterise the conduct of the workmen in no measured terms; every word he spoke rendering their looks more livid, their glaring eyes more fierce. One among them would have spoken, but checked himself, in obedience to the stern glance and pressure on his arm received from the leader. Mr. Carson sat down, and a friend instantly got up to second the motion. It was carried, but far from unanimously. The chairman announced it to the delegates (who had been once more turned out of the room for a division). They received it with deep brooding silence, but spoke never a word, and left the room without even a bow.

Now there had been some by-play at this meeting, not recorded in the Manchester newspapers, which gave an account of the more regular part of the transaction.

While the men had stood grouped near the door, on their first entrance, Mr. Harry Carson had taken out his silver pencil and had drawn an admirable caricature of them—lank, ragged, dispirited, and famine-stricken. Underneath he wrote a hasty quotation from the fat knight's well-known speech in *Henry IV*. He passed it to one of his neighbours, who acknowledged the likeness instantly, and by him it was sent round to others, who all smiled and nodded their heads. When it came back to its owner, he tore the back of the letter on which it was drawn in two, twisted them up and flung them into the fire-place; but, careless whether they reached their aim or not, he did not look to see that they fell just short of any consuming cinders.

This proceeding was closely observed by one of the men.

He watched the masters as they left the hotel (laughing, some of them were, at passing jokes), and when all had gone he re-entered. He went to the waiter, who recognised him.

"There's a bit on a picture up yonder, as one o' the gentlemen threw away; I've a little lad at home as dearly loves a picture; by your leave I'll go up for it."

The waiter, good-natured and sympathetic, accompanied him up-stairs; saw the paper picked up and untwisted, and then being convinced by a hasty glance at its contents that it was only what the man had called it, "a bit of a picture," he allowed him to bear away his prize.

Towards seven o'clock that evening, many operatives began to assemble in a room in the Weavers' Arms public-house, a room appropriated for "festive occasions," as the landlord, in his circular on opening the premises, had described it. But, alas! it was on no festive occasion that they met there this night. Starved, irritated, despairing men, they were assembling to hear the answer that morning given by their masters to the delegates; after which, as was stated in the notice, a gentleman from London would have the honour of addressing the meeting on the present state of affairs between the employers and the employed, or (as he chose to term them) the idle and the industrious classes. The room was not large, but its bareness of furniture made it appear so. Unshaded gas flared down upon the lean and unwashed artisans as they entered, their eyes blinking at the excess of light.

They took their seats on benches, and awaited the deputation. The latter, gloomily and ferociously, delivered the masters' ultimatum, adding thereto not one word of their own; and it sank all the deeper into the sore hearts of the listeners for their forbearance.

Then the "gentleman from London" (who had been previously informed of the masters' decision) entered. You would have been puzzled to define his exact position, or what was the state of his mind as regarded education. He looked so self-conscious, so far from earnest, among the group of eager, fierce, absorbed men, among whom he now stood. He might have been a disgraced medical student of the Bob Sawyer class, or an unsuccessful actor, or a flashy shopman. The impression he would have given you would have been unfavourable, and yet there was much about him that could only be characterised as doubtful.

He smirked in acknowledgment of their uncouth greetings and sat down; then glancing round, he inquired whether it would not be agreeable to the gentlemen present to have pipes and liquor handed round, adding that he would stand treat.

As the man who has had his taste educated to love reading falls devouringly upon books after a long abstinence, so these poor fellows, whose tastes had been left to educate themselves into a liking for tobacco, beer, and similar gratifications, gleamed up at the proposal of the London delegate. Tobacco and drink deaden the pangs of hunger and make one forget the miserable home, the desolate future.

They were now ready to listen to him with approbation. He felt it; and rising like a great orator, with his right arm outstretched, his left in the breast of his waistcoat, he began to declaim with a forced theatrical voice.

After a burst of eloquence, in which he blended the deeds of the elder and the younger Brutus, and magnified the resistless might of the "millions of Manchester," the Londoner descended to matter-of-fact business, and in his capacity this way he did not belie the good judgment of those who had sent him as delegate. Masses of people, when left to their own free choice, seem to have discretion in distinguishing men of natural talent; it is a pity they so little regard temper and principles. He rapidly dictated resolutions and suggested measures. He wrote out a stirring placard for the walls. He proposed sending delegates to entreat the assistance of other Trades Unions in other towns. He headed the list of subscribing Unions by a liberal donation from that with which he was especially connected in London; and what was more, and more uncommon, he paid down the money in real, clinking, blinking, golden sovereigns! The money, alas! was cravingly required; but before alleviating any private necessities on the morrow, small sums were handed to each of the delegates, who were in a day or two to set out on their expeditions to Glasgow, Newcastle, Nottingham, etc. These men were most of them members of the deputation who had that morning waited upon the masters. After he had drawn up some letters and spoken a few more stirring words, the gentleman from London withdrew, previously shaking hands all round; and many speedily followed him out of the room and out of the house.

The newly appointed delegates and one or two others, remained behind to talk over their respective missions, and to give and exchange opinions in more homely and natural language than they dared to use before the London orator.

"He's a rare chap, yon," began one, indicating the departed delegate by a jerk of his thumb towards the door. "He's getten the gift of the gab, anyhow!"

"Ay! ay! he knows what he's about. See how he poured it into us about that there Brutus. He were pretty hard, too, to kill his own son!"

"I could kill mine if he took part with the masters; to be sure, he's but a stepson, but that makes no odds," said another.

But now tongues were hushed, and all eyes were directed towards the member of the deputation who had that morning returned to the hotel to obtain possession of Harry Carson's clever caricature of the operatives.

The heads clustered together to gaze at and detect the likenesses.

"That's John Slater! I'd ha' known him anywhere, by his big nose. Lord! how like; that's me, by G—d, it's the very way I'm obligated to pin my waistcoat up, to hide that I've getten no shirt. That is a shame, and I'll not stand it."

"Well!" said John Slater, after having acknowledged his nose and his likeness; "I could laugh at a jest as well as e'er the best on 'em, though it did tell agen mysel, if I were not clemming" (his eyes filled with tears; he was a poor, pinched, sharp-featured man, with a gentle and melancholy expression of countenance), "and if I could keep from thinking of them at home as is clemming; but with their cries for food ringing in my ears, and making me afeard of going home, and wonder if I should hear 'em wailing out, if I lay cold and drowned at th' bottom o' th' canal, there; why, man, I cannot laugh at aught. It seems to make me sad that there is any as can make game on what they've never knowed; as can make such laughable pictures on men whose very hearts within 'em are so raw and sore as ours were and are God help us."

John Barton began to speak; they turned to him with great attention. "It makes me more than sad, it makes my heart burn within me, to see that folk can make a jest of striving men; of chaps who comed to ask for a bit o' fire for th' old granny as shivers i' th' cold; for a bit o' bedding, and some warm clothing to the poor wife who lies in labour on th' damp flags; and for victuals for the childer, whose little voices are getting too faint and weak to cry aloud wi' hunger. For, brothers, is not them the things we ask for when we ask for more wage? We donnot want dainties, we want bellyfuls; we donnot want gimcrack coats and waistcoats, we want warm clothes; and so that we get 'em, we'd not quarrel wi' what they're made on. We donnot want their grand houses, we want a roof to cover us from the rain, and the snow, and the storm; ay, and not alone to cover us, but the helpless ones that cling to us in the keen wind, and ask us with their eyes why we brought 'em into th' world to suffer?" He lowered his deep voice almost to a whisper:

"I've seen a father who had killed his child rather than let it clem before his eyes; and he were a tender-hearted man."

He began again in his usual tone, "We come to th' masters wi' full hearts to ask for them things I named afore. We know that they've getten money, as we've earned for 'em; we know trade is mending and they've large orders, for which they'll be well paid; we ask for our share o' th' payment; for, say we, if th' masters get our share of payment it will only go to keep servants and horses—to more dress and pomp. Well and good, if yo choose to be fools we'll not hinder you, so long as you're just; but our share we must and will have; we'll not be cheated. *We* want it for daily bread, for life itself; and not for our own lives neither (for there's many a one here, I know by mysel, as would be glad and thankful to lie down and die out o' this weary world), but for the lives of them little ones, who don't yet know what life is, and are afeard of death. Well, we come before the masters to state what we want and what we must have, afore we'll set shoulder to their work; and they say 'No.' One would think that would be enough of hard-heartedness, but it isn't. They go and make jesting pictures on us! I could laugh at mysel, as well as poor John Slater there; but then I must be easy in my mind to laugh. Now I only know that I would give the last drop of my blood to avenge us on yon chap, who had so little feeling in him as to make game on earnest, suffering men!"

A low angry murmur was heard among the men, but it did not yet take form or words. John continued:

"You'll wonder, chaps, how I came to miss the time this morning; I'll just tell you what I was a-doing. Th' chaplin at the New Bailey sent and gived me an order to see Jonas Higginbotham; him as was taken up last week for throwing vitriol in a knob-stick's face. Well, I couldn't help but go; and I didn't reckon it would ha' kept me so late. Jonas were like one crazy when I got to him; he said he could na' get rest night or day for th' face of the poor fellow he had damaged; then he thought on his weak, clemmed look, as he tramped, footsore into town; and Jonas thought, maybe, he had left them at home as would look for news, and hope and get none, but, haply, tidings of his death. Well, Jonas had thought on these things till he could not rest, but walked up and down continually like a wild beast in his cage. At last he bethought him on a way to help a bit, and he got the chaplain to send for me; and he tell'd me this; and that th' man were lying in the Infirmary, and he bade me go (to-day's the day as folk may be admitted into th' Infirmary) and get his silver watch, as was his mother's, and sell it as well as I could, and take the money, and bid the poor knob-stick send it to his friends beyond Burnley; and I were to take him Jonas's kind regards, and he humbly axed him to forgive him. So I did what Jonas wished. But, bless your life, none of us would ever throw vitriol again (at least at a knob-stick) if they could see the sight I saw to-day. The man lay, his face all wrapped in cloths, so I didn't see *that*; but not a limb, nor a bit of a limb, could keep from quivering with pain. He would ha' bitten his hands to keep down his moans, but couldn't, his face hurt him so if he moved it e'er so little. He could scarce mind me when I telled him about Jonas; he did squeeze my hand when I jingled the money, but when I axed his wife's name, he shrieked out, 'Mary, Mary, shall I never see you again? Mary, my darling, they've made me blind because I wanted to work for you and our own baby; O Mary, Mary!' Then the nurse came, and said he were raving, and that I had made him worse. And I'm afeard it was true; yet I were loth to go without knowing where to send the money…. So that kept me beyond my time, chaps."

"Did you hear where the wife lived at last?" asked many anxious voices.

"No! he went on talking to her, till his words cut my heart like a knife. I axed the nurse to find out who she was, and where she lived. But what I'm more especial naming it now for is this—for one thing, I wanted you all to know why I weren't at my post this morning; for another, I wish to say, that I, for one, ha' seen enough of what comes of attacking knob-sticks, and I'll ha' nought to do with it no more."

There were some expressions of disapprobation, but John did not mind them.

"Nay! I'm no coward," he replied, "and I'm true to th' back-bone. What I would like, and what I would do, would be to fight the masters. There's one among yo called me a coward. Well! every man has a right to his opinion; but since I've thought on th' matter to-day, I've thought we han all on us been more like cowards in attacking the poor like ourselves; them as has none to help, but mun choose between vitriol and starvation. I say we're more cowardly in doing that than leaving them alone. No! what I would do is this: Have at the masters!" Again he shouted, "Have at the masters!" He spoke lower; all listened with hushed breath:

"It's the masters as has wrought this woe; it's the masters as should pay for it. Him as called me coward just now, may try if I am one or not. Set me to serve out the masters, and see if there's aught I'll stick at."

"It would give the masters a bit on a fright if one of them were beaten within an inch of his life," said one.

"Ay! or beaten till no life were left in him," growled another.

And so with words, or looks that told more than words, they built up a deadly plan. Deeper and darker grew the import of their speeches, as they stood hoarsely muttering their meaning out, and glaring, with eyes that told the terror their own thoughts were to them, upon their neighbours. Their clenched fists, their set teeth, their livid looks, all told the suffering which their minds were voluntarily undergoing in the contemplation of crime, and in familiarising themselves with its details.

Then came one of those fierce, terrible oaths which bind members of Trades Unions to any given purpose. Then, under the flaring gaslight, they met together to consult further. With the distrust of guilt, each was suspicious of his neighbour; each dreaded the treachery of another. A number of pieces of paper (the identical letter on which the caricature had been drawn that very morning) were torn up, and *one was marked*. Then all were folded up again, looking exactly alike. They were shuffled together in a hat. The gas was extinguished; each drew out a paper. The gas was relighted. Then each went as far as he could from his fellows, and examined the paper he had drawn without saying a word, and with a countenance as stony and immovable as he could make it.

Then, still rigidly silent, they each took up their hats and went every one his own way.

He who had drawn the marked paper, had drawn the lot of the assassin! and he had sworn to act according to his drawing! But no one, save God and his own conscience, knew who was the appointed murderer.

John Barton Joins the Chartists

From *Mary Barton*, 1848

WE must return to John Barton. Poor John! He never got over his disappointing journey to London. The deep mortification he then experienced (with, perhaps, as little selfishness for its cause as mortification ever had) was of no temporary nature; indeed, few of his feelings were.

Then came a long period of bodily privation; of daily hunger after food; and though he tried to persuade himself he could bear want himself with stoical indifference, and did care about it as little as most men, yet the body took its revenge for its uneasy feelings. The mind became soured and morose, and lost much of its equipoise. It was no longer elastic, as in the days of youth, or in times of comparative happiness; it ceased to hope. And it is hard to live on when one can no longer hope.

The same state of feeling which John Barton entertained, if belonging to one who had had leisure to think of such things, and physicians to give names to them, would have been called monomania, so haunting, so incessant were the thoughts that pressed upon him. I have somewhere read a forcibly described punishment among the Italians, worthy of a Borgia. The supposed or real criminal was shut up in a room, supplied with every convenience and luxury; and at first mourned little over his imprisonment. But day by day he became aware that the space between the walls of his apartment was narrowing, and then he understood the end. Those painted walls would come into hideous nearness, and at last crush the life out of him.

And so day by day, nearer and nearer, came the diseased thoughts of John Barton. They excluded the light of heaven, the cheering sounds of earth. They were preparing his death.

It is true much of their morbid power might be ascribed to the use of opium. But before you blame too harshly this use, or rather abuse, try a hopeless life, with daily cravings of the body for food. Try, not alone being without hope yourself, but seeing all around you reduced to the same despair, arising from the same circumstances; all around you telling (though they use no words or language), by their looks and feeble actions, that they are suffering and sinking under the pressure of want. Would you not be glad to forget life, and its burdens? And opium gives forgetfulness for a time.

It is true they who thus purchase it pay dearly for their oblivion; but can you expect the uneducated to count the cost of their whistle? Poor wretches! They pay a heavy price. Days of oppressive weariness and languor, whose realities have the feeble sickliness of dreams; nights, whose dreams are fierce realities of agony; sinking health, tottering frames, incipient madness, and worse, the *consciousness* of incipient madness: this is the price of their whistle. But have you taught them the science of consequences?

John Barton's overpowering thought, which was to work out his fate on earth, was—rich and poor. Why are they so separate, so distinct, when God has made them all? It is not His will that their interests are so far apart. Whose doing is it?

And so on into the problems and mysteries of life, until, bewildered and lost, unhappy and suffering, the only feeling that remained clear and undisturbed in the tumult of his heart was hatred to the one class, and keen sympathy with the other.

But what availed his sympathy? No education had given him wisdom; and without wisdom, even love, with all its effects, too often works but harm. He acted to the best of his judgment, but it was a widely erring judgment.

The actions of the uneducated seem to me typified in those of Frankenstein, that monster of many human qualities, ungifted with a soul, a knowledge of the difference between good and evil.

The people rise up to life; they irritate us, they terrify us, and we become their enemies. Then, in the sorrowful moment of our triumphant power, their eyes gaze on us with mute reproach. Why have we made them what they are; a powerful monster, yet without the inner means for peace and happiness?

John Barton became a Chartist, a Communist, all that is commonly called wild and visionary. Ay! but being visionary is something. It shows a soul, a being not altogether sensual; a creature who looks forward for others, if not for himself.

And with all his weakness he had a sort of practical power, which made him useful to the bodies of men to whom he belonged. He had a ready kind of rough Lancashire eloquence, arising out of the fullness of his heart, which was very stirring to men similarly circumstanced, who liked to hear their feelings put into words. He had a pretty clear head at times for method and arrangement, a necessary talent to large combinations of men. And what perhaps more than all made him relied upon and valued, was the consciousness which everyone who came in contact with him felt, that he was actuated by no selfish motives; that his class, his order, was what he stood by, not the rights of his own paltry self. For even in great and noble men, as soon as self comes into prominent existence, it becomes a mean and paltry thing.

A little time before this there had come one of those occasions for deliberation among the employed, which deeply interested John Barton, and the discussions concerning which had caused his frequent absence from home of late.

I am not sure if I can express myself in the technical terms of either masters or workmen, but I will try simply to state the case on which the latter deliberated.

An order for coarse goods came in from a new foreign market. It was a large order, giving employment to all the mills engaged in that species of manufacture; but it was necessary to execute it speedily, and at as low prices as possible, as the masters had reason to believe that a duplicate order had been sent to one of the Continental manufacturing towns, where there were no restrictions on food, no taxes on building or machinery, and where consequently they dreaded that the goods could be made at a much lower price than they could afford them for; and that, by so acting and charging, the rival manufacturers would obtain undivided possession of the market. It was clearly their interest to buy cotton as cheaply, and to beat down wages as low as possible. And in the long run the interests of the workmen would have been thereby benefited. Distrust each other as they may, the employers and the employed must rise or fall together. There may be some difference as to chronology, none as to fact.

But the masters did not choose to make all these circumstances known. They stood upon being the masters, and that they had a right to order work at their own prices, and they believed that in the present depression of trade, and unemployment of hands, there would be no great difficulty in getting it done.

Now let us turn to the workmen's view of the question. The masters (of the tottering foundation of whose prosperity they were ignorant) seemed doing well, and, like gentlemen, "lived at home in ease," while they were starving, gasping on from day to day; and there was a foreign order to be executed, the extent of which, large as it was, was greatly exaggerated; and it was to be done speedily. Why were the masters offering such low wages under these circumstances? Shame upon them! It was taking advantage of their workpeople being almost starved; but they would starve entirely rather than come into such terms. It was bad enough to be poor, while by the labour of their thin hands, the sweat of their brows, the masters were made rich; but they would not be utterly ground down to dust. No! they would fold their hands and sit idle, and smile at the masters, whom even in death they could baffle. With Spartan endurance they determined to let the employers know their power, by refusing to work.

So class distrusted class, and their want of mutual confidence wrought sorrow to both. The masters would not be bullied, and compelled to reveal why they felt it wisest and best to offer only such low wages; they would not be made to tell that they were even sacrificing capital to obtain a decisive victory over the Continental manufacturers. And the workmen sat silent and stern, with folded hands, refusing to work for such pay. There was a strike in Manchester.

Of course, it was succeeded by the usual consequences. Many other Trades Unions, connected with different branches of business, supported with money, countenance, and encouragement of every kind, the stand which the Manchester power-loom weavers were making against their masters. Delegates from Glasgow, from Nottingham, and other towns were sent to Manchester, to keep up the spirit of resistance; a committee was formed, and all the requisite officers elected—chairman, treasurer, honorary secretary; among them was John Barton.

The masters, meanwhile, took their measures. They placarded the walls with advertisements for power-loom weavers. The workmen replied by a placard in still larger letters, stating their grievances. The masters met daily in town, to mourn over the time (so fast slipping away) for the fulfilment of the foreign orders; and to strengthen each other in their resolution not to yield. If they gave up now, they might give up always. It would never do. And amongst the most energetic of the masters, the Carsons, father and son, took their places. It is well known that there is no religionist so zealous as a convert; no masters so stern, and regardless of the interests of their workpeople, as those who have risen from such a station themselves. This would account for the elder Mr. Carson's determination not to be bullied into yielding; not even to be bullied into giving reasons for acting as the masters did. It was the employer's will, and that should be enough for the employed. Harry Carson did not trouble himself much about the grounds for his conduct. He liked the excitement of the affair. He liked the attitude of resistance. He was brave, and he liked the idea of personal danger, with which some of the more cautious tried to intimidate the violent among the masters.

Meanwhile the power-loom weavers living in the more remote parts of Lancashire, and the neighbouring counties, heard of the masters' advertisements for workmen; and in their solitary dwellings grew weary of starvation, and resolved to come to Manchester. Foot-sore, way-worn, half-starved-looking men they were, as they tried to steal into town in the early dawn, before people were astir, or in the dusk of the evening. And now began the real wrong-doing of the Trades Unions. As to their decision to work or not at such a particular rate of wages, that was either wise or unwise; an error of judgment, at the worst. But they had no right to tyrannise over others, and tie them down to their own Procrustean bed. Abhorring what they considered oppression in their masters, why did they oppress others? Because, when men get excited, they know not what they do. Judge, then, with something of the mercy of the Holy One, whom we all love.

In spite of policemen, set to watch over the safety of the poor country weavers—in spite of magistrates and prisons and severe punishments—the poor depressed men tramping in from Burnley, Padiham, and other places, to work at the condemned "Starvation Prices," were waylaid, and beaten, and left by the roadside almost for dead. The police broke up every lounging knot of men: they separated quietly to reunite half a mile out of town.

Of course the feeling between the masters and workmen did not improve under these circumstances.

Combination is an awful power. It is like the equally mighty agency of steam; capable of almost unlimited good or evil. But to obtain a blessing on its labours, it must work under the direction of a high and intelligent will, not being misled by passion or excitement. The will of the operatives had not been guided to the calmness of wisdom.

So much for generalities.

The Trial for Murder causes Mary Barton to Confess her Love for the Prisoner at the Bar

From Mary Barton, 1848

AS soon as he could bring his distracted thoughts to bear upon the present scene, he perceived that the trial of James Wilson for the murder of Henry Carson was just commencing. The clerk was gabbling over the indictment, and in a minute or two there was the accustomed question, "How say you, Guilty or not Guilty?"

Although but one answer was expected—was customary in all cases—there was a pause of dead silence, an interval of solemnity even in this hackneyed part of the proceeding; while the prisoner at the bar stood with compressed lips, looking at the judge with his outward eyes, but with far other and different scenes presented to his mental vision; a sort of rapid recapitulation of his life—remembrances of his childhood—his father (so proud of him, his first-born child)—his sweet little playfellow, Mary—his hopes, his love—his despair, yet still, yet ever and ever, his love—the blank, wide world it had been without her love—his mother—his childless mother—but not long to be so—not long to be away from all she loved—nor during that time to be oppressed with doubt as to his innocence, sure and secure of her darling's heart;—he started from his instant's pause, and said in a low, firm voice:

"Not guilty, my lord."

The circumstances of the murder, the discovery of the body, the causes of suspicion against Jem, were as well known to most of the audience as they are to you, so there was some little buzz of conversation going on among the people while the leading counsel for the prosecution made his very effective speech.

"That's Mr. Carson, the father, sitting behind Serjeant Wilkinson!"

"What a noble-looking old man he is! so stern and inflexible, with such classical features! Does he not remind you of some of the busts of Jupiter?"

"I am more interested by watching the prisoner. Criminals always interest me. I try to trace in the features common to humanity some expression of the crimes by which they have distinguished themselves from their kind. I have seen a good number of murderers in my day, but I have seldom seen one with such marks of Cain on his countenance as the man at the bar."

"Well, I am no physiognomist, but I don't think his face strikes me as bad. It certainly is gloomy and depressed, and not unnaturally so, considering his situation."

"Only look at his low, resolute brow, his downcast eye, his white compressed lips. He never looks up—just watch him."

"His forehead is not so low if he had that mass of black hair removed, and is very square, which some people say is a good sign. If others are to be influenced by such trifles as you are, it would have been much better if the prison barber had cut his hair a little previous to the trial; and as for downcast eye and compressed lip, it is all part and parcel of his inward agitation just now; nothing to do with character, my good fellow."

Poor Jem! His raven hair (his mother's pride, and so often fondly caressed by her fingers), was that, too, to have its influence against him?

The witnesses were called. At first they consisted principally of policemen, who, being much accustomed to giving evidence, knew what were the material points they were called on to prove, and did not lose the time of the court in listening to anything unnecessary.

"Clear as day against the prisoner," whispered one attorney's clerk to another.

"Black as night, you mean," replied his friend; and they both smiled.

"Jane Wilson! who's she? Some relation, I suppose, from the name."

"The mother—she that is to prove the gun part of the case."

"Oh, ay—I remember! Rather hard on her, too, I think."

They both were silent, as one of the officers of the court ushered Mrs. Wilson into the witness-box. I have often called her the "old woman," and "an old woman," because, in truth, her appearance was so much beyond her years, which could not be many above fifty. But partly owing to her accident in early life, which left a stamp of pain upon her face, partly owing to her anxious temper, partly to her sorrows, and partly to her limping gait, she always gave me the idea of age. But now she might have seemed more than seventy; her lines were so set and deep, her features so sharpened, and her walk so feeble. She was trying to check her sobs into composure, and (unconsciously) was striving to behave as she thought would best please her poor boy, whom she knew she had often grieved by her uncontrolled impatience. He had buried his face in his arms, which rested on the front of the dock (an attitude he retained during the greater part of his trial, and which prejudiced many against him).

The counsel began the examination.

"Your name is Jane Wilson, I believe?"

"Yes, sir."

"The mother of the prisoner at the bar?"

"Yes, sir," with quivering voice, ready to break out into weeping, but earning respect by the strong effort at self-control, prompted as I have said before, by her earnest wish to please her son by her behaviour.

The barrister now proceeded to the important part of the examination, tending to prove that the gun found on the scene of the murder was the prisoner's. She had committed herself so fully to the policeman that she could not well retract; so without much delay in bringing the question round to the desired point, the gun was produced in court, and the inquiry made:

"That gun belongs to your son, does it not?"

She clenched the sides of the witness-box in her efforts to make her parched tongue utter words. At last she moaned forth:

"Oh! Jem, Jem! what mun I say?"

Every one bent forward to hear the prisoner's answer; although, in fact, it was of little importance to the issue of the trial. He lifted up his head; and with a face brimming full of pity for his mother, yet resolved into endurance, said:

"Tell the truth, mother!"

And so she did, and with the fidelity of a little child. Every one felt that she did; and the little colloquy between mother and son did them some slight service in the opinion of the audience. But the awful judge sat unmoved; and the jurymen changed not a muscle of their countenances; while the counsel for the prosecution went triumphantly through this part of the case, including the fact of Jem's absence from home on the night of the murder, and bringing every admission to bear right against the prisoner.

It was over. She was told to go down. But she could no longer compel her mother's heart to keep silence, and suddenly turning towards the judge (with whom she imagined the verdict to rest), she thus addressed him with her choking voice:

"And now, sir, I've told you the whole truth, as *he* bid me; but don't you let what I have said go for to hang him; oh, my lord judge, take my word for it, he's as innocent as the child as has yet to be born. For sure, I, who am his mother, and have nursed him on my knee, and been gladdened by the sight of him every day since, ought to know him better than yon pack of fellows" (indicating the jury, while she strove against her heart to render her words distinct and clear for her dear son's sake), "who, I'll go bail, never saw him before this morning in all their born days. My lord judge, he's so good I often wondered what harm there was in him; many is the time when I've been fretted (for I'm frabbit enough at times), when I've scold't myself, and said, 'You ungrateful thing, the Lord God has given you Jem, and isn't that blessing enough for you?' But He has seen fit to punish me. If Jem is—if Jem is—taken from me, I shall be a childless woman; and very poor, having nought left to love on earth, and I cannot say 'His will be done.' I cannot, my lord judge, oh, I cannot!"

While sobbing out these words she was led away by the officers of the court, but tenderly and reverently, with the respect which great sorrow commands.

The stream of evidence went on and on, gathering fresh force from every witness who was examined, and threatening to overwhelm poor Jem. Already they had proved that the gun was his, that he had been heard not many days before the commission of the deed to threaten the deceased; indeed that the police had, at that time, been obliged to interfere, to prevent some probable act of violence. It only remained to bring forward a sufficient motive for the threat and the murder. The clue to this had been furnished by the policeman, who had overheard Jem's angry language to Mr. Carson; and his report in the first instance had occasioned the subpœna to Mary.

And now she was to be called on to bear witness. The court was by this time almost as full as it could hold; but fresh attempts were being made to squeeze in at all the entrances, for many were anxious to see and hear this part of the trial.

Old Mr. Carson felt an additional beat at his heart at the thought of seeing the fatal Helen, the cause of all—a kind of interest and yet repugnance, for was not she beloved by the dead; nay, perhaps in her way, loving and mourning for the same being that he himself was so bitterly grieving over? And yet he felt as if he abhorred her and her rumoured loveliness, as if she were the curse against him; and he grew jealous of the love with which she had inspired his son, and would fain have deprived her of even her natural right of sorrowing over her lover's untimely end; for, you see, it was a fixed idea in the minds of all that the handsome, bright, gay, rich young gentleman must have been beloved in preference to the serious, almost stern-looking smith, who had to toil for his daily bread.

Hitherto the effect of the trial had equalled Mr. Carson's most sanguine hopes, and a severe look of satisfaction came over the face of the avenger— over that countenance whence a smile had departed, never more to return.

All eyes were directed to the door through which the witnesses entered. Even Jem looked up to catch one glimpse, before he hid his face from her look of aversion. The officer had gone to fetch her.

She was in exactly the same attitude as when Job Legh had seen her two hours before through the half-open door. Not a finger had moved. The officer summoned her, but she did not stir. She was so still, he thought she had fallen asleep, and he stepped forward and touched her. She started up in an instant, and followed him with a kind of rushing, rapid motion into the court, into the witness-box.

And amid all that sea of faces, misty and swimming before her eyes, she saw but two clear bright spots, distinct and fixed: the judge, who might have to condemn; and the prisoner, who might have to die.

The mellow sunlight streamed down that high window on her head, and fell on the rich treasure of her golden hair, stuffed away in masses under her little bonnet-cap; and in those warm beams the motes kept dancing up and down. The wind had changed—had changed almost as soon as she had given up her watching; the wind had changed, and she heeded it not.

Many who were looking for mere flesh and blood beauty, mere colouring, were disappointed; for her face was deadly white, and almost set in its expression, while a mournful, bewildered soul looked out of the depths of those soft, deep grey eyes. But others recognised a higher and a stranger kind of beauty; one that would keep its hold on the memory for many after years.

I was not there myself; but one who was, told me that her look, and indeed her whole face, was more like the well-known engraving from Guido's picture of "Beatrice Cenci" than anything else he could give me an idea of. He added that her countenance haunted him, like the remembrance of some wild sad melody, heard in childhood; that it would perpetually recur with its mute imploring agony.

With all the court reeling before her (always save and except those awful two) she heard a voice speak, and answered the simple inquiry (something about her name) mechanically, as if in a dream. So she went on for two or three more questions with a strange wonder in her brain, at the reality of the terrible circumstances in which she was placed.

Suddenly she was roused, she knew not how or by what. She was conscious that all was real, that hundreds were looking at her, that true-sounding words were being extracted from her; that that figure, so bowed down, with the face concealed with both hands, was really Jem. Her face flushed scarlet, and then paler than before. But in dread of herself with the tremendous secret imprisoned within her, she exerted every power she had to keep in the full understanding of what was going on, of what she was asked, and of what she answered. With all her faculties preternaturally alive and sensitive, she heard the next question from the pert young barrister, who was delighted to have the examination of this witness.

"And pray, may I ask, which was the favoured lover? You say you knew both these young men. Which was the favoured lover? Which did you prefer?"

And who was he, the questioner, that he should dare so lightly to ask of her heart's secrets? That he should dare to ask her to tell, before that multitude assembled there, what woman usually whispers with blushes and tears, and many hesitations, to one ear alone?

So, for an instant, a look of indignation contracted Mary's brow, as she steadily met the eyes of the impertinent counsellor. But, in that instant, she saw the hands removed from a face beyond, behind; and a countenance revealed of such intense love and woe—such a deprecating dread of her answer; and suddenly her resolution was taken. The present was everything; the future, that vast shroud, it was maddening to think upon; but *now* she might own her fault, but *now* she might even own her love. Now, when the beloved stood thus, abhorred of men, there would be no feminine shame to stand between her and her avowal. So she also turned towards the judge, partly to mark that her answer was not given to the monkeyfied man who questioned her, and likewise that the face might be averted from, and her eyes not gaze upon, the form that contracted with the dread of the words he anticipated.

"He asks me which of them two I liked best. Perhaps I liked Mr. Harry Carson once—I don't know—I've forgotten; but I loved James Wilson, that's now on trial, above what tongue can tell—above all else on earth put together; and I love him now better than ever, though he has never known a word of it till this minute. For you see, sir, mother died before I was thirteen, before I could know right from wrong about some things; and I was giddy and vain, and ready to listen to any praise of my good looks; and this poor young Mr. Carson fell in with me, and told me he loved me; and I was foolish enough to think he meant me marriage: a mother is a pitiful loss to a girl, sir; and so I used to fancy I could like to be a lady, and rich, and never know want any more. I never found out how dearly I loved another till one day, when James Wilson asked me to marry him, and I was very hard and sharp in my answer—for, indeed, sir, I'd a deal to bear just then—and he took me at my word and left me; and from that day to this, I've never spoken a word to him, or set eyes on him; though I'd fain have done so, to try and show him we had both been too hasty; for he'd not been gone out of my sight above a minute, before I knew I loved—far above my life," said she, dropping her voice as she came to this second confession of the strength of her attachment. "But if the gentleman asks me which I loved the best, I make answer, I was flattered by Mr. Carson, and pleased with his flattery; but James Wilson, I——"

She covered her face with her hands, to hide the burning scarlet blushes, which even dyed her fingers.

John Barton's Confession of the Murder of young Mr. Carson

From *Mary Barton*, 1848

"AND have I heard you aright?" began Mr. Carson, with his deep quivering voice. "Man! have I heard you aright? Was it you, then, that killed my boy? my only son?"—(he said these last few words almost as if appealing for pity, and then he changed his tone to one more vehement and fierce). "Don't dare to think that I shall be merciful, and spare you, because you have come forward to accuse yourself. I tell you I will not spare you the least pang the law can inflict—you, who did not show pity on my boy, shall have none from me."

"I did not ask for any," said John Barton, in a low voice.

"Ask, or not ask, what care I? You shall be hanged—hanged—man!" said he, advancing his face, and repeating the word with slow grinding emphasis, as if to infuse some of the bitterness of his soul into it.

John Barton gasped, but not with fear. It was only that he felt it terrible to have inspired such hatred as was concentrated into every word, every gesture of Mr. Carson's.

"As for being hanged, sir, I know it's all right and proper. I dare say it's bad enough; but I tell you what, sir," speaking with an outburst, "if you'd hanged me the day after I'd done the deed, I would have gone down on my knees and blessed you. Death! Lord, what is it to Life? To such a life as I've been leading this fortnight past. Life at best is no great thing; but such a life as I have dragged through since that night," he shuddered at the thought. "Why, sir, I've been on the point of killing myself this many a time to get away from my own thoughts. I didn't! and I'll tell you why. I didn't know but that I should be more haunted than ever with the recollection of my sin. Oh! God above only can tell the agony with which I've repented me of it, and part perhaps because I feared He would think I were impatient of the misery He sent as punishment—far, far worse misery than any hanging, sir." He ceased from excess of emotion.

Then he began again.

"Sin' that day (it may be very wicked, sir, but it's the truth) I've kept thinking and thinking if I were but in that world where they say God is, He would, maybe, teach me right from wrong, even if it were with many stripes. I've been sore puzzled here. I would go through hell-fire if I could but get free from sin at last, it's an awful thing. As for hanging, that's just nought at all."

His exhaustion compelled him to sit down. Mary rushed to him. It seemed as if till then he had been unaware of her presence.

"Ay, ay, wench!" said he feebly, "is it thee? Where's Jem Wilson?"

Jem came forward. John Barton spoke again, with many a break and gasping pause:

"Lad! thou hast borne a deal for me. It's the meanest thing I ever did to leave thee to bear the brunt. Thou, who wert as innocent of any knowledge of it as the babe unborn. I'll not bless thee for it. Blessing from such as me would not bring thee any good. Thou'lt love Mary, though she is my child."

He ceased, and there was a pause for a few seconds.

Then Mr. Carson turned to go. When his hand was on the latch of the door, he hesitated for an instant.

"You can have no doubt for what purpose I go. Straight to the police-office, to send men to take care of you, wretched man, and your accomplice. To-morrow morning your tale shall be repeated to those who can commit you to gaol, and before long you shall have the opportunity of trying how desirable hanging is."

"O sir!" said Mary, springing forward and catching hold of Mr. Carson's arm, "my father is dying. Look at him, sir. If you want Death for Death, you have it. Don't take him away from me these last hours. He must go alone through Death, but let me be with him as long as I can. O, sir! if you have any mercy in you, leave him here to die."

John himself stood up, stiff and rigid, and replied:

"Mary, wench! I owe him summat. I will go die, where, and as he wishes me. Thou hast said true, I am standing side by side with Death; and it matters little where I spend the bit of time left of life. That time I must pass wrestling with my soul for a character to take into the other world. I'll go where you see fit, sir. He's innocent," faintly indicating Jem, as he fell back in the chair.

"Never fear! They cannot touch him," said Job Legh, in a low voice.

But as Mr. Carson was on the point of leaving the house with no sign of relenting about him, he was again stopped by John Barton, who had risen once more from his chair, and stood supporting himself on Jem while he spoke.

"Sir, one word! My hairs are grey with suffering, and yours with years——"

"And have I had no suffering?" asked Mr. Carson, as if appealing for sympathy, even to the murderer of his child.

And the murderer of his child answered to the appeal, and groaned in spirit over the anguish he had caused.

"Have I had no inward suffering to blanch these hairs? Have not I toiled and struggled even to these years with hopes in my heart that all centred in my boy! I did not speak of them, but were they not there? I seemed hard and cold; and so I might be to others, but not to him!—who shall ever imagine the love I bore to him? Even he never dreamed how my heart leapt up at the sound of his footstep, and how precious he was to his poor old father. And he is gone—killed—out of the hearing of all loving words—out of my sight for ever. He was my sunshine, and now it is night! Oh, my God! comfort me, comfort me!" cried the old man aloud.

The eyes of John Barton grew dim with tears. Rich and poor, masters and men, were then brothers in the deep suffering of the heart; for was not this the very anguish he had felt for little Tom, in years so long gone by that they seemed like another life!

The mourner before him was no longer the employer; a being of another race, eternally placed in antagonistic attitude; going through the world glittering like gold, with a stony heart within, which knew no sorrow but through the accidents of Trade; no longer the enemy, the oppressor, but a very poor and desolate old man.

The sympathy for suffering, formerly so prevalent a feeling with him, again filled John Barton's heart, and almost impelled him to speak (as best he could) some earnest tender words to the stern man, shaking in his agony.

But who was he that he should utter sympathy or consolation? The cause of all this woe.

Oh, blasting thought! Oh, miserable remembrance! He had forfeited all right to bind up his brother's wounds.

Stunned by the thought, he sank upon the seat, almost crushed with the knowledge of the consequences of his own action; for he had no more imagined to himself the blighted home, and the miserable parents, than does the soldier, who discharges his musket, picture to himself the desolation of the wife, and the pitiful cries of the helpless little ones, who are in an instant to be made widowed and fatherless.

To intimidate a class of men, known only to those below them as desirous to obtain the greatest quantity of work for the lowest wages—at most, to remove an overbearing partner from an obnoxious firm, who stood in the way of those who struggled as well as they were able to obtain their rights— this was the light in which John Barton had viewed his deed; and even so viewing it, after the excitement had passed away, the Avenger, the sure Avenger, had found him out.

But now he knew that he had killed a man and a brother—now he knew that no good thing could come out of this evil, even to the sufferers whose cause he had so blindly espoused.

He lay across the table, broken-hearted. Every fresh quivering sob of Mr. Carson's stabbed him to his soul.

He felt execrated by all; and as if he could never lay bare the perverted reasonings which had made the performance of undoubted sin appear a duty. The longing to plead some faint excuse grew stronger and stronger. He feebly raised his head, and looking at Job Legh, he whispered out:

"I did not know what I was doing, Job Legh; God knows I didn't! O, sir!" said he wildly, almost throwing himself at Mr. Carson's feet, "say you forgive me the anguish I now see I have caused you. I care not for pain, or death; you know I don't; but oh, man! forgive me the trespass I have done!"

"Forgive us our trespasses as we forgive them that trespass against us," said Job, solemnly and low, as if in prayer: as if the words were suggested by those John Barton had used.

Mr. Carson took his hands away from his face. I would rather see death than the ghastly gloom which darkened that countenance.

"Let my trespasses be unforgiven, so that I may have vengeance for my son's murder."

There are blasphemous actions as well as blasphemous words: all unloving, cruel deeds are acted blasphemy.

Mr. Carson left the house. And John Barton lay on the ground as one dead.

They lifted him up, and almost hoping that that deep trance might be to him the end of all earthly things, they bore him to his bed.

For a time they listened with divided attention to his faint breathings; for in each hasty hurried step that echoed in the street outside they thought they heard the approach of the officers of justice.

When Mr. Carson left the house he was dizzy with agitation; the hot blood went careering through his frame. He could not see the deep blue of the night heavens for the fierce pulses which throbbed in his head. And partly to steady and calm himself, he leaned against a railing, and looked up into those calm majestic depths with all their thousand stars.

And by-and-by his own voice returned upon him, as if the last words he had spoken were being uttered through all that infinite space; but in their echoes there was a tone of unutterable sorrow.

"Let my trespasses be unforgiven, so that I may have vengeance for my son's murder."

He tried to shake off the spiritual impression made by this imagination. He was feverish and ill—and no wonder.

So he turned to go homewards; not, as he had threatened, to the police-office. After all (he told himself) that would do in the morning. No fear of the man escaping, unless he escaped to the grave.

So he tried to banish the phantom voices and shapes which came unbidden to his brain, and to recall his balance of mind by walking calmly and slowly, and noticing everything which struck his senses.

It was a warm soft evening in spring, and there were many persons in the streets. Among others a nurse with a little girl in her charge, conveying her home from some children's gaiety—a dance most likely, for the lovely little creature was daintily decked out in soft, snowy muslin; and her fairy feet tripped along by her nurse's side as if to the measure of some tune she had lately kept time to.

Suddenly, up behind her there came a rough, rude errand-boy, nine or ten years of age; a giant he looked by the fairy-child as she fluttered along. I don't know how it was, but in some awkward way he knocked the poor little girl down upon the hard pavement as he brushed rudely past, not much caring whom he hurt so that he got along.

The child arose, sobbing with pain; and not without cause, for blood was dropping down from the face but a minute before so fair and bright— dropping down on the pretty frock, making those scarlet marks so terrible to little children.

The nurse, a powerful woman, had seized the boy just as Mr. Carson (who had seen the whole transaction) came up.

"You naughty little rascal! I'll give you to a policeman, that I will! Do you see how you've hurt the little girl? Do you?" accompanying every sentence with a violent jerk of passionate anger.

The lad looked hard and defying; but withal terrified at the threat of the policeman, that ogre of our streets to all unlucky urchins. The nurse saw it, and began to drag him along, with a view of making what she called "a wholesome impression."

His terror increased, and with it his irritation; when the little sweet face, choking away its sobs, pulled down nurse's head, and said—

"Please, dear nurse, I'm not much hurt; it was very silly to cry, you know. He did not mean to do it. *He did not know what he was doing*, did you, little boy? Nurse won't call a policeman, so don't be frightened." And she put up her little mouth to be kissed by her injurer, just as she had been taught to do at home to "make peace."

"That lad will mind, and be more gentle for the time to come, I'll be bound, thanks to that little lady," said a passer by, half to himself and half to Mr. Carson, whom he had observed to notice the scene.

The latter took no apparent heed of the remark, but passed on. But the child's pleading reminded him of the low, broken voice he had so lately heard, penitently and humbly urging the same extenuation of his great guilt.

"I did not know what I was doing."

He had some association with those words; he had heard or read of that plea somewhere before. Where was it?

Could it be——?

He would look when he got home. So when he entered his house he went straight and silently upstairs to his library, and took down the large handsome Bible, all grand and golden, with its leaves adhering together from the bookbinder's press, so little had it been used.

On the first page (which fell open to Mr. Carson's view) were written the names of his children, and his own.

"Henry John, son of the above John
and Elizabeth Carson
Born, Sept. 29th, 1815."

To make the entry complete, his death should now be added. But the page became hidden by the gathering mist of tears.

Thought upon thought, and recollection upon recollection, came crowding in, from the remembrance of the proud day when he had purchased the costly book in order to write down the birth of the little babe of a day old.

He laid his head down on the open page, and let the tears fall slowly on the spotless leaves.

His son's murderer was discovered; had confessed his guilt; and yet (strange to say) he could not hate him with the vehemence of hatred he had felt when he had imagined him a young man, full of lusty life defying all laws, human and divine. In spite of his desire to retain the revengeful feeling he considered as a duty to his dead son, something of pity would steal in for the poor, wasted skeleton of a man, the smitten creature, who had told him of his sin, and implored his pardon that night.

In the days of his childhood and youth, Mr. Carson had been accustomed to poverty, but it was honest, decent poverty; not the grinding, squalid misery he had remarked in every part of John Barton's house, and which contrasted strangely with the pompous sumptuousness of the room in which he now sat. Unaccustomed wonder filled his mind at the reflection of the different lots of the brethren of mankind.

Then he roused himself from his reverie, and turned to the object of his search—the Gospel, where he half expected to find the tender pleading: "They know not what they do."

It was murk midnight by this time, and the house was still and quiet. There was nothing to interrupt the old man in his unwonted study.

Years ago the Gospel had been his task-book in learning to read. So many years ago that he had become familiar with the events before he could comprehend the Spirit that made the Life.

He fell to the narrative now afresh, with all the interest of a little child. He began at the beginning, and read on almost greedily, understanding for the first time the full meaning of the story. He came to the end; the awful End. And there were the haunting words of pleading.

He shut the book and thought deeply.

All night long, the Archangel combated with the Demon.

All night long others watched by the bed of Death. John Barton had revived a fitful intelligence. He spoke at times with even something of his former energy, and in the racy Lancashire dialect he had always used when speaking freely.

"You see, I've so often been hankering after the right way; and it's a hard one for a poor man to find. At least it's been so to me. No one learned me, and no one telled me. When I was a little chap they taught me to read, and then they never gave no books; only I heard say the Bible was a good book. So when I grew thoughtful and puzzled, I took to it. But you'd never believe black was black, or night was night, when you saw all about you acting as if black was white, and night was day. It's not much I can say for myself in t'other world, God forgive me; but I can say this, I would fain have gone after the Bible rules if I'd seen folk credit it; they all spoke up for it, and went and did clean contrary. In those days I would ha' gone about wi' my Bible, like a little child, my finger in th' place, and asking the meaning of this or that text, and no one telled me. Then I took out two or three texts as clear as glass, and I tried to do what they bid me do. But I don't know how it was, masters and men, all alike cared no more for minding those texts than I did for th' Lord Mayor of London; so I grew to think it must be a sham put upon poor ignorant folk, women, and such like.

"It was not long I tried to live Gospelwise, but it was liker heaven than any other bit of earth has been. I'd old Alice to strengthen me; but everyone else said, 'Stand up for thy rights, or thou'lt never get them;' and wife and children never spoke, but their helplessness cried aloud, and I was driven to do as others did—and then Tom died. You know all about that—I'm getting scant o' breath, and blind like."

Then again he spoke, after some minutes of hushed silence.

"All along it came natural to love folk, though now I am what I am. I think one time I could e'en have loved the masters if they'd ha' letten me; that was in my Gospel-days, afore my child died o' hunger. I was tore in two oftentimes, between my sorrow for poor, suffering folk, and my trying to love them as caused their sufferings (to my mind).

"At last I gave it up in despair, trying to make folks' actions square wi' th' Bible; and I thought I'd no longer labour at following th' Bible mysel'. I've said all this afore, maybe. But from that time I've dropped down, down— down."

After that he only spoke in broken sentences.

"I did not think he'd been such an old man—oh, that he had but forgiven me!" and then came earnest, passionate, broken words of prayer.

Job Legh had gone home like one struck down with the unexpected shock. Mary and Jem together waited the approach of death; but as the final struggle drew on, and morning dawned, Jem suggested some alleviation to the gasping breath, to purchase which he left the house in search of a druggist's shop which should be open at that early hour.

During his absence, Barton grew worse; he had fallen across the bed, and his breathing seemed almost stopped; in vain did Mary strive to raise him, her sorrow and exhaustion had rendered her too weak.

So, on hearing someone enter the house-place below, she cried out for Jem to come to her assistance.

A step, which was not Jem's, came up the stairs.

Mr. Carson stood in the doorway. In one instant he comprehended the case.

He raised up the powerless frame; and the departing soul looked out of the eyes with gratitude. He held the dying man propped in his arms. John Barton folded his hands as if in prayer.

"Pray for us," said Mary, sinking on her knees, and forgetting in that solemn hour all that had divided her father and Mr. Carson.

No other words would suggest themselves than some of those he had read only a few hours before:

"God be merciful to us sinners.—Forgive us our trespasses as we forgive them that trespass against us."

And when the words were said, John Barton lay a corpse in Mr. Carson's arms.

So ended the tragedy of a poor man's life.

Job Legh Defends John Barton

From *Mary Barton*, 1848

"JOHN BARTON was not a man to take counsel with people; nor did he make many words about his doings. So I can only judge from his way of thinking and talking in general, never having heard him breathe a syllable concerning this matter in particular. You see, he were sadly put about to make great riches and great poverty square with Christ's Gospel"—Job paused in order to try and express what was clear enough in his own mind as to the effect produced on John Barton by the great and mocking contrasts presented by the varieties of human condition. Before he could find suitable words to explain his meaning, Mr. Carson spoke.

"You mean he was an Owenite; all for equality and community of goods, and that kind of absurdity."

"No, no! John Barton was no fool. No need to tell him that were all men equal to-night, some would get the start by rising an hour earlier to-morrow. Nor yet did he care for goods, nor wealth; no man less, so that he could get daily bread for him and his; but what hurt him sore, and rankled in him as long as I knew him (and, sir, it rankles in many a poor man's heart far more than the want of any creature comforts, and puts a sting into starvation itself), was that those who wore finer clothes and ate better food, and had more money in their pockets, kept him at arm's length, and cared not whether his heart was sorry or glad; whether he lived or died—whether he was bound for heaven or hell. It seemed hard to him that a heap of gold should part him and his brother so far asunder. For he was a loving man before he grew mad with seeing such as he was slighted, as if Christ Himself had not been poor. At one time, I've heard him say, he felt kindly towards every man, rich or poor, because he thought they were all men alike. But latterly he grew aggravated with the sorrows and suffering that he saw, and which he thought the masters might help if they would."

"That's the notion you've all of you got," said Mr. Carson. "Now, how in the world can we help it? We cannot regulate the demand for labour. No man or set of men can do it. It depends on events which God alone can control. When there is no market for our goods we suffer just as much as you can do."

"Not as much, I'm sure, sir; though I'm not given to Political Economy, I know that much. I'm wanting in learning, I'm aware; but I can use my eyes. I never see the masters getting thin and haggard for want of food; I hardly ever see them making much change in their way of living, though I don't doubt they've got to do it in bad times. But it's in things for show they cut short; while for such as me, it's in things for life we've to stint. For sure, sir, you'll own it's come to a hard pass when a man would give aught in the world for work to keep his children from starving, and can't get a bit, if he's ever so willing to labour. I'm not up to talking as John Barton would have done, but that's clear to me at any rate."

"My good man, just listen to me. Two men live in a solitude; one produces loaves of bread, the other coats—or what you will. Now, would it not be hard if the bread-producer were forced to give bread for the coats, whether he wanted them or not, in order to furnish employment to the other: that is the simple form of the case; you've only to multiply the numbers. There will come times of great changes in the occupation of thousands when improvements in manufactures and machinery are made. It's all nonsense talking—it must be so!"

Job Legh pondered a few moments.

"It's true it was a sore time for the hand-loom weavers when power-looms came in; them new-fangled things make a man's life like a lottery; and yet I'll never misdoubt that power-looms, and railways, and all such-like inventions are the gifts of God. I have lived long enough, too, to see that it is a part of His plan to send suffering to bring out a higher good; but surely it's also a part of His plan that so much of the burden of the suffering as can be should be lightened by those whom it is His pleasure to make happy and content in their own circumstances. Of course, it would take a deal more thought and wisdom than me or any other man has to settle out of hand how this should be done. But I'm clear about this, when God gives a blessing to be enjoyed, He gives it with a duty to be done; and the duty of the happy is to help the suffering to bear their woe."

"Still facts have proved, and are daily proving, how much better it is for every man to be independent of help, and self-reliant," said Mr. Carson thoughtfully.

"You can never work facts as you would fixed quantities, and say, given two facts, and the product is so and so. God has given men feelings and passions which cannot be worked into the problem, because they are for ever changing and uncertain. God has also made some weak; not in any one way, but in all. One is weak in body, another in mind, another in steadiness of purpose, a fourth can't tell right from wrong, and so on; or if he can tell the right, he wants strength to hold by it. Now, to my thinking, them that is strong in any of God's gifts is meant to help the weak—be hanged to the facts! I ask your pardon, sir; I can't rightly explain the meaning that is in me. I'm like a tap as won't run, but keeps letting it out drop by drop, so that you've no notion of the force of what's within."

Job looked and felt very sorrowful at the want of power in his words, while the feeling within him was so strong and clear.

"What you say is very true, no doubt," replied Mr. Carson; "but how would you bring it to bear upon the masters' conduct—on my particular case?" added he gravely.

"I'm not learned enough to argue. Thoughts come into my head that I'm sure are as true as Gospel, though maybe they don't follow each other like the Q.E.D. of a Proposition. The masters has it on their own conscience—you have it on yours, sir, to answer for to God whether you've done, and are doing, all in your power to lighten the evils that seem always to hang on the trades by which you make your fortunes. It's no business of mine, thank God. John Barton took the question in hand, and his answer to it was NO! Then he grew bitter and angry, and mad; and in his madness he did a great sin, and wrought a great woe; and repented him with tears of blood, and will go through his penance humbly and meekly in t'other place, I'll be bound. I never seed such bitter repentance as his that last night."

There was a silence of many minutes. Mr. Carson had covered his face, and seemed utterly forgetful of their presence; and yet they did not like to disturb him by rising to leave the room.

At last he said, without meeting their sympathetic eyes:

"Thank you both for coming—and for speaking candidly to me. I fear, Legh, neither you nor I have convinced each other, as to the power, or want of power, in the masters to remedy the evils the men complain of."

"I'm loth to vex you, sir, just now; but it was not the want of power I was talking on; what we all feel sharpest is the want of inclination to try and help the evils which come like blights at times over the manufacturing places, while we see the masters can stop work and not suffer. If we saw the masters try for our sakes to find a remedy—even if they were long about it—even if they could find no help, and at the end of all could only say, 'Poor fellows, our hearts are sore for ye; we've done all we could, and can't find a cure'— we'd bear up like men through bad times. No one knows till they have tried what power of bearing lies in them, if once they believe that men are caring for their sorrows and will help if they can. If fellow-creatures can give nought but tears and brave words, we take our trials straight from God, and we know enough of His love to put ourselves blind into His hands. You say our talk has done no good. I say it has. I see the view you take of things from the place where you stand. I can remember that when the time comes for judging you; I shan't think any longer, does he act right on my views of a thing, but does he act right on his own. It has done me good in that way. I'm an old man, and may never see you again; but I'll pray for you, and think on you and your trials, both of your great wealth, and of your son's cruel death, many and many a day to come; and I'll ask God to bless you both now and for evermore. Amen. Farewell!"

Jem had maintained a manly and dignified reserve ever since he had made his open statement of all he knew. Now both the men rose, and bowed low, looking at Mr. Carson with the deep human interest they could not fail to take in one who had endured and forgiven a deep injury; and who struggled hard, as it was evident he did, to bear up like a man under his affliction.

He bowed low in return to them. Then he suddenly came forward and shook them by the hand; and thus, without a word more, they parted.

There are stages in the contemplation and endurance of great sorrow which endow men with the same earnestness and clearness of thought that in some of old took the form of Prophecy. To those who have large capability of loving and suffering, united with great power of firm endurance, there comes a time in their woe when they are lifted out of the contemplation of their individual case into a searching inquiry into the nature of their calamity, and the remedy (if remedy there be) which may prevent its recurrence to others as well as to themselves.

Hence the beautiful, noble efforts which are from time to time brought to light, as being continuously made by those who have once hung on the cross of agony, in order that others may not suffer as they have done; one of the grandest ends which sorrow can accomplish; the sufferer wrestling with God's messenger until a blessing is left behind, not for one alone but for generations.

It took time before the stern nature of Mr. Carson was compelled to the recognition of this secret of comfort, and that same sternness prevented his reaping any benefit in public estimation from the actions he performed; for the character is more easily changed than the habits and manners originally formed by that character, and to his dying day Mr. Carson was considered hard and cold by those who only casually saw him, or superficially knew him. But those who were admitted into his confidence were aware that the wish that lay nearest to his heart was that none might suffer from the cause from which he had suffered; that a perfect understanding, and complete confidence and love, might exist between masters and men; that the truth might be recognised that the interests of one were the interests of all, and as such required the consideration and deliberation of all, that hence it was most desirable to have educated workers, capable of judging, not mere machines of ignorant men; and to have them bound to their employers by the ties of respect and affection, not by mere money bargains alone; in short, to acknowledge the Spirit of Christ as the regulating law between both parties.

Many of the improvements now in practice in the system of employment in Manchester owe their origin to short earnest sentences spoken by Mr. Carson. Many and many yet to be carried into execution take their birth from that stern, thoughtful mind which submitted to be taught by suffering.

A Manchester Strike in the "Hungry Forties"

From *North and South*, 1855

Writing of *North and South* Mrs. Gaskell said: "I tried to make both the story and the writing as quiet as I could, in order that people might not say that they could not see what the writer felt to be a plain and earnest truth for romantic incident or exaggerated writing." The earlier chapters of *North and South* contain some of Mrs. Gaskell's best work.

SHE desired me to apologise to you as it is. Perhaps you know my brother has imported hands from Ireland, and it has irritated the Milton people excessively—as if he hadn't a right to get labour where he could; and the stupid wretches here wouldn't work for him; and now they've frightened these poor Irish starvelings so with their threats, that we daren't let them out. You may see them huddled in that top room in the mill—and they're to sleep there, to keep them safe from those brutes, who will neither work nor let them work.

"They're at the gates! Call John, Fanny—call him in from the mill! They're at the gates! They'll batter them in! Call John, I say!"

And simultaneously, the gathering tramp—to which she had been listening, instead of heeding Margaret's words—was heard just right outside the wall, and an increasing din of angry voices raged behind the wooden barrier, which shook as if the unseen maddened crowd made battering-rams of their bodies, and retreated a short space only to come with more united steady impetus against it, till their great beats made the strong gates quiver like reeds before the wind.

The women gathered round the windows, fascinated to look on the scene which terrified them. Mrs. Thornton, the women-servants, Margaret—all were there. Fanny had returned, screaming upstairs as if pursued at every step, and had thrown herself in hysterical sobbing on the sofa. Mrs. Thornton watched for her son, who was still in the mill. He came out, looked up at them—the pale cluster of faces—and smiled good courage to them, before he locked the factory-door. Then he called to one of the women to come down and undo his own door, which Fanny had fastened behind her in her mad flight. Mrs. Thornton herself went. And the sound of his well-known and commanding voice seemed to have been like the taste of blood to the infuriated multitude outside. Hitherto they had been voiceless, wordless, needing all their breath for their hard-labouring efforts to break down the gates. But now, hearing him speak inside, they set up such a fierce unearthly groan, that even Mrs. Thornton was white with fear as she preceded him into the room. He came in a little flushed, but his eyes gleaming, as in answer to the trumpet-call of danger, and with a proud look of defiance on his face, that made him a noble, if not a handsome man. Margaret had always dreaded lest her courage should fail her in any emergency, and she should be proved to be, what she dreaded lest she was—a coward. But now, in this real great time of reasonable fear and nearness of terror, she forgot herself, and felt only an intense sympathy—intense to painfulness—in the interests of the moment.

Mr. Thornton came frankly forwards:

"I'm sorry, Miss Hale, you have visited us at this unfortunate moment, when, I fear, you may be involved in whatever risk we have to bear. Mother! hadn't you better go into the back rooms? I'm not sure whether they may not have made their way from Pinner's Lane into the stable-yard; but if not, you will be safer there than here. Go, Jane!" continued he, addressing the upper servant. And she went, followed by the others.

"I stop here!" said his mother. "Where you are, there I stay." And, indeed, retreat into the back rooms was of no avail; the crowd had surrounded the out-buildings at the rear, and were sending forth their awful threatening roar behind. The servants retreated into the garrets, with many a cry and shriek. Mr. Thornton smiled scornfully as he heard them. He glanced at Margaret, standing all by herself at the window nearest the factory. Her eyes glittered, her colour was deepened on cheek and lip. As if she felt his look, she turned to him and asked a question that had been for some time in her mind:

"Where are the poor imported work-people? In the factory there?"

"Yes! I left them cowered up in a small room, at the head of a back flight of stairs; bidding them run all risks, and escape down there, if they heard any attack made on the mill-doors. But it is not them—it is me they want."

"When can the soldiers be here?" asked his mother, in a low but not unsteady voice.

He took out his watch with the same measured composure with which he did everything. He made some little calculation:

"Supposing Williams got straight off when I told him, and hadn't to dodge about amongst them—it must be twenty minutes yet."

"Twenty minutes!" said his mother, for the first time showing her terror in the tones of her voice.

"Shut down the windows instantly, mother," exclaimed he: "the gates won't bear such another shock. Shut down that window, Miss Hale."

Margaret shut down her window, and then went to assist Mrs. Thornton's trembling fingers.

From some cause or other, there was a pause of several minutes in the unseen street. Mrs. Thornton looked with wild anxiety at her son's countenance, as if to gain the interpretation of the sudden stillness from him. His face was set into rigid lines of contemptuous defiance; neither hope nor fear could be read there. Fanny raised herself up:

"Are they gone?" asked she, in a whisper.

"Gone!" replied he. "Listen!"

She did listen; they all could hear the one great straining breath; the creak of wood slowly yielding; the wrench of iron; the mighty fall of the ponderous gates. Fanny stood up tottering—made a step or two towards her mother, and fell forwards into her arms in a fainting fit. Mrs. Thornton lifted her up with a strength that was as much that of the will as of the body, and carried her away.

"Thank God!" said Mr. Thornton, as he watched her out. "Had you not better go upstairs, Miss Hale?"

Margaret's lips formed a "No"!—but he could not hear her speak, for the tramp of innumerable steps right under the very wall of the house, and the fierce growl of low, deep, angry voices that had a ferocious murmur of satisfaction in them, more dreadful than their baffled cries not many minutes before.

"Never mind!" said he, thinking to encourage her. "I am very sorry you should have been entrapped into all this alarm; but it cannot last long now; a few minutes more, and the soldiers will be here."

"Oh, God!" cried Margaret suddenly; "there is Boucher. I know his face, though he is livid with rage—he is fighting to get to the front—look! look!"

"Who is Boucher?" asked Mr. Thornton coolly, and coming close to the window to discover the man in whom Margaret took such an interest. As soon as they saw Mr. Thornton, they set up a yell—to call it not human is nothing—it was as the demoniac desire of some terrible wild beast for the food that is withheld from his ravening. Even he drew back for a moment, dismayed at the intensity of hatred he had provoked.

"Let them yell!" said he. "In five minutes more———. I only hope my poor Irishmen are not terrified out of their wits by such a fiend-like noise. Keep up your courage for five minutes, Miss Hale."

"Don't be afraid for me," she said hastily. "But what in five minutes? Can you do nothing to soothe these poor creatures? It is awful to see them."

"The soldiers will be here directly, and that will bring them to reason."

"To reason!" said Margaret quickly. "What kind of reason?"

"The only reason that does with men that make themselves into wild beasts. By Heaven! they've turned to the mill-door!"

"Mr. Thornton," said Margaret, shaking all over with her passion, "go down this instant, if you are not a coward. Go down and face them like a man. Save these poor strangers, whom you have decoyed here. Speak to your workmen as if they were human beings. Speak to them kindly. Don't let the soldiers come in and cut down poor creatures who are driven mad. I see one there who is. If you have any courage or noble quality in you, go out and speak to them, man to man."

He turned and looked at her while she spoke. A dark cloud came over his face while he listened. He set his teeth as he heard her words.

"I will go. Perhaps I may ask you to accompany me downstairs, and bar the door behind me; my mother and sister will need that protection."

"Oh! Mr. Thornton! I do not know—I may be wrong—only——"

But he was gone; he was downstairs in the hall; he had unbarred the front door; all she could do, was to follow him quickly, and fasten it behind him, and clamber up the stairs again with a sick heart and a dizzy head. Again she took her place by the farthest window. He was on the steps below; she saw that by the direction of a thousand angry eyes; but she could neither see nor hear anything save the savage satisfaction of the rolling angry murmur. She threw the window wide open. Many in the crowd were mere boys; cruel and thoughtless—cruel because they were thoughtless; some were men, gaunt as wolves, and mad for prey. She knew how it was; they were like Boucher—with starving children at home—relying on ultimate success in their efforts to get higher wages, and enraged beyond measure at discovering that Irishmen were to be brought in to rob their little ones of bread. Margaret knew it all; she read it in Boucher's face, forlornly desperate and livid with rage. If Mr. Thornton would but say something to them—let them hear his voice only—it seemed as if it would be better than this wild beating and raging against the stony silence that vouchsafed them no word, even of anger or reproach. But perhaps he was speaking now; there was a momentary hush of their noise, inarticulate as that of a troup of animals. She tore her bonnet off; and bent forwards to hear. She could only see; for if Mr. Thornton had indeed made the attempt to speak, the momentary instinct to listen to him was past and gone, and the people were raging worse than ever. He stood with his arms folded; still as a statue; his face pale with repressed excitement. They were trying to intimidate him—to make him flinch; each was urging the other on to some immediate act of personal violence. Margaret felt intuitively that in an instant all would be uproar; the first touch would cause an explosion, in which, among such hundreds of infuriated men and reckless boys, even Mr. Thornton's life would be unsafe—that in another instant the stormy passions would have passed their bounds, and swept all barriers of reason, or apprehension of consequence. Even while she looked she saw lads in the background stooping to take off their heavy wooden clogs—the readiest missile they could find; she saw it was the spark to the gunpowder, and, with a cry, which no one heard, she rushed out of the room, downstairs—she had lifted the great iron bar of the door with an imperious force—had thrown the door open wide—and was there, in face of that angry sea of men, her eyes smiting them with flaming arrows of reproach. The clogs were arrested in the hands that held them—the countenances, so fell not a moment before, now looked irresolute, and as if asking what this meant. For she stood between them and their enemy. She could not speak, but held out her arms towards them till she could recover breath.

"Oh, do not use violence! He is one man, and you are many;" but her words died away, for there was no tone in her voice; it was but a hoarse whisper. Mr. Thornton stood a little on one side; he had moved away from behind her, as if jealous of anything that should come between him and danger.

"Go!" said she, once more (and now her voice was like a cry). "The soldiers are sent for—are coming. Go peaceably. Go away. You shall have relief from your complaints, whatever they are."

"Shall them Irish blackguards be packed back again?" asked one from out the crowd, with fierce threatening in his voice.

"Never, for your bidding!" exclaimed Mr. Thornton. And instantly the storm broke. The hootings rose and filled the air—but Margaret did not hear them. Her eye was on the group of lads who had armed themselves with their clogs some time before. She saw their gesture—she knew its meaning—she read their aim. Another moment, and Mr. Thornton might be smitten down—he whom she had urged and goaded to come to this perilous place. She only thought how she could save him. She threw her arms around him; she made her body into a shield from the fierce people beyond. Still, with his arms folded, he shook her off.

"Go away," said he, in his deep voice. "This is no place for you."

"It is!" said she. "You did not see what I saw." If she thought her sex would be a protection—if, with shrinking eyes, she had turned away from the terrible anger of these men, in any hope that ere she looked again they would have paused and reflected, and slunk away, and vanished—she was wrong. Their reckless passion had carried them too far to stop—at least had carried some of them too far; for it is always the savage lads, with their love of cruel excitement, who head the riot—reckless to what bloodshed it may lead. A clog whizzed through the air. Margaret's fascinated eyes watched its progress; it missed its aim, and she turned sick with affright, but changed not her position, only hid her face on Mr. Thornton's arm. Then she turned and spoke again:

"For God's sake! do not damage your cause by this violence. You do not know what you are doing." She strove to make her words distinct.

A sharp pebble flew by her, grazing forehead and cheek, and drawing a blinding sheet of light before her eyes. She lay like one dead on Mr. Thornton's shoulder. Then he unfolded his arms, and held her encircled in one for an instant:

"You do well!" said he. "You come to oust the innocent stranger. You fall— you hundreds—on one man; and when a woman comes before you, to ask you for your own sakes to be reasonable creatures, your cowardly wrath falls upon her! You do well!" They were silent while he spoke. They were watching, open-eyed and open-mouthed, the thread of dark-red blood which wakened them up from their trance of passion. Those nearest the gate stole out ashamed; there was a movement through all the crowd—a retreating movement. Only one voice cried out:

"Th' stone were meant for thee; but thou wert sheltered behind a woman!"

Mr. Thornton quivered with rage. The blood-flowing had made Margaret conscious—dimly, vaguely conscious. He placed her gently on the doorstep, her head leaning against the frame.

"Can you rest there?" he asked. But without waiting for her answer, he went slowly down the steps right into the middle of the crowd. "Now kill me, if it is your brutal will. There is no woman to shield me here. You may beat me to death—you will never move me from what I have determined upon—not you!" He stood amongst them, with his arms folded, in precisely the same attitude as he had been in on the steps.

But the retrograde movement towards the gate had begun—as unreasoningly, perhaps as blindly, as the simultaneous anger. Or, perhaps, the idea of the approach of the soldiers, and the sight of that pale, upturned face, with closed eyes, still and sad as marble, though the tears welled out of the long entanglement of eyelashes, and dropped down; and, heavier, slower plash than even tears, came the drip of blood from her wound. Even the most desperate—Boucher himself—drew back, faltered away, scowled, and finally went off, muttering curses on the master, who stood in his unchanging attitude, looking after their retreat with defiant eyes. The moment that retreat had changed into a flight (as it was sure from its very character to do), he darted up the steps to Margaret.

She tried to rise without his help.

"It is nothing," she said, with a sickly smile. "The skin is grazed, and I was stunned at the moment. Oh, I am so thankful they are gone!" And she cried without restraint.

North *versus* South

From *North and South*.

Mrs. Gaskell was undecided about a title for her novel, when Charles Dickens, reading the following, came to the conclusion that *North and South* would be most suitable. Mrs. Gaskell was inclined to give the name of the heroine, Margaret Hale, as the title.

MARGARET liked this smile; it was the first thing she had admired in this new friend of her father's; and the opposition of character, shown in all these details of appearance she had just been noticing, seemed to explain the attraction they evidently felt towards each other.

She arranged her mother's worsted-work, and fell back into her own thoughts—as completely forgotten by Mr. Thornton as if she had not been in the room, so thoroughly was he occupied in explaining to Mr. Hale the magnificent power, yet delicate adjustment of the might of the steam-hammer, which was recalling to Mr. Hale some of the wonderful stories of subservient genii in the *Arabian Nights*—one moment stretching from earth to sky and filling all the width of the horizon, at the next obediently compressed into a vase small enough to be borne in the hand of a child.

"And this imagination of power, this practical realisation of a gigantic thought, came out of one man's brain in our good town. That very man has it within him to mount, step by step, on each wonder he achieves to higher marvels still. And I'll be bound to say, we have many among us who, if he were gone, could spring into the breach and carry on the war which compels, and shall compel, all material power to yield to science."

"Your boast reminds me of the old lines:

'I've a hundred captains in England,' he said,

'As good as ever was he.'"

At her father's quotation Margaret looked suddenly up, with inquiring wonder in her eyes. How in the world had they got from cog-wheels to Chevy Chace?

"It is no boast of mine," replied Mr. Thornton; "it is plain matter-of-fact. I won't deny that I am proud of belonging to a town—or perhaps I should rather say a district—the necessities of which give birth to such grandeur of conception. I would rather be a man toiling, suffering—nay, failing and successless—here, than lead a dull prosperous life in the old worn grooves of what you call more aristocratic society down in the South, with their slow days of careless ease. One may be clogged with honey and unable to rise and fly."

"You are mistaken," said Margaret, roused by the aspersion on her beloved South to a fond vehemence of defence, that brought the colour into her cheeks and the angry tears into her eyes. "You do not know anything about the South. If there is less adventure or less progress—I suppose I must not say less excitement—from the gambling spirit of trade, which seems requisite to force out these wonderful inventions, there is less suffering also. I see men here going about in the streets who look ground down by some pinching sorrow or care—who are not only sufferers but haters. Now, in the South we have our poor, but there is not that terrible expression in their countenances of a sullen sense of injustice which I see here. You do not know the South, Mr. Thornton," she concluded, collapsing into a determined silence, and angry with herself for having said so much.

"And may I say you do not know the North?" asked he, with an inexpressible gentleness in his tone, as he saw that he had really hurt her. She continued resolutely silent; yearning after the lovely haunts she had left far away in Hampshire, with a passionate longing that made her feel her voice would be unsteady and trembling if she spoke.

"At any rate, Mr. Thornton," said Mrs. Hale, "you will allow that Milton is a much more smoky, dirty town than you will ever meet with in the South."

"I'm afraid I must give up its cleanliness," said Mr. Thornton, with the quick gleaming smile. "But we are bidden by Parliament to burn our own smoke; so I suppose, like good little children, we shall do as we are bid—some time."

Nicholas Higgins Discusses Religion with the Retired Clergyman

From *North and South*.

The Rev. William Gaskell, who, along with his gifted wife, did so much during the "Hungry Forties" as a peacemaker between the masters and the men, was often to be found in the homes of the Manchester poor listening to their tale of woe, and like Mr. Hale, he always treated the poor with marked courtesy and kindness.

SHE wondered how her father and Higgins had got on.

In the first place, the decorous, kind-hearted, simple, old-fashioned gentleman had unconsciously called out, by his own refinement and courteousness of manner, all the latent courtesy in the other.

Mr. Hale treated all his fellow creatures alike; it never entered into his head to make any difference because of their rank. He placed a chair for Nicholas: stood up till he, at Mr. Hale's request, took a seat; and called him, invariably, "Mr. Higgins," instead of the curt "Nicholas" or "Higgins," to which the "drunken infidel weaver" had been accustomed. But Nicholas was neither an habitual drunkard nor a thorough infidel. He drank to drown care, as he would have himself expressed it; and he was infidel so far as he had never yet found any form of faith to which he could attach himself, heart and soul.

Margaret was a little surprised, and very much pleased, when she found her father and Higgins in earnest conversation—each speaking with gentle politeness to the other, however their opinions might clash. Nicholas—clean, tidied (if only at the pump trough), and quiet spoken—was a new creature to her, who had only seen him in the rough independence of his own hearthstone. He had "slicked" his hair down with the fresh water; he had adjusted his neck-handkerchief, and borrowed an odd candle-end to polish his clogs with; and there he sat, enforcing some opinion on her father, with a strong Darkshire accent, it is true, but with a lowered voice, and a good, earnest composure on his face. Her father, too, was interested in what his companion was saying. He looked round as she came in, smiled, and quietly gave her his chair, and then sat down afresh as quickly as possible, and with a little bow of apology to his guest for the interruption. Higgins nodded to her as a sign of greeting; and she softly adjusted her working materials on the table, and prepared to listen.

"As I was a-sayin', sir, I reckon yo'd not ha' much belief in yo' if yo' lived here—if yo'd been bred here. I ax your pardon if I use wrong words; but what I mean by belief just now, is a-thinking on sayings and maxims and promises made by folk yo' never saw, about the things and the life yo' never saw, nor no one else. Now, yo' say these are true things, and true sayings, and a true life. I just say, where's the proof? There's many and many a one wiser, and scores better learned than I am around me—folk who've had time to think on these things—while my time has had to be gi'en up to getting my bread. Well, I sees these people. Their lives is pretty much open to me. They're real folk. They don't believe i' the Bible—not they. They may say they do, for form's sake; but Lord, sir, dy'e think their first cry i' th' morning is, 'What shall I do to get hold on eternal life?' or 'What shall I do to fill my purse this blessed day? Where shall I go? What bargains shall I strike?' The purse and the gold and the notes is real things; things as can be felt and touched; them's realities; and eternal life is all a talk, very fit for—I ax your pardon, sir; yo'r a parson out o' work, I believe. Well! I'll never speak disrespectful of a man in the same fix as I'm in mysel'. But I'll just ax yo' another question, sir, and I dunnot want yo' to answer it, only to put in yo'r pipe, and smoke it, afore yo' go for to set down us, who only believe in what we see, as fools and noddies. If salvation, and life to come, and what not, was true—not in men's words, but in men's hearts' core—dun yo' not think they'd din us wi' it as they do wi' political 'conomy? They're mighty anxious to come round us wi' that piece o' wisdom; but t'other would be a greater convarsion, if it were true."

"But the masters have nothing to do with your religion. All that they are connected with you in is trade—so they think—and all that it concerns them, therefore, to rectify your opinions in is the science of trade."

"I'm glad, sir," said Higgins, with a curious wink of his eye, "that yo' put in, 'so they think.' I'd ha' thought yo' a hypocrite, I'm afeard, if yo' hadn't, for all yo'r a parson, or rayther because yo'r a parson. Yo' see, if yo'd spoken o' religion as a thing that, if it was true, it didn't concern all men to press on all men's attention, above everything else in this 'varsal earth, I should ha' thought yo' a knave for to be a parson; and I'd rather think yo' a fool than a knave. No offence, I hope, sir."

"None at all. You consider me mistaken, and I consider you far more fatally mistaken. I don't expect to convince you in a day—not in one conversation; but let us know each other, and speak freely to each other about these things, and the truth will prevail. I should not believe in God if I did not believe that. Mr. Higgins, I trust, whatever else you have given up, you believe" (Mr. Hale's voice dropped low in reverence)—"you believe in Him."

Nicholas Higgins suddenly stood straight, stiff up. Margaret started to her feet—for she thought, by the working of his face, he was going into convulsions. Mr. Hale looked at her dismayed. At last Higgins found words:

"Man! I could fell yo' to the ground for tempting me. Whatten business have yo' to try me wi' your doubts? Think o' her lying theere, after the life hoo's led; and think then how yo'd deny me the one sole comfort left—that there is a God, and that He set her her life. I dunnot believe she'll ever live again," said he, sitting down, and drearily going on, as if to the unsympathising fire. "I dunnot believe in any other life than this, in which she dreed such trouble, and had such never-ending care; and I cannot bear to think it were all a set o' chances, that might ha' been altered wi' a breath o' wind. There's many a time when I've thought I didna believe in God, but I've never put if fair out before me in words, as many men do. I may ha' laughed at those who did, to brave it out like—but I have looked round at after, to see if He heard me, if so be there was a He; but to-day, when I'm left desolate, I wunnot listen to yo' wi' yo'r questions, and yo'r doubts. There's one thing steady and quiet i' all this reeling world, and, reason or no reason, I'll cling to that."

Humorous

The New Mamma—Mrs. Gibson

From *Wives and Daughters*, 1866

Writing of *Wives and Daughters*, Madame Mohl said: "The Hamleys are delightful, and Mrs. Gibson! oh, the tricks are delicious; but I am not up to Cynthia yet. Molly is the best heroine you have had yet. Everyone says it is the best thing you ever did."

ON Tuesday afternoon Molly returned home—to the home which was already strange, and what Warwickshire people would call "unked," to her. New paper, new colours; grim servants dressed in their best, and objecting to every change—from their master's marriage to the new oilcloth in the hall, "which tripped 'em up, and threw 'em down, and was cold to the feet, and smelt just abominable." All these complaints Molly had to listen to, and it was not a cheerful preparation for the reception which she already felt to be so formidable.

The sound of their carriage-wheels was heard at last, and Molly went to the front door to meet them. Her father got out first, and took her hand and held it while he helped his bride to alight. Then he kissed her fondly, and passed her on to his wife; but her veil was so securely (and becomingly) fastened down, that it was some time before Mrs. Gibson could get her lips clear to greet her new daughter. Then there was luggage to be seen about; and both the travellers were occupied in this, while Molly stood by trembling with excitement, unable to help, and only conscious of Betty's rather cross looks, as heavy box after heavy box jammed up the passage.

"Molly, my dear, show—your mamma to her room!"

Mr. Gibson had hesitated, because the question of the name by which Molly was to call her new relation had never occurred to him before. The colour flashed into Molly's face. Was she to call her "mamma"?—the name long appropriated in her mind to someone else—to her own dead mother. The rebellious heart rose against it, but she said nothing. She led the way upstairs,

Mrs. Gibson turning round from time to time with some fresh direction as to which bag or trunk she needed most. She hardly spoke to Molly till they were both in the newly-furnished bedroom, where a small fire had been lighted by Molly's orders.

"Now, my love, we can embrace each other in peace. O dear, how tired I am!"—(after the embrace had been accomplished). "My spirits are so easily affected with fatigue; but your dear papa has been kindness itself. Dear! what an old-fashioned bed! And what a—But it doesn't signify. By and by we'll renovate the house—won't we, my dear? And you'll be my little maid to-night, and help me to arrange a few things, for I'm just worn out with the day's journey."

"I've ordered a sort of tea-dinner to be ready for you," said Molly. "Shall I go and tell them to send it in?"

"I'm not sure if I can go down again to-night. It would be very comfortable to have a little table brought in here, and sit in my dressing-gown by this cheerful fire. But, to be sure, there's your dear papa! I really don't think he would eat anything if I were not there. One must not think about oneself, you know. Yes, I'll come down in a quarter of an hour."

But Mr. Gibson had found a note awaiting him, with an immediate summons to an old patient, dangerously ill; and, snatching a mouthful of food while his horse was being saddled, he had to resume at once his old habits of attention to his profession above everything.

As soon as Mrs. Gibson found that he was not likely to miss her presence— he had eaten a very tolerable lunch of bread and cold meat in solitude, so her fears about his appetite in her absence were not well founded—she desired to have her meal upstairs in her own room; and poor Molly, not daring to tell the servants of this whim, had to carry up first a table, which, however small, was too heavy for her; and afterwards all the choice portions of the meal, which she had taken great pains to arrange on the table, as she had seen such things done at Hamley, intermixed with fruit and flowers that had that morning been sent in from various great houses where Mr. Gibson was respected and valued. How pretty Molly had thought her handiwork an hour or two before! How dreary it seemed, at last released from Mrs. Gibson's conversation, she sat down in solitude to cold tea and the drumsticks of the chicken! No one to look at her preparations and admire her deft-handedness and taste! She had thought that her father would be gratified by it, and then he had never seen it. She had meant her cares as an offering of goodwill to her stepmother, who even now was ringing her bell to have the tray taken away and Miss Gibson summoned to her bedroom.

Molly hastily finished her meal, and went upstairs again.

"I feel so lonely, darling, in this strange house; do come and be with me, and help me to unpack. I think your dear papa might have put off his visit to Mr. Craven Smith for just this one evening."

"Mr. Craven Smith couldn't put off his dying," said Molly, bluntly.

"You droll girl!" said Mrs. Gibson, with a faint laugh. "But if this Mr. Smith is dying, as you say, what's the use of your father's going off to him in such a hurry? Does he expect any legacy, or anything of that kind?"

Molly bit her lips to prevent herself from saying something disagreeable. She only answered:

"I don't quite know that he is dying. The man said so; and papa can sometimes do something to make the last struggle easier. At any rate, it's always a comfort to the family to have him."

"What dreary knowledge of death you have learned for a girl of your age! Really, if I had heard all these details of your father's profession, I doubt if I could have brought myself to have him!"

"He doesn't make the illness or the death; he does his best against them. I call it a very fine thing to think of what he does or tries to do. And you will think so, too, when you see how he is watched for, and how people welcome him!"

"Well, don't let us talk any more of such gloomy things, to-night! I think I shall go to bed at once, I am so tired, if you will only sit by me till I get sleepy, darling. If you will talk to me, the sound of your voice will soon send me off."

Molly got a book and read her stepmother to sleep, preferring that to the harder task of keeping up a continual murmur of speech.

Then she stole down and went into the dining-room, where the fire was gone out; purposely neglected by the servants, to mark their displeasure at their new mistress's having had her tea in her own room. Molly managed to light it, however, before her father came home, and collected and rearranged some comfortable food for him. Then she knelt down again on the hearth-rug, gazing into the fire in a dreamy reverie, which had enough of sadness about it to cause the tear to drop unnoticed from her eyes. But she jumped up, and shook herself into brightness at the sound of her father's step.

"How is Mr. Craven Smith?" said she.

"Dead. He just recognised me. He was one of my first patients on coming to Hollingford."

Mr. Gibson sat down in the arm-chair made ready for him, and warmed his hands at the fire, seeming neither to need food nor talk, as he went over a train of recollections. Then he roused himself from his sadness, and looking round the room, he said, briskly enough:

"And where's the new mamma?"

"She was tired, and went to bed early. Oh, papa! must I call her 'mamma'?"

"I should like it," replied he, with a slight contraction of the brows.

Molly was silent. She put a cup of tea near him; he stirred it, and sipped it, and then he recurred to the subject.

"Why shouldn't you call her 'mamma'? I'm sure she means to do the duty of a mother to you. We all may make mistakes, and her ways may not be quite all at once our ways; but at any rate let us start with a family bond between us."

What would Roger say was right?—that was the question that rose to Molly's mind. She had always spoken of her father's new wife as Mrs. Gibson, and had once burst out at Miss Brownings' with a protestation that she would never call her "mamma." She did not feel drawn to her new relation by their intercourse that evening. She kept silence, though she knew her father was expecting an answer. At last he gave up his expectation and turned to another subject; told about their journey, questioned her as to the Hamleys, the Brownings, Lady Harriet, and the afternoon they had passed together at the Manor-house. But there was a certain hardness and constraint in his manner, and in hers a heaviness and absence of mind. All at once she said:

"Papa, I will call her 'mamma'!"

He took her hand and grasped it tight; but for an instant or two he did not speak. Then he said:

"You won't be sorry for it, Molly, when you come to lie as poor Craven Smith did to-night."

Calf-Love

From Wives and Daughters.

Lady Ritchie says: "To people of an elder generation re-reading *Wives and Daughters*, now, strong, gentle, and full of fun and wisdom, all youth seems to be in it; it is rest to live again in the merry touching pages" (*Blackstick Papers*, 1908).

ONE day, for some reason or other, Mr. Gibson came home unexpectedly. He was crossing the hall, having come in by the garden door—the garden communicated with the stable-yard, where he had left his horse—when the kitchen door opened, and the girl who was underling in the establishment came quickly into the hall with a note in her hand, and made as if she was taking it upstairs; but on seeing her master she gave a little start, and turned back as if to hide herself in the kitchen. If she had not made this movement, so conscious of guilt, Mr. Gibson, who was anything but suspicious, would never have taken any notice of her. As it was, he stepped quickly forwards, opened the kitchen door, and called out "Bethia" so sharply that she could not delay coming forwards.

"Give me that note," he said. She hesitated a little.

"It's for Miss Molly," she stammered out.

"Give it to me!" he repeated more quickly than before. She looked as if she would cry; but still she kept the note tight held behind her back.

"He said as I was to give it into her own hands; and I promised as I would, faithful."

"Cook, go and find Miss Molly. Tell her to come here at once."

He fixed Bethia with his eyes. It was of no use trying to escape: she might have thrown it into the fire, but she had not presence of mind enough. She stood immovable, only her eyes looked any way rather than encounter her master's steady gaze. "Molly, my dear!"

"Papa! I did not know you were at home," said innocent, wondering Molly.

"Bethia, keep your word. Here is Miss Molly; give her the note."

"Indeed, miss, I couldn't help it!"

Molly took the note, but before she could open it, her father said: "That's all, my dear; you need not read it. Give it to me. Tell those who sent you, Bethia, that all letters for Miss Molly must pass through my hands. Now be off with you, goosey, and go back to where you came from."

"Papa, I shall make you tell me who my correspondent is."

"We'll see about that, by and by."

She went a little reluctantly, with ungratified curiosity, upstairs to Miss Eyre, who was still her daily companion, if not her governess. He turned into the empty dining-room, shut the door, broke the seal of the note, and began to read it. It was a flaming love-letter from Mr. Coxe; who professed himself unable to go on seeing her day after day without speaking to her of the passion she had inspired—an "eternal passion," he called it; on reading which Mr. Gibson laughed a little. Would she not look kindly at him? would she not think of him whose only thought was of her? and so on, with a very proper admixture of violent compliments to her beauty. She was fair, not pale; her eyes were lode-stars, her dimples marks of Cupid's fingers, etc.

Mr. Gibson finished reading it; and began to think about it in his own mind. "Who would have thought the lad had been so poetical? but, to be sure, there's a *Shakespeare* in the surgery library: I'll take it away and put *Johnson's Dictionary* instead. One comfort is the conviction of her perfect innocence—ignorance, I should rather say—for it is easy to see it's the first "confession of his love," as he calls it. But it's an awful worry—to begin with lovers so early. Why, she's only just seventeen—not seventeen, indeed, till July; not for six weeks yet. Sixteen and three-quarters! Why, she's quite a baby. To be sure—poor Jeanie was not so old, and how I did love her!" (Mrs. Gibson's name was Mary, so he must have been referring to someone else). Then his thoughts wandered back to other days, though he still held the open note in his hand. By and by his eyes fell upon it again, and his mind came back to bear upon the present time. "I'll not be hard upon him. I'll give him a hint; he is quite sharp enough to take it. Poor laddie! if I send him away, which would be the wisest course, I do believe he's got no home to go to."

After a little more consideration in the same strain, Mr. Gibson went and sat down at the writing-table and wrote the following formula:

Master Coxe

("That 'master' will touch him to the quick," said Mr. Gibson to himself as he wrote the word).

R.   Verecundiae ℨj.

        Fidelitatis Domesticae ℨj.

        Reticentiae gr. iij.

M.   Capiat hanc dosim ter die in aquâ purâ.

Mr. Gibson smiled a little sadly as he re-read his words. "Poor Jeanie," he said aloud. And then he chose out an envelope, enclosed the fervid love-letter, and the above prescription; sealed it with his own sharply-cut seal-ring, R. G., in old English letters, and then paused over the address.

"He'll not like *Master* Coxe outside; no need to put him to unnecessary shame." So the direction on the envelope was:

Then Mr. Gibson applied himself to the professional business which had brought him home so opportunely and unexpectedly, and afterwards he went back through the garden to the stables; and just as he had mounted his horse, he said to the stable-man—"Oh! by the way, here's a letter for Mr. Coxe. Don't send it through the women; take it round yourself to the surgery door, and do it at once."

The slight smile upon his face, as he rode out of the gates, died away as soon as he found himself in the solitude of the lanes. He slackened his speed, and began to think. It was very awkward, he considered, to have a motherless girl growing up into womanhood in the same house with two young men, even if she only met them at meal-times, and all the intercourse they had with each other was merely the utterance of such words as, "May I help you to potatoes?" or, as Mr. Wynne would persevere in saying, "May I assist you to potatoes?"—a form of speech which grated daily more and more upon Mr. Gibson's ears. Yet Mr. Coxe, the offender in this affair which had just occurred, had to remain for three years more as a pupil in Mr. Gibson's family. He should be the very last of the race. Still there were three years to be got over; and if this stupid passionate calf-love of his lasted, what was to be done? Sooner or later Molly would become aware of it. The contingencies of the affair were so excessively disagreeable to contemplate, that Mr. Gibson determined to dismiss the subject from his mind by a good strong effort. He put his horse to a gallop, and found that the violent shaking over the lanes— paved as they were with round stones, which had been dislocated by the wear and tear of a hundred years—was the very best thing for the spirits, if not for the bones. He made a long round that afternoon, and came back to his home imagining that the worse was over, and that Mr. Coxe would have taken the hint conveyed in the prescription. All that would be needed was to find a safe place for the unfortunate Bethia, who had displayed such a daring aptitude for intrigue. But Mr. Gibson reckoned without his host. It was the habit of the young men to come in to tea with the family in the dining-room, to swallow two cups, munch their bread and toast, and then disappear. This night Mr. Gibson watched their countenances furtively from under his long eyelashes, while he tried against his wont to keep up a *dégagé* manner, and a brisk conversation on general subjects. He saw that Mr. Wynne was on the point of breaking out into laughter, and that red-haired, red-faced Mr. Coxe was redder and fiercer than ever, while his whole aspect and ways betrayed indignation and anger.

"He will have it, will he?" thought Mr. Gibson to himself; and he girded up his loins for the battle. He did not follow Molly and Miss Eyre into the drawing-room as he usually did. He remained where he was, pretending to read the newspaper, while Bethia, her face swelled up with crying, and with an aggrieved and offended aspect, removed the tea-things. Not five minutes after the room was cleared, came the expected tap at the door. "May I speak to you, sir?' said the invisible Mr. Coxe, from outside.

"To be sure. Come in, Mr. Coxe. I was rather wanting to talk to you about that bill of Corbyn's. Pray sit down."

"It is about nothing of that kind, sir, that I wanted—that I wished—No, thank you—I would rather not sit down." He, accordingly, stood in offended dignity. "It is about that letter, sir—that letter with the insulting prescription, sir."

"Insulting prescription! I am surprised at such a word being applied to any prescription of mine—though, to be sure, patients are sometimes offended at being told the nature of their illnesses; and, I daresay, they may take offence at the medicines which their cases require."

"I did not ask you to prescribe for me."

"Oh, no! Then you are the Master Coxe who sent the note through Bethia! Let me tell you it has cost her her place, and was a very silly letter into the bargain."

"It was not the conduct of a gentleman, sir, to intercept it, and to open it, and to read words never addressed to you, sir."

"No!" said Mr. Gibson, with a slight twinkle in his eye and a curl on his lips, not unnoticed by the indignant Mr. Coxe. "I believe I was once considered tolerably good-looking, and I daresay I was as great a coxcomb as anyone at twenty; but I don't think that even then I should quite have believed that all those pretty compliments were addressed to myself."

"It was not the conduct of a gentleman, sir," repeated Mr. Coxe, stammering over his words—he was going on to say something more, when Mr. Gibson broke in.

"And let me tell you, young man," replied Mr. Gibson, with a sudden sternness in his voice, "that what you have done is only excusable in consideration of your youth and extreme ignorance of what are considered the laws of domestic honour. I receive you into my house as a member of the family—you induce one of my servants—corrupting her with a bribe, I have no doubt——"

"Indeed, sir! I never gave her a penny."

"Then you ought to have done. You should always pay those who do your dirty work."

"Just now, sir, you called it corrupting with a bribe," muttered Mr. Coxe.

Mr. Gibson took no notice of this speech, but went on—"Inducing one of my servants to risk her place, without offering her the slightest equivalent, by begging her to convey a letter clandestinely to my daughter—a mere child."

"Miss Gibson, sir, is nearly seventeen! I heard you say so only the other day," said Mr. Coxe, aged twenty. Again Mr. Gibson ignored the remark.

"A letter which you were unwilling to have seen by her father, who had tacitly trusted to your honour, by receiving you as an inmate of this house. Your father's son—I know Major Coxe well—ought to have come to me, and have said out openly, 'Mr. Gibson, I love—or I fancy that I love—your daughter; I do not think it right to conceal this from you, although unable to earn a penny; and with no prospect of an unassisted livelihood, even for myself, for several years, I shall not say a word about my feelings—or fancied feelings—to the very young lady herself.' That is what your father's son ought to have said; if, indeed, a couple of grains of reticent silence would not have been better still."

"And if I had said it, sir—perhaps I ought to have said it," said Mr. Coxe, in a hurry of anxiety, "what would have been your answer? Would you have sanctioned my passion, sir?"

"I would have said, most probably—I will not be certain of my exact words in a supposititious case—that you were a young fool, but not a dishonourable young fool, and I should have told you not to let your thoughts run upon a calf-love until you had magnified it into a passion. And I daresay, to make up for the mortification I should have given you, I should have prescribed your joining the Hollingford Cricket Club, and set you at liberty as often as I could, on the Saturday afternoons. As it is, I must write to your father's agent in London, and ask him to remove you out of my household, repaying the premium, of course, which will enable you to start afresh in some other doctor's surgery."

"It will so grieve my father," said Mr. Coxe, startled into dismay, if not repentance.

"I see no other course open. It will give Major Coxe some trouble (I shall take care that he is at no extra expense), but what I think will grieve him the most is the betrayal of confidence; for I trusted you, Edward, like a son of my own!" There was something in Mr. Gibson's voice when he spoke seriously, especially when he referred to any feeling of his own—he who so rarely betrayed what was passing in his heart—that was irresistible to most people: the change from joking and sarcasm to tender gravity.

Mr. Coxe hung his head a little, and meditated.

"I do love Miss Gibson," said he, at length. "Who could help it?"

"Mr. Wynne, I hope!" said Mr. Gibson.

"His heart is pre-engaged," replied Mr. Coxe. "Mine was free as air till I saw her."

"Would it tend to cure your—well! passion, we'll say—if she wore blue spectacles at meal-times? I observe you dwell much on the beauty of her eyes."

"You are ridiculing my feelings, Mr. Gibson. Do you forget that you yourself were young once?"

"Poor Jeanie" rose before Mr. Gibson's eyes; and he felt a little rebuked.

"Come, Mr. Coxe, let us see if we can't make a bargain," said he, after a minute or so of silence. "You have done a really wrong thing, and I hope you are convinced of it in your heart, or that you will be when the heat of this discussion is over, and you come to think a little about it. But I won't lose all respect for your father's son. If you will give me your word that, as long as you remain a member of my family—pupil, apprentice, what you will—you won't again try to disclose your passion—you see I am careful to take your view of what I should call a mere fancy—by word or writing, looks or acts, in any manner whatever, to my daughter, or to talk about your feelings to anyone else, you shall remain here. If you cannot give me your word, I must follow out the course I named, and write to your father's agent."

Mr. Coxe stood irresolute.

"Mr. Wynne knows all I feel for Miss Gibson, sir. He and I have no secrets from each other."

"Well, I suppose he must represent the reeds. You know the story of King Midas's barber, who found out that his royal master had the ears of an ass beneath his hyacinthine curls. So the barber, in default of a Mr. Wynne, went to the reeds that grew on the shores of a neighbouring lake and whispered to them, 'King Midas has the ears of an ass.' But he repeated it so often that the reeds learnt the words, and kept on saying them all day long, till at last the secret was no secret at all. If you keep on telling your tale to Mr. Wynne, are you sure he won't repeat it in his turn?"

"If I pledge my word as a gentleman, sir, I pledge it for Mr. Wynne as well."

"I suppose I must run the risk. But remember how soon a young girl's name may be breathed upon, and sullied. Molly has no mother, and for that very reason she ought to move among you all as unharmed as Una herself."

"Mr. Gibson, if you wish it, I'll swear it on the Bible," cried the excitable young man.

"Nonsense. As if your word, if it's worth anything, was not enough! We'll shake hands upon it, if you like."

Mr. Coxe came forward eagerly, and almost squeezed Mr. Gibson's ring into his finger.

As he was leaving the room, he said, a little uneasily, "May I give Bethia a crown-piece?"

"No, indeed! Leave Bethia to me. I hope you won't say another word to her while she is here. I shall see that she gets a respectable place when she goes away."

Heart Trouble

From Mr. Harrison's Confessions, *The Ladies' Companion*, 1851

MISS CAROLINE always received me, and kept me talking in her washed-out style, after I had seen my patient. One day she told me she thought she had a weakness about the heart, and would be glad if I would bring my stethoscope the next time, which I accordingly did! and, while I was on my hands and knees listening to the pulsations, one of the young ladies came in. She said:

"Oh, dear! I never! I beg your pardon, ma'am," and scuttled out. There was not much the matter with Miss Caroline's heart: a little feeble in action or so, a mere matter of weakness and general languor. When I went down I saw two or three of the girls peeping out of the half-closed schoolroom door, but they shut it immediately, and I heard them laughing. The next time I called, Miss Tomkinson was sitting in state to receive me.

"Miss Tyrrell's throat does not seem to make much progress. Do you understand the case, Mr. Harrison, or should we have further advice. I think Mr. Morgan would probably know more about it."

I assured her it was the simplest thing in the world; that it always implied a little torpor in the constitution, and that we preferred working through the system, which of course was a slow process; and that the medicine the young lady was taking (iodide of iron) was sure to be successful, although the progress would not be rapid. She bent her head and said, "It might be so; but she confessed she had more confidence in medicines which had some effect."

She seemed to expect me to tell her something; but I had nothing to say, and accordingly I bade good-bye. Somehow, Miss Tomkinson always managed to make me feel very small, by a succession of snubbings; and, whenever I left her I had always to comfort myself under her contradictions by saying to myself, "Her saying it is so, does not make it so." Or I invented good retorts which I might have made to her brusque speeches, if I had but thought of them at the right time. But it was provoking that I had not had the presence of mind to recollect them just when they were wanted.

The Young Doctor's Dilemma

From Mr. Harrison's Confessions, *The Ladies' Companion.*

A FEW days after the sale, I was in the consulting-room. The servant must have left the folding-doors a little ajar, I think. Mrs. Munton came to call on Mrs. Rose; and the former being deaf, I heard all the speeches of the latter lady, as she was obliged to speak very loud in order to be heard. She began:

"This is a great pleasure, Mrs. Munton, so seldom as you are well enough to go out."

Mumble, mumble, mumble, through the door.

"Oh, very well, thank you. Take this seat, and then you can admire my new work-table, ma'am; a present from Mr. Harrison."

Mumble, mumble.

"Who could have told you, ma'am? Miss Horsman? Oh, yes, I showed it Miss Horsman."

Mumble, mumble.

"I don't quite understand you, ma'am."

Mumble, mumble.

"I'm not blushing, I believe, I really am quite in the dark as to what you mean."

Mumble, mumble.

"Oh, yes, Mr. Harrison and I are most comfortable together. He reminds me so of my dear Mr. Rose—just as fidgety and anxious in his profession."

Mumble, mumble.

"I'm sure you are joking now, ma'am." Then I heard a pretty loud:

"Oh, no;" mumble, mumble, mumble, for a long time.

"Did he really? Well, I'm sure I don't know, I should be sorry to think he was doomed to be unfortunate in so serious an affair; but you know my undying regard for the late Mr. Rose."

Another long mumble.

"You're very kind, I'm sure. Mr. Rose always thought more of my happiness than his own"—a little crying—"but the turtle-dove has always been my ideal, ma'am."

Mumble, mumble.

"No one could have been happier than I. As you say, it is a compliment to matrimony."

Mumble.

"Oh, you must not repeat such a thing! Mr. Harrison would not like it. He can't bear to have his affairs spoken about."

Then there was a change of subject; an inquiry after some poor person, I imagine. I heard Mrs. Rose say:

"She has got a mucous membrane, I'm afraid, ma'am."

A commiserating mumble.

"Not always fatal. I believe Mr. Rose knew some cases that lived for years after it was discovered that they had a mucous membrane." A pause. Then Mrs. Rose spoke in a different tone.

"Are you sure, ma'am, there is no mistake about what he said?"

Mumble.

"Pray don't be so observant, Mrs. Munton; you find out too much. One can have no little secrets."

The call broke up; and I heard Mrs. Munton say in the passage, "I wish you joy, ma'am, with all my heart. There's no use denying it; for I've seen all along what would happen."

When I went in to dinner, I said to Mrs. Rose:

"You've had Mrs. Munton here, I think. Did she bring any news?" To my surprise, she bridled and simpered, and replied, "Oh, you must not ask, Mr. Harrison; such foolish reports!"

I did not ask, as she seemed to wish me not, and I knew there were silly reports always about. Then I think she was vexed that I did not ask.

Altogether she went on so strangely that I could not help looking at her; and then she took up a hand-screen, and held it between me and her. I really felt rather anxious.

"Are you not feeling well?" said I innocently.

"Oh, thank you, I believe I'm quite well; only the room is rather warm, is it not?"

"Let me put the blinds down for you? The sun begins to have a good deal of power." I drew down the blinds.

"You are so attentive, Mr. Harrison. Mr. Rose himself never did more for my little wishes than you do."

"I wish I could do more—I wish I could show you how much I feel"—her kindness to John Brouncker, I was going to say; but I was just then called out to a patient. Before I went I turned back, and said:

"Take care of yourself, my dear Mrs. Rose; you had better rest a little."

"For your sake I will," she said tenderly.

I did not care for whose sake she did it. Only I really thought she was not quite well, and required rest. I thought she was more affected than usual at tea-time; and could have been angry with her nonsensical ways once or twice, but that I knew the real goodness of her heart. She said she wished she had the power to sweeten my life as she could my tea. I told her what a comfort she had been during my late time of anxiety; and then I stole out to try if I could hear the evening singing at the vicarage, by standing close to the garden wall.

"Oh, Mr. Harrison," said she, "if you have really loved Caroline, do not let a little paltry money make you desert her for another."

I was struck dumb. Loved Miss Caroline! I loved Miss Tomkinson a great deal better, and yet I disliked her. She went on:

"I have saved nearly three thousand pounds. If you think you are too poor to marry without money, I will give it all to Caroline. I am strong, and can go on working; but she is weak, and this disappointment will kill her." She sat down suddenly, and covered her face with her hands. Then she looked up.

"You are unwilling, I see. Don't suppose I would have urged you if it had been for myself; but she has had so much sorrow." And now she fairly cried aloud. I tried to explain; but she would not listen, but kept saying, "Leave the house, sir! leave the house!" But I would be heard.

"I have never had any feeling warmer than respect for Miss Caroline, and I have never shown any different feeling. I never for an instant thought of making her my wife, and she has had no cause in my behaviour to imagine I entertained any such intention."

"This is adding insult to injury," said she. "Leave the house, sir, this instant!"

I went, and sadly enough. In a small town such an occurrence is sure to be talked about, and to make a great deal of mischief. When I went home to dinner I was so full of it, and foresaw so clearly that I should need some advocate soon to set the case in its right light, that I determined on making a confidante of good Mrs. Rose. I could not eat. She watched me tenderly, and sighed when she saw my want of appetite.

"I am sure you have something on your mind, Mr. Harrison. Would it be—would it not be—a relief to impart it to some sympathising friend?"

It was just what I wanted to do.

"My dear kind Mrs. Rose," said I, "I must tell you, if you will listen."

She took up the hand-screen, and held it, as yesterday between me and her.

"The most unfortunate misunderstanding has taken place. Miss Tomkinson thinks that I have been paying attentions to Miss Caroline; when, in fact—may I tell you, Mrs. Rose?—my affections are placed elsewhere. Perhaps you have found it out already?" for indeed I thought I had been too much in love to conceal my attachment to Sophy from anyone who knew my movements as well as Mrs. Rose.

She hung down her head, and said she believed she had found out my secret.

"Then only think how miserably I am situated. If I have any hope—oh, Mrs. Rose, do you think I have any hope—?"

She put the hand-screen still more before her face, and after some hesitation she said she thought "If I persevered—in time—I might have hope." And then she suddenly got up, and left the room.

That afternoon I met Mr. Bullock in the street. My mind was so full of the affair with Miss Tomkinson that I should have passed him without notice, if he had not stopped me short, and said that he must speak to me; about my wonderful five hundred pounds, I supposed. But I did not care for that now.

"What is this I hear," he said severely, "about your engagement with Mrs. Rose?"

"With Mrs. Rose!" said I, almost laughing, although my heart was heavy enough.

"Yes! with Mrs. Rose!" said he sternly.

"I'm not engaged to Mrs. Rose," I replied. "There is some mistake."

"I'm glad to hear it, sir," he answered, "very glad. It requires some explanation, however. Mrs. Rose has been congratulated, and has acknowledged the truth of the report. It is confirmed by many facts. The work-table you bought, confessing your intention of giving it to your future wife, is given to her. How do you account for these things, sir?"

I said I did not pretend to account for them. At present a good deal was inexplicable; and, when I could give an explanation, I did not think I should feel myself called upon to give it to him....

He looked as if he would like to horsewhip me.

"Once for all, I am not engaged to anybody. Till you have seen your daughter, and learnt the truth from her, I will wish you farewell."

I bowed in a stiff, haughty manner and walked off homewards. But when I got to my own door, I remembered Mrs. Rose, and all that Mr. Bullock had said about her acknowledging the truth of the report of my engagement to her. Where could I go to be safe? Mrs. Rose, Miss Bullock, Miss Caroline— they lived, as it were, at the three points of an equilateral triangle; here was I in the centre. I would go to Mr. Morgan's, and drink tea with him. There, at any rate, I was secure from anyone wanting to marry me; and I might be as professionally bland as I liked, without being misunderstood. But there, too, a contretemps awaited me.

Mr. Morgan was looking grave. After a minute or two of humming and hawing, he said:

"I have been sent for to Miss Caroline Tomkinson. Mr. Harrison, I am sorry to hear of this. I am grieved to find that there seems to have been some trifling with the affections of a very worthy lady. Miss Tomkinson, who is in sad distress, tells me that they had every reason to believe that you were attached to her sister. May I ask if you do not intend to marry her?"

I said nothing was farther from my thoughts.

"My dear sir," said Mr. Morgan, rather agitated, "do not express yourself so strongly and vehemently. It is derogatory to the sex to speak so. It is more respectful to say, in these cases, that you do not venture to entertain a hope; such a manner is generally understood and does not sound like such positive objection."

"I cannot help it, sir; I must talk in my own natural manner. I would not speak disrespectfully of any woman; but nothing should induce me to marry Miss Caroline Tomkinson; not if she were Venus herself, and Queen of England in the bargain. I cannot understand what has given rise to the idea."

"Indeed, sir; I think that is very plain. You have a trifling case to attend to in the house, and you invariably make it a pretext for seeing and conversing with the lady."

"That was her doing, not mine!" said I vehemently.

"But, my dear sir, I had no idea that you would carry it out to such consequences. 'Philandering,' Miss Tomkinson called it. That is a hard word, sir. My manner has been always tender and sympathetic, but I am not aware that I ever excited any hopes; there never was any report about me. I believe no lady was ever attached to me. You must strive after this happy medium, sir."

I was still distressed. Mr. Morgan had only heard of one, but there were three ladies (including Miss Bullock) hoping to marry me. He saw my annoyance.

"Don't be too much distressed about it, my dear sir; I was sure you were too honourable a man from the first. With a conscience like yours, I would defy the world."

I was very cowardly. I positively dared not go home; but at length I was obliged to. I had done all I could to console Mr. Morgan, but he refused to be comforted. I went at last. I rang the bell. I don't know who opened the door, but I think it was Mrs. Rose. I kept a handkerchief to my face, and, muttering something about having a dreadful toothache, I flew up to my room and bolted the door. I had no candle; but what did that signify. I was safe. I could not sleep; and when I did fall into a sort of doze, it was ten times worse waking up. I could not remember whether I was engaged or not. If I was engaged, who was the lady? I had always considered myself as rather plain than otherwise; but surely I had made a mistake. Fascinating I certainly must be; but perhaps I was handsome. As soon as day dawned, I got up to ascertain the fact at the looking-glass. Even with the best disposition to be convinced, I could not see any striking beauty in my round face, with an unshaven beard and a nightcap like a fool's cap at the top. No! I must be content to be plain, but agreeable. All this I tell you in confidence. I would not have my little bit of vanity known for the world.

Family Prayer at Hope Farm

From Cousin Phillis, 1865

AS soon as supper was done, the household assembled for prayer. It was a long impromptu evening prayer; and it would have seemed desultory enough had I not had a glimpse of the kind of day that preceded it, and so been able to find a clue to the thoughts that preceded the disjointed utterances; for he kept there kneeling down in the centre of a circle, his eyes shut, his outstretched hands pressed palm to palm—sometimes with a long pause of silence, as if waiting to see if there was anything else he wished to "lay before the Lord" (to use his own expression) before he concluded with the blessing. He prayed for the cattle and live creatures, rather to my surprise; for my attention had begun to wander, till it was recalled by the familiar words.

And here I must not forget to name an odd incident at the conclusion of the prayer, and before we had risen from our knees (indeed, before Betty was well awake, for she made a nightly practice of having a sound nap, her weary head lying on her stalwart arms); the minister, still kneeling in our midst, with his eyes wide open, and his arms dropped by his side, spoke to the elder man, who turned round on his knees to attend. "John, didst see that Daisy had her warm mash to-night? for we must not neglect the means, John—two quarts of gruel, a spoonful of ginger, and a gill of beer—the poor beast needs it, and I fear it slipped out of my mind to tell thee; and here was I asking a blessing and neglecting the means, which is a mockery," said he, dropping his voice.

Before he went to bed, he told me he should see little or nothing more of me during my visit, which was to end on Sunday evening, as he always gave up both Saturday and Sabbath to his work in the ministry. I remembered that the landlord at the inn had told me this on the day when I first inquired about these new relations of mine; and I did not dislike the opportunity which I saw would be afforded me of becoming more acquainted with Cousin Holman and Phillis, though I earnestly hoped that the latter would not attack me on the subject of the dead languages.

Miss Galindo Nearly Becomes an Authoress

From *My Lady Ludlow*, 1859

NO one knows how great a trial it was to her when she thought of Sally, unchecked and unscolded for three hours every morning. But all she said was:

"'Sally, go to the Deuce.' I beg your pardon, my lady, if I was talking to myself; it's a habit I have got into of keeping my tongue in practice, and I am not quite aware when I do it. Three hours every morning! I shall be only too proud to do what I can for your ladyship; and I hope Mr. Horner will not be too impatient with me at first. You know, perhaps, that I was nearly being an authoress once, and that seems as if I was destined to 'employ my time in writing.'"

"No, indeed; we must return to the subject of the clerkship afterwards, if you please. An authoress, Miss Galindo! You surprise me!"

"But, indeed, I was. All was quite ready. Doctor Burney used to teach me music; not that I ever could learn, but it was a fancy of my poor father's. And his daughter wrote a book, and they said she was but a very young lady, and nothing but a music-master's daughter; so why should not I try?"

"Well?"

"Well! I got paper and half-a-hundred good pens, a bottle of ink, all ready."

"And then——"

"Oh, it ended in my having nothing to say, when I sat down to write. But sometimes, when I get hold of a book, I wonder why I let such a poor reason stop me. It does not others."

"But I think it was very well it did, Miss Galindo," said her ladyship. "I am extremely against women usurping men's employments, as they are very apt to do. But perhaps, after all, the notion of writing a book improved your hand. It is one of the most legible I ever saw."

"I despise z's without tails," said Miss Galindo, with a good deal of gratified pride at my lady's praise. Presently, my lady took her to look at a curious old cabinet, which Lord Ludlow had picked up at the Hague; and, while they were out of the room on this errand, I suppose the question of remuneration was settled, for I heard no more of it.

And the most delicate dainty work of all was done by Miss Galindo, as Lady Ludlow very well knew. Yet, for all their fine sewing, it sometimes happened that Miss Galindo's patterns were of an old-fashioned kind; and the dozen night-caps, maybe, on the materials for which she had expended *bona-fide* money, and on the making-up, no little time and eyesight, would lie for months in a yellow neglected heap; and at such times, it was said, Miss Galindo was more amusing than usual, more full of dry drollery and humour; just as at times when an order came in to X (the initial she had chosen) for a stock of well-paying things, she sat and stormed at her servant as she stitched away. She herself explained her practice in this way:

"When everything goes wrong, one would give up breathing if one could not lighten one's heart by a joke. But when I've to sit from morning to night, I must have something to stir my blood, or I should go off into an apoplexy; so I set to, and quarrel with Sally."

Such were Miss Galindo's means and manner of living in her own house. Out of doors, and in the village, she was not popular, although she would have been sorely missed had she left the place. But she asked too many home questions (not to say impertinent) respecting the domestic economies (for even the very poor liked to spend their bit of money in their own way), and would open cupboards to find out hidden extravagances, and question closely respecting the weekly amount of butter; till one day she met with what would have been a rebuff to any other person, but was by her rather enjoyed than otherwise.

She was going into a cottage, and in the doorway met the good woman chasing out a duck, and apparently unconscious of her visitor.

"Get out, Miss Galindo!" she cried, addressing the duck. "Get out! Oh, I ask your pardon," she continued as if seeing the lady for the first time. "It's only that weary duck will come in. Get out, Miss Gal——" (to the duck).

"And so you call it after me, do you?" inquired her visitor.

"Oh, yes, ma'am; my master would have it so; for, he said, sure enough the unlucky bird was always poking herself where she was not wanted."

"Ha, ha! very good! And so your master is a wit, is he? Well! tell him to come up and speak to me to-night about my parlour chimney; for there is no one like him for chimney doctoring."

And the master went up, and was so won over by Miss Galindo's merry ways, and sharp insight into the mysteries of his various kinds of business (he was a mason, chimney-sweeper and rat-catcher), that he came home and abused his wife the next time she called the duck the name by which he himself had christened her.

London as John Barton Saw It

From *Mary Barton*, 1848

"DO tell us all about London, dear father," asked Mary, who was sitting at her old post by her father's knee.

"How can I tell yo' a' about it when I never see'd one-tenth of it. It's as big as six Manchesters they told me. One-sixth may be made up o' grand palaces, and three-sixths o' middling kind, an' th' rest o' holes o' iniquity and filth, such as Manchester knows nought on, I'm glad to say."

"Well, father, but did you see the Queen?"

"I believe I didn't, though one day I thought I'd seen her many a time. You see," said he, turning to Job Legh, "there were a day appointed for us to go to Parliament House. We were most on us biding at a public-house in Holborn, where they did very well for us. Th' morning of taking our petition we had such a spread for breakfast as th' Queen hersel' might ha' sitten down to. I suppose they thought we wanted putting in heart. There were mutton kidneys, and sausages, and broiled ham and fried beef and onions; more like a dinner nor a breakfast. Many on our chaps though, I could see, could eat but little. Th' food stuck in their throats when they thought o' them at home, wives and little ones, as had, maybe at that very time, nought to eat. Well, after breakfast, we were all set to walk in procession, and a time it took to put us in order, two and two, and the petition, as was yards long, carried by the foremost pairs. The men looked grave enough yo' may ye sure; and such a set of thin, wan, wretched-looking chaps as they were!"

"Yourself is none to boast on."

"Ay, but I were fat and rosy to many a one. Well, we walked on and on through many a street, much the same as Deansgate. We had to walk slowly, slowly, for th' carriages an' cabs as thronged th' streets. I thought by-and-by we should maybe get clear on 'em, but as the streets grew wider they grew worse, and at last we were fairly blocked up at Oxford Street. We getten across it after a while though, and my eyes! the grand streets we were in then! They're sadly puzzled how to build houses though in London; there'd be an opening for a good steady master builder there, as know'd his business. For yo see the houses are many on 'em built without any proper shape for a body to live in; some on 'em they've after thought would fall down, so they've stuck great ugly pillars out before 'em. And some on 'em (we thought they must be th' tailors' sign) had getten stone men and women as wanted clothes stuck on 'em. I were like a child, I forgot a' my errand in looking about me. By this it were dinnertime, or better, as we could tell by the sun, right above our heads, and we were dusty and tired, going a step now and a step then. Well, at last we getten into a street grander nor all, leading to th' Queen's palace, and there it were I thought I saw th' Queen. Yo've seen th' hearses wi' white plumes, Job?"

Job assented.

"Well, them undertaker folk are driving a pretty trade in London. Wellnigh every lady we saw in a carriage had hired one o' them plumes for the day, and had it niddle noddling on her head. It were th' Queen's drawing-room, they said, and th' carriages went bowling along towards her house, some wi' dressed-up gentlemen like circus folk in 'em, and rucks o' ladies in others. Carriages themselves were great shakes too. Some o' th' gentlemen as couldn't get inside hung on behind, wi' nosegays to smell at, and sticks to keep off folks as might splash their silk stockings. I wonder why they didn't hire a cab rather than hang on like a whip-behind boy; but I suppose they wished to keep wi' their wives, Darby and Joan like. Coachmen were little squat men, wi' wigs like th' oud-fashioned parsons'. Well, we could na get on for these carriages, though we waited and waited. Th' horses were too fat to move quick; they never known want o' food, one might tell by their sleek coats; and police pushed us back when we tried to cross. One or two of 'em struck wi' their sticks, and coachmen laughed, and some officers as stood nigh put their spy-glasses in their eye, and left 'em sticking there like mountebanks. One o' th' police struck me. 'Whatten business have you to do that?' said I.

"'You're frightening them horses,' says he, in his mincing way (for Londoners are mostly all tongue-tied, and can't say their a's and i's properly), 'and it's our business to keep you from molesting the ladies and gentlemen going to her Majesty's drawing-room.'

"'And why are we to be molested,' asked I, 'going decently about our business, which is life and death to us, and many a little one clemming at home in Lancashire? Which business is of most consequence i' the sight o' God, think yo, our'n or them grand ladies and gentlemen as yo think so much on?'

"But I might as well ha' held my peace, for he only laughed."

John ceased. After waiting a little, to see if he would go on himself, Job said:

"Well, but that's not a' your story, man. Tell us what happened when you got to th' Parliament House."

After a little pause, John answered:

"If you please, neighbour, I'd rather say nought about that. It's not to be forgotten or forgiven either, by me or many another; but I canna tell of our down-casting just as a piece of London news. As long as I live, our rejection of that day will abide in my heart; and as long as I live I shall curse them as so cruelly refused to hear us; but I'll not speak of it no more."

Major Jenkyns Visits Cranford

From *Cranford*, 1853

MAJOR JENKYNS wrote to propose that he and his wife should spend a night at Cranford, on his way to Scotland—at the inn, if it did not suit Miss Matilda to receive them into her house; in which case they should hope to be with her as much as possible during the day. Of course, it *must* suit her, as she said; for all Cranford knew that she had her sister's bedroom at liberty; but I am sure she wished the Major had stopped in India and forgotten his cousins out and out.

"Oh! how must I manage?" asked she helplessly. "If Deborah had been alive, she would have known what to do with the gentleman-visitor. Must I put razors in his dressing-room? Dear! dear! and I've got none. Deborah would have had them. And slippers and coat-brushes?" I suggested that probably he would bring all these things with him. "And after dinner, how am I to know when to get up, and leave him to his wine? Deborah would have done it so well; she would have been quite in her element. Will he want coffee, do you think?" I undertook the management of the coffee, and told her I would instruct Martha in the art of waiting, in which it must be owned she was terribly deficient; and that I had no doubt Major and Mrs. Jenkyns would understand the quiet mode in which a lady lived by herself in a country town. But she was sadly flustered. I made her empty her decanters, and bring up two fresh bottles of wine. I wished I could have prevented her being present at my instructions to Martha; for she frequently cut in with some fresh direction, muddling the poor girl's mind, as she stood open-mouthed, listening to us both.

"Hand the vegetables round," said I (foolishly, I see now—for it was aiming at more than we could accomplish with quietness and simplicity): and then, seeing her look bewildered, I added, "Take the vegetables round to people, and let them help themselves."

"And mind you go first to the ladies," put in Miss Matilda. "Always go to the ladies before gentlemen, when you are waiting."

"I'll do it as you tell me, ma'am," said Martha; "but I like lads best."

We felt very uncomfortable and shocked at this speech of Martha's; yet I don't think she meant any harm; and, on the whole, she attended very well to our directions, except that she "nudged" the Major, when he did not help himself as soon as she expected, to the potatoes, while she was handing them round.

The Major and his wife were quiet, unpretending people enough when they did come; languid, as all East Indians are, I suppose. We were rather dismayed at their bringing two servants with them, a Hindoo body-servant for the Major, and a steady elderly maid for his wife; but they slept at the inn, and took off a good deal of the responsibility by attending carefully to their master's and mistress's comfort. Martha, to be sure, had never ended her staring at the East Indian's white turban and brown complexion, and I saw that Miss Matilda shrunk away from him a little as he waited at dinner. Indeed, she asked me, when they were gone, if he did not remind me of Blue Beard? On the whole, the visit was most satisfactory, and is a subject of conversation even now with Miss Matilda; at the time, it greatly excited Cranford, and even stirred up the apathetic and Honourable Mrs. Jamieson to some expression of interest, when I went to call and thank her for the kind answers she had vouchsafed to Miss Matilda's inquiries as to the arrangement of a gentleman's dressing-room—answers which I must confess she had given in the wearied manner of the Scandinavian prophetess:

"Leave me, leave me to repose."

Mrs. Gibson Visits Lady Cumnor

From *Wives and Daughters*, 1866

It has been suggested that a statue might be erected in Hollingford [Knutsford] to Mrs. Gibson if all the people who have been amused by her were to subscribe.

THEN, finally, Mrs. Gibson was to go to the Towers next day to lunch; Lady Cumnor had written a little note by Lady Harriet to beg her to come; if Mrs. Gibson could manage to find her way to the Towers, one of the carriages in use should bring her back to her own home in the course of the afternoon.

"The dear countess!" said Mrs Gibson, with soft affection. It was a soliloquy, uttered after a minute's pause, at the end of all this information.

And all the rest of that day her conversation had an aristocratic perfume hanging about it. One of the few books she had brought with her into Mr. Gibson's house was bound in pink, and in it she studied, "Menteith, Duke of, Adolphus George," etc. etc., till she was fully up in all the duchess's connections, and probable interests. Mr. Gibson made his mouth up into a droll whistle when he came home at night, and found himself in a Towers' atmosphere. Molly saw the shade of annoyance through the drollery; she was beginning to see it oftener than she liked, not that she reasoned upon it, or that she consciously traced the annoyance to its source; but she could not help feeling uneasy in herself when she knew that her father was in the least put out.

Of course a fly was ordered for Mrs. Gibson. In the early afternoon she came home. If she had been disappointed in her interview with the countess she never told her woe, nor revealed the fact that when she first arrived at the Towers she had to wait for an hour in Lady Cumnor's morning-room, uncheered by any companionship save that of her old friend, Mrs. Bradley, till suddenly, Lady Harriet coming in, she exclaimed, "Why, Clare! you dear woman! are you here all alone? Does mamma know?" And, after a little more affectionate conversation, she rushed to find her ladyship, who was perfectly aware of the fact, but too deep in giving the duchess the benefit of her wisdom and experience in trousseaux to be at all mindful of the length of time Mrs. Gibson had been passing in patient solitude. At lunch Mrs. Gibson was secretly hurt by my lord's supposing it to be her dinner, and calling out his urgent hospitality from the very bottom of the table, giving as a reason for it, that she must remember it was her dinner. In vain she piped out in her soft, high voice, "Oh, my lord! I never eat meat in the middle of the day; I can hardly eat anything at lunch." Her voice was lost, and the duchess might go away with the idea that the Hollingford doctor's wife dined early; that is to say, if her grace ever condescended to have any idea on the subject at all; which presupposes that she was cognisant of the fact of there being a doctor at Hollingford, and that he had a wife, and that his wife was the pretty, faded, elegant-looking woman, sending away her plate of untasted food—food which she longed to eat, for she was really desperately hungry after her drive and her solitude.

And then after lunch there did come a *tête-à-tête* with Lady Cumnor, which was conducted after this wise:

"Well, Clare! I am really glad to see you. I once thought I should never get back to the Towers, but here I am! There was such a clever man at Bath—a Doctor Snape—he cured me at last—quite set me up. I really think if ever I am ill again I shall send for him: it is such a thing to find a really clever medical man. Oh, by the way, I always forget you've married Mr. Gibson— of course he is very clever, and all that. (The carriage to the door in ten minutes, Brown, and desire Bradley to bring my things down.) What was I asking you? Oh! how do you get on with the step-daughter? She seemed to me to be a young lady with a pretty stubborn will of her own. I put a letter for the post down somewhere, and I cannot think where; do help me look for it, there's a good woman. Just run to my room, and see if Brown can find it, for it is of great consequence."

Off went Mrs. Gibson, rather unwillingly; for there were several things she wanted to speak about, and she had not heard half of what she had expected to learn of the family gossip. But all chance was gone; for, when she came back from her fruitless errand, Lady Cumnor and the duchess were in full talk, the former with the missing letter in her hand, which she was using something like a baton to enforce her words.

"Every iota from Paris! Every i-o-ta!"

Lady Cumnor was too much of a lady not to apologise for useless trouble, but they were nearly the last words she spoke to Mrs Gibson, for she had to go out and drive with the duchess; and the brougham to take "Clare" (as she persisted in calling Mrs. Gibson) back to Hollingford followed the carriage to the door. Lady Harriet came away from her entourage of young men and young ladies, all prepared for some walking expedition, to wish Mrs. Gibson good-bye.

"We shall see you at the ball," she said. "You'll be there with your two girls, of course, and I must have a little talk with you there; with all these visitors in the house, it has been impossible to see anything of you to-day, you know."

Such were the facts, but rose-colour was the medium through which they were seen by Mrs. Gibson's household listeners on her return.

"There are many visitors staying at the Towers—oh, yes! a great many: the duchess and Lady Alice, and Mr. and Mrs. Grey, and Lord Albert Monson and his sister, and my old friend Captain James of the Blues—many more, in fact. But of course I preferred going to Lady Cumnor's own room, where I could see her and Lady Harriet quietly, and where we were not disturbed by the bustle downstairs. Of course we were obliged to go down to lunch, and then I saw my old friends, and renewed pleasant acquaintances. But I really could hardly get any connected conversation with anyone. Lord Cumnor seemed so delighted to see me there again: though there were six or seven between us, he was always interrupting with some civil or kind speech especially addressed to me. And after lunch Lady Cumnor asked me all sorts of questions about my new life with as much interest as if I had been her daughter. To be sure, when the duchess came in we had to leave off, and talk about the trousseau she is preparing for Lady Alice. Lady Harriet made such a point of our meeting at the ball; she is such a good, affectionate creature, is Lady Harriet!"

This last was said in a tone of meditative appreciation.

Mrs. Gibson's Little Dinner Party

From Wives and Daughters.

MRS. Gibson intended the Hamleys to find this dinner pleasant; and they did. Mr. Gibson was fond of the two young men, both for their parents' sake and their own, for he had known them since boyhood; and to those whom he liked Mr. Gibson could be remarkably agreeable. Mrs. Gibson really gave them a welcome—and cordiality in a hostess is a very becoming mantle for any other deficiencies there may be. Cynthia and Molly looked their best, which was all the duty Mrs. Gibson absolutely required of them, as she was willing enough to take her full share in the conversation. Osborne fell to her lot, of course, and for some time he and she prattled on with all the ease of manner and commonplaceness of meaning which go so far to make the "art of polite conversation." Roger, who ought to have made himself agreeable to one or the other of the young ladies, was exceedingly interested in what Mr. Gibson was telling him of a paper on comparative osteology in some foreign journal of science, which Lord Hollingford was in the habit of forwarding to his friend the country surgeon. Yet every now and then while he listened he caught his attention wandering to the face of Cynthia, who was placed between his brother and Mr. Gibson. She was not particularly occupied with attending to anything that was going on; her eyelids were carelessly dropped, as she crumbled her bread on the tablecloth, and her beautiful long eyelashes were seen on the clear tint of her oval cheek. She was thinking of something else; Molly was trying to understand with all her might. Suddenly Cynthia looked up, and caught Roger's gaze of intent admiration too fully for her to be unaware that he was staring at her. She coloured a little; but, after the first moment of rosy confusion at his evident admiration of her, she flew to the attack, diverting his confusion at thus being caught, to the defence of himself from her accusation.

"It is quite true!" she said to him. "I was not attending: you see I don't know even the A B C of science. But, please, don't look so severely at me, even if I am a dunce!"

"I didn't know—I didn't mean to look severely, I am sure," replied he, not knowing well what to say.

"Cynthia is not a dunce either," said Mrs. Gibson, afraid lest her daughter's opinion of herself might be taken seriously. "But I have always observed that some people have a talent for one thing and some for another. Now Cynthia's talents are not for science and the severer studies. Do you remember, love, what trouble I had to teach you the use of the globes?"

"Yes; and I don't know longitude from latitude now; and I'm always puzzled as to which is perpendicular and which is horizontal."

"Yet, I do assure you," her mother continued, rather addressing herself to Osborne, "that her memory for poetry is prodigious. I have heard her repeat the 'Prisoner of Chillon' from beginning to end."

"It would be rather a bore to have to hear her, I think," said Mr. Gibson, smiling at Cynthia, who gave him back one of her bright looks of mutual understanding.

"Ah, Mr. Gibson, I have found out before now that you have no soul for poetry; and Molly there is your own child. She reads such deep books—all about facts and figures: she'll be quite a blue-stocking by and by."

"Mamma," said Molly, reddening, "you think it was a deep book because there were the shapes of the different cells of bees in it! but it was not at all deep. It was very interesting."

"Never mind, Molly," said Osborne. "I stand up for blue-stockings."

"And I object to the distinction implied in what you say," said Roger. "It was not deep, *ergo*, it was very interesting. Now, a book may be both deep and interesting."

"Oh, if you are going to chop logic and use Latin words, I think it is time for us to leave the room," said Mrs. Gibson.

"Don't let us run away as if we were beaten, mamma," said Cynthia. "Though it may be logic, I for one can understand what Mr. Roger Hamley said just now; and I read some of Molly's books; and whether it was deep or not, I found it very interesting—more so than I should think the 'Prisoner of Chillon' nowadays. I've displaced the Prisoner to make room for Johnnie Gilpin as my favourite poem."

"How could you talk such nonsense, Cynthia!" said Mrs. Gibson, as the girls followed her upstairs. "You know you are not a dunce. It is all very well not to be a blue-stocking, because gentle-people don't like that kind of woman; but running yourself down, and contradicting all I said about your liking for Byron, and poets and poetry—to Osborne Hamley of all men, too!"

Mrs. Gibson spoke quite crossly for her.

"But, mamma," Cynthia replied, "I am either a dunce, or I am not. If I am, I did right to own it; if I am not, he's a dunce if he doesn't find out I was joking."

"Well," said Mrs. Gibson, a little puzzled by this speech, and wanting some elucidatory addition.

"Only that if he's a dunce his opinion of me is worth nothing. So, any way, it doesn't signify."

"You really bewilder me with your nonsense, child. Molly is worth twenty of you."

"I quite agree with you, mamma," said Cynthia, turning round to take Molly's hand.

"Yes; but she ought not to be," said Mrs. Gibson, still irritated. "Think of the advantages you've had."

"I'm afraid I had rather be a dunce than a blue-stocking," said Molly; for the term had a little annoyed her, and the annoyance was rankling still.

"Hush; here they are coming: I hear the dining-room door! I never meant you were a blue-stocking, dear, so don't look vexed—Cynthia, my love, where did you get those lovely flowers—anemones, are they? They suit your complexion so exactly."

"Come, Molly, don't look so grave and thoughtful," exclaimed Cynthia. "Don't you perceive mamma wants us to be smiling and amiable?"

A Visit to an Old Bachelor

From *Cranford*, 1853

A FEW days after, a note came from Mr. Holbrook, asking us—impartially asking both of us—in a formal, old-fashioned style, to spend a day at his house—a long June day—for it was June now. He named that he had also invited his cousin, Miss Pole; so that we might join in a fly, which could be put up at his house.

I expected Miss Matty to jump at this invitation; but, no! Miss Pole and I had the greatest difficulty in persuading her to go. She thought it was improper; and was even half annoyed when we utterly ignored the idea of any impropriety in her going with two other ladies to see her old lover. Then came a more serious difficulty. She did not think Deborah would have liked her to go. This took us half a day's good hard talking to get over; but, at the first sentence of relenting, I seized the opportunity, and wrote and dispatched an acceptance in her name—fixing day and hour, that all might be decided and done with.

The next morning she asked me if I would go down to the shop with her; and there, after much hesitation, we chose out three caps to be sent home and tried on, that the most becoming might be selected to take with us on Thursday.

She was in a state of silent agitation all the way to Woodley. She had evidently never been there before; and, although she little dreamt I knew anything of her early story, I could perceive she was in a tremor at the thought of seeing the place which might have been her home, and round which it is probable that many of her innocent girlish imaginations had clustered. It was a long drive there, through paved jolting lanes. Miss Matilda sat bolt upright, and looked wistfully out of the windows, as we drew near the end of our journey. The aspect of the country was quiet and pastoral. Woodley stood among fields; and there was an old-fashioned garden, where roses and currant-bushes touched each other, and where the feathery asparagus formed a pretty background to the pinks and gillyflowers; there was no drive up to the door: we got out at a little gate, and walked up a straight box-edged path.

"My cousin might make a drive, I think," said Miss Pole, who was afraid of earache, and had only her cap on.

"I think it is very pretty," said Miss Matty, with a soft plaintiveness in her voice, and almost in a whisper; for just then Mr. Holbrook appeared at the door, rubbing his hands in very effervescence of hospitality. He looked more like my idea of Don Quixote than ever, and yet the likeness was only external. His respectable housekeeper stood modestly at the door to bid us welcome; and while she led the elder ladies upstairs to a bedroom, I begged to look about the garden. My request evidently pleased the old gentleman; who took me all round the place, and showed me his six-and-twenty cows, named after the different letters of the alphabet. As we went along, he surprised me occasionally by repeating apt and beautiful quotations from the poets, ranging easily from Shakspeare and George Herbert to those of our own day. He did this as naturally as if he were thinking aloud, and their true and beautiful words were the best expression he could find for what he was thinking or feeling. To be sure, he called Byron "my Lord Byrron," and pronounced the name of Goethe strictly in accordance with the English sound of the letters—"As Goëthe says, 'Ye ever-verdant palaces,'" etc. Altogether, I never met with a man, before or since, who had spent so long a life in a secluded and not impressive country, with ever-increasing delight in the daily and yearly change of season and beauty.

When he and I went in, we found that dinner was nearly ready in the kitchen—for so I suppose the room ought to be called, as there were oak dressers and cupboards all round, all over by the side of the fireplace, and only a small Turkey carpet in the middle of the flag-floor. The room might have been easily made into a handsome dark oak dining-parlour, by removing the oven, and a few other appurtenances of a kitchen, which were evidently never used; the real cooking place being at some distance. The room in which we were expected to sit was a stiffly furnished, ugly apartment; but that in which we did sit was what Mr. Holbrook called the counting-house, when he paid his labourers their weekly wages, at a great desk near the door. The rest of the pretty sitting-room—looking into the orchard, and all covered over with dancing tree-shadows—was filled with books. They lay on the ground, they covered the walls, they strewed the table. He was evidently half-ashamed and half proud of his extravagance in this respect. They were of all kinds, poetry and wild weird tales prevailing. He evidently chose his books in accordance with his own tastes, not because such and such were classical, or established favourites.

"Ah!" he said, "we farmers ought not to have much time for reading; yet somehow one can't help it."

"What a pretty room!" said Miss Matty, *sotto voce*.

"What a pleasant place!" said I, aloud, almost simultaneously.

"Nay! if you like it," replied he; "but can you sit on these great black leather three-cornered chairs? I like it better than the best parlour; but I thought ladies would take that for the smarter place."

It was the smarter place; but, like most smart things, not at all pretty, or pleasant, or home-like; so, while we were at dinner, the servant girl dusted and scrubbed the counting-house chairs, and we sat there all the rest of the day.

We had pudding before meat; and I thought Mr. Holbrook was going to make some apology for his old-fashioned ways, for he began:

"I don't know whether you like new-fangled ways."

"Oh! not at all!" said Miss Matty.

"No more do I," said he. "My housekeeper *will* have these in her new fashion; or else I tell her, that when I was a young man, we used to keep strictly to my father's rule, 'No broth, no ball; no ball, no beef'; and always began dinner with broth. Then we had suet puddings, boiled in the broth with the beef and then the meat itself. If we did not sup our broth, we had no ball, which we liked a deal better; and the beef came last of all, and only those had it who had done justice to the broth and the ball. Now folks begin with sweet things, and turn their dinners topsy-turvy."

When the ducks and green peas came, we looked at each other in dismay; we had only two-pronged, black-handled forks. It is true, the steel was as bright as silver; but what were we to do? Miss Matty picked up her peas, one by one, on the point of the prongs, much as Aminé ate her grains of rice after her previous feast with the Ghoul. Miss Pole sighed over her delicate young peas as she left them on one side of her plate untasted; for they *would* drop between the prongs. I looked at my host: the peas were going wholesale into his capacious mouth, shovelled up by his large round-ended knife. I saw, I imitated, I survived! My friends, in spite of my precedent, could not muster up courage enough to do an ungenteel thing; and, if Mr. Holbrook had not been so heartily hungry, he would probably have seen that the good peas went away almost untouched.

After dinner, a clay pipe was brought in, and a spittoon; and, asking us to retire to another room, where he would soon join us, if we disliked tobacco-smoke, he presented his pipe to Miss Matty, and requested her to fill the bowl. This was a compliment to a lady in his youth; but it was rather inappropriate to propose it as an honour to Miss Matty, who had been trained by her sister to hold smoking of every kind in utter abhorrence. But if it was a shock to her refinement, it was also a gratification to her feelings to be thus selected; so she daintily stuffed the strong tobacco into the pipe; and then we withdrew.

"It is very pleasant dining with a bachelor," said Miss Matty, softly, as we settled ourselves in the counting-house. "I only hope it is not improper; so many pleasant things are!"

Marriage

From Cranford.

BUT when she was gone, Miss Pole began a long congratulation to Miss Matty that so far they had escaped marriage, which she noticed always made people credulous to the last degree; indeed, she thought it argued great natural credulity in a woman if she could not keep herself from being married; and in what Lady Glenmire had said about Mr. Hoggins's robbery, we had a specimen of what people came to, if they gave way to such a weakness; evidently, Lady Glenmire would swallow anything, if she could believe the poor vamped-up story about a neck of mutton and a pussy, with which he had tried to impose on Miss Pole, only she had always been on her guard against believing too much of what men said.

We were thankful, as Miss Pole desired us to be, that we had never been married; but I think, of the two, we were even more thankful that the robbers had left Cranford; at least I judge so from a speech of Miss Matty's that evening, as we sat over the fire, in which she evidently looked upon a husband as a great protector against thieves, burglars, and ghosts; and said, that she did not think that she should dare to be always warning young people against matrimony, as Miss Pole did continually;—to be sure, marriage was a risk, as she saw now she had had some experience; but she remembered the time when she had looked forward to being married as much as anyone.

"Not to any particular person, my dear," said she, hastily checking herself up as if she were afraid of having admitted too much; "only the old story, you know, of ladies always saying, '*When* I marry,' and gentlemen, '*If* I marry.'" It was a joke spoken in rather a sad tone, and I doubt if either of us smiled; but I could not see Miss Matty's face by the flickering firelight. In a little while she continued:

"But after all I have not told you the truth. It is so long ago, and no one ever knew how much I thought of it at the time, unless, indeed, my dear mother guessed; but I may say that there was a time when I did not think I should have been only Miss Matty Jenkyns all my life; for even if I did meet anyone who wished to marry me now (and, as Miss Pole says, one is never too safe), I could not take him—I hope he would not take it too much to heart, but I could *not* take him—or any one but the person I once thought I should be married to, and he is dead and gone, and he never knew how it all came about that I said 'No,' when I had thought many and many a time——Well, it's no matter what I thought. God ordains it all, and I am very happy, my dear. No one has such kind friends as I," continued she, taking my hand and holding it in hers.

If I had never known of Mr. Holbrook, I could have said something in this pause, but as I had, I could not think of anything that would come in naturally, and so we both kept silence for a little time.

"My father once made us," she began, "keep a diary, in two columns; on one side we were to put down in the morning what we thought would be the course and events of the coming day, and at night we were to put down on the other side what really had happened. It would be to some people rather a sad way of telling their lives"—(a tear dropped upon my hand at these words)—"I don't mean that mine has been sad, only so very different to what I expected. I remember, one winter's evening, sitting over our bedroom fire with Deborah—I remember it as if it were yesterday—and we were planning our future lives—both of us were planning, though only she talked about it. She said she should like to marry an archdeacon, and write his charges; and you know, my dear, she never was married, and, for aught I know, she never spoke to an unmarried archdeacon in her life. I never was ambitious, nor could I have written charges, but I thought I could manage a house (my mother used to call me her right hand), and I was always so fond of little children—the shyest babies would stretch out their little arms to come to me; when I was a girl, I was half my leisure time nursing in the neighbouring cottages—but I don't know how it was, when I grew sad and grave—which I did a year or two after this time—the little things drew back from me, and I am afraid I lost the knack, though I am just as fond of children as ever, and have a strange yearning at my heart whenever I see a mother with a baby in her arms. Nay, my dear"—(and by a sudden blaze which sprang up from a fall of the unstirred coals, I saw that her eyes were full of tears—gazing intently on some vision of what might have been)—"do you know, I dream sometimes that I have a little child—always the same—a little girl of about two years old; she never grows older, though I have dreamt about her for many years. I don't think I ever dream of any words or sound she makes; she is very noiseless and still, but she comes to me when she is very sorry or very glad, and I have wakened with the clasp of her dear little arms round my neck. Only last night—perhaps because I had gone to sleep thinking of this ball for Phoebe—my little darling came in my dream, and put up her mouth to be kissed, just as I have seen real babies do to real mothers before going to bed. But all this is nonsense, dear! only don't be frightened by Miss Pole from being married. I can fancy it may be a very happy state, and a little credulity helps one on through life very smoothly—better than always doubting and doubting, and seeing difficulties and disagreeables in everything."

A Love Affair of Long Ago

From *Cranford*.

AND *now* I come to the love affair.

It seems that Miss Pole had a cousin, once or twice removed, who had offered to Miss Matty long ago. Now, this cousin lived four or five miles from Cranford on his own estate; but his property was not large enough to entitle him to rank higher than a yeoman; or rather, with something of the "pride which apes humility," he had refused to push himself on, as so many of his class had done, into the ranks of the squires. He would not allow himself to be called Thomas Holbrook, *Esq.*: he even sent back letters with this address, telling the postmistress at Cranford that his name was *Mr.* Thomas Holbrook, yeoman.

He despised every refinement which had not its root deep down in humanity. If people were not ill, he saw no necessity for moderating his voice. He spoke the dialect of the country in perfection, and constantly used it in conversation; although Miss Pole (who gave me these particulars) added, that he read aloud more beautifully and with more feeling than anyone she had ever heard, except the late Rector.

"And how came Miss Matilda not to marry him?" asked I.

"Oh, I don't know. She was willing enough, I think; but you know Cousin Thomas would not have been enough of a gentleman for the Rector, and Miss Jenkyns."

"Well! but they were not to marry him," said I, impatiently.

"No; but they did not like Miss Matty to marry below her rank. You know she was the Rector's daughter, and somehow they are related to Sir Peter Arley: Miss Jenkyns thought a deal of that."

"Poor Miss Matty!" said I.

"Nay, now, I don't know anything more than that he offered and was refused. Miss Matty might not like him—and Miss Jenkyns might never have said a word—it is only a guess of mine."

"Has she never seen him since?"

"No, I think not. You see, Woodley, Cousin Thomas's house, lies half-way between Cranford and Misselton; and I know he made Misselton his market town very soon after he had offered to Miss Matty; and I don't think he has been into Cranford above once or twice since—once, when I was walking with Miss Matty, in High Street; and suddenly she darted from me, and went up Shire Lane. A few minutes after, I was startled by meeting Cousin Thomas."

"How old is he?" I asked, after a pause of castle-building.

"He must be about seventy, I think, my dear," said Miss Pole, blowing up my castle, as if by gunpowder, into small fragments.

Very soon after—at least during my long visit to Miss Matilda—I had the opportunity of seeing Mr. Holbrook; seeing, too, his first encounter with his former love, after thirty or forty years' separation. I was helping to decide whether any of the new assortment of coloured silks which they had just received at the shop, would do to match a grey and black mousseline-de-laine that wanted a new breadth, when a tall, thin, Don Quixote-looking old man came into the shop for some woollen gloves. I had never seen the person (who was rather striking) before, and I watched him rather attentively, while Miss Matty listened to the shopman. The stranger wore a blue coat with brass buttons, drab breeches, and gaiters, and drummed with his fingers on the counter until he was attended to. When he answered the shop-boy's question, "What can I have the pleasure of showing you to-day, Sir?" I saw Miss Matilda start, and then suddenly sit down; and instantly I guessed who it was. She had made some enquiry which had to be carried round to the other shopman.

"Miss Jenkyns wants the black sarsenet two-and-twopence the yard"; and Mr. Holbrook had caught the name, and was across the shop in two strides.

"Matty—Miss Matilda—Miss Jenkyns! God bless my soul! I should not have known you. How are you? how are you?" He kept shaking her hand in a way which proved the warmth of his friendship; but he repeated so often, as if to himself, "I should not have known you!" that any sentimental romance which I might be inclined to build, was quite done away with by his manner.

However, he kept talking to us all the time we were in the shop; and then waving the shopman with the unpurchased gloves on one side, with "Another time, sir! another time!" he walked home with us. I am happy to say my client, Miss Matilda, also left the shop in an equally bewildered state, not having purchased either green or red silk. Mr. Holbrook was evidently full with honest, loud-spoken joy at meeting his old love again; he touched on the changes that had taken place; he even spoke of Miss Jenkyns as "Your poor sister! Well, well! we have all our faults"; and bade us good-bye with many a hope that he should soon see Miss Matty again. She went straight to her room; and never came back till our early tea-time, when I thought she looked as if she had been crying.

The Cat and the Lace

From *Cranford*.

MRS. FORRESTER related a curious little fact to Lady Glenmire—an anecdote known to the circle of her intimate friends, but of which even Mrs. Jamieson was not aware. It related to some fine old lace, the sole relic of better days, which Lady Glenmire was admiring on Mrs. Forrester's collar.

"Yes," said that lady, "such lace cannot be got now for either love or money; made by the nuns abroad they tell me. They say that they can't make it now, even there. But perhaps they can now they've passed the Catholic Emancipation Bill. I should not wonder. But, in the meantime, I treasure up my lace very much. I daren't even trust the washing of it to my maid" (the little charity school-girl I have named before, but who sounded well as "my maid"). "I always wash it myself. And once it had a narrow escape. Of course, your ladyship knows that such lace must never be starched or ironed. Some people wash it in sugar and water; and some in coffee, to make it the right yellow colour; but I myself have a very good recipe for washing it in milk, which stiffens it enough, and gives it a very good creamy colour. Well, ma'am, I had tacked it together (and the beauty of this fine lace is, that when it is wet, it goes into a very little space), and put it to soak in milk, when, unfortunately, I left the room; on my return, I found pussy on the table, looking very like a thief, but gulping very uncomfortably, as if she was half-choked with something she wanted to swallow, and could not. And, would you believe it? At first, I pitied her, and said, 'Poor pussy! poor pussy!' till, all at once, I looked and saw the cup of milk empty—cleaned out! 'You naughty cat!' said I; and I believe I was provoked enough to give her a slap, which did no good, but only helped the lace down—just as one slaps a choking child on the back. I could have cried, I was so vexed; but I determined I would not give the lace up without a struggle for it. I hoped the lace might disagree with her at any rate; but it would have been too much for Job, if he had seen, as I did, that cat come in, quite placid and purring, not a quarter of an hour after, and almost expecting to be stroked. 'No, pussy!' said I; 'if you have any conscience, you ought not to expect that!' And then a thought struck me; and I rang the bell for my maid, and sent her to Mr. Hoggins, with my compliments, and would he be kind enough to lend me one of his top-boots for an hour? I did not think there was anything odd in the message; but Jenny said, the young men in the surgery laughed as if they would be ill, at my wanting a top boot. When it came, Jenny and I put pussy in, with her fore-feet straight down, so that they were fastened, and could not scratch, and we gave her a teaspoonful of currant-jelly, in which (your ladyship must excuse me) I had mixed some tartar emetic. I shall never forget how anxious I was for the next half hour. I took pussy to my own room, and spread a clean towel on the floor. I could have kissed her when she returned the lace to sight, very much as it had gone down. Jenny had boiling water ready, and we soaked it and soaked it, and spread it on a lavender bush in the sun, before I could touch it again, even to put it in milk. But now, your ladyship would never guess that it had been in pussy's inside."

Small Economies

From Cranford

I HAVE often noticed that almost everyone has his own individual small economies—careful habits of saving fractions of pennies in some one peculiar direction—any disturbance of which annoys him more than spending shillings or pounds on some real extravagance. An old gentleman of my acquaintance, who took the intelligence of the failure of a Joint-Stock Bank, in which some of his money was invested, with stoical mildness, worried his family all through a long summer's day, because one of them had torn (instead of cutting) out the written leaves of his now useless bank-book; of course, the corresponding pages at the other end came out as well; and this little unnecessary waste of paper (his private economy) chafed him more than all the loss of his money. Envelopes fretted his soul terribly when they first came in; the only way in which he could reconcile himself to such waste of his cherished article, was by patiently turning inside out all that were sent to him, and so making them serve again. Even now, though tamed by age, I see him casting wistful glances at his daughters when they send a whole inside of a half sheet of note-paper, with the three lines of acceptance to an invitation, written on only one of the sides. I am not above owning that I have this human weakness myself. String is my foible. My pockets get full of little hanks of it, picked up and twisted together, ready for uses that never come. I am seriously annoyed if anyone cuts the string of a parcel, instead of patiently and faithfully undoing it fold by fold. How people can bring themselves to use india-rubber rings, which are a sort of deification of string, as lightly as they do, I cannot imagine. To me an india-rubber ring is a precious treasure. I have one which is not new; one that I picked up off the floor, nearly six years ago. I have really tried to use it; but my heart failed me, and I could not commit the extravagance.

Small pieces of butter grieve others. They cannot attend to conversation, because of the annoyance occasioned by the habit which some people have of invariably taking more butter than they want. Have you not seen the anxious look (almost mesmeric) which such persons fix on the article? They would feel it a relief if they might bury it out of their sight by popping it into their own mouths and swallowing it down; and they are really made happy if the person on whose plate it lies unused, suddenly breaks off a piece of toast (which he does not want at all) and eats up his butter. They think that this is not waste.

Now Miss Matty Jenkyns was chary of candles. We had many devices to use as few as possible. In the winter afternoons she would sit knitting for two or three hours; she could do this in the dark, or by firelight; and when I asked if I might not ring for candles to finish stitching my wristbands, she told me to "keep blind man's holiday." They were usually brought in with tea; but we only burnt one at a time. As we lived in constant preparation for a friend who might come in any evening (but who never did), it required some contrivance to keep our two candles of the same length, ready to be lighted, and to look as if we burnt two always. The candles took it in turns; and, whatever we might be talking about or doing, Miss Matty's eyes were habitually fixed upon the candle, ready to jump up and extinguish it, and to light the other before they had become too uneven in length to be restored to equality in the course of the evening.

One night, I remember, this candle economy particularly annoyed me. I had been very much tired of my compulsory "blind man's holiday,"—especially as Miss Matty had fallen asleep, and I did not like to stir the fire and run the risk of awakening her; so I could not even sit on the rug and scorch myself with sewing by fire-light, according to my usual custom. I fancied Miss Matty must be dreaming of her early life; for she spoke one or two words, in her uneasy sleep, bearing reference to persons who were dead long before. When Martha brought in the lighted candle and tea, Miss Matty started into wakefulness, with a strange bewildered look around, as if we were not the people she expected to see about her. There was a little sad expression that shadowed her face as she recognised me; but immediately afterwards she tried to give me her usual smile.

Elegant Economy

From *Cranford*

I IMAGINE that a few of the gentlefolks of Cranford were poor, and had some difficulty in making both ends meet; but they were like the Spartans, and concealed their smart under a smiling face. We none of us spoke of money, because that subject savoured of commerce and trade, and though some might be poor, we were all aristocratic. The Cranfordians had that kindly *esprit de corps* which made them overlook all deficiencies in success when some among them tried to conceal their poverty. When Mrs. Forrester, for instance, gave a party in her baby-house of a dwelling, and the little maiden disturbed the ladies on the sofa by a request that she might get the tea-tray out from underneath, everyone took this novel proceeding as the most natural thing in the world; and talked on about household forms and ceremonies, as if we all believed that our hostess had a regular servants' hall, second table, with housekeeper and steward, instead of the one little charity-school maiden, whose short ruddy arms could never have been strong enough to carry the tray upstairs, if she had not been assisted in private by her mistress, who now sat in state, pretending not to know what cakes were sent up; though she knew, and we knew, and she knew that we knew, she had been busy all the morning making tea-bread and sponge-cakes.

There were one or two consequences arising from this general but unacknowledged poverty, and this very much acknowledged gentility, which were not amiss, and which might be introduced into many circles of society to their great improvement. For instance, the inhabitants of Cranford kept early hours, and clattered home in their pattens, under the guidance of a lantern-bearer, about nine o'clock at night; and the whole town was abed and asleep by half-past ten. Moreover, it was considered "vulgar" (a tremendous word in Cranford) to give anything expensive, in the way of eatable or drinkable, at the evening entertainments. Wafer bread-and-butter and sponge-biscuits were all that the Honourable Mrs. Jamieson gave; and she was sister-in-law to the late Earl of Glenmire, although she did practise such "elegant economy."

"Elegant economy!" How naturally one falls back into the phraseology of Cranford! There, economy was always "elegant," and money-spending always "vulgar and ostentatious"; a sort of sour-grapeism, which made us very peaceful and satisfied. I never shall forget the dismay felt when a certain Captain Brown came to live at Cranford, and openly spoke about his being poor—not in a whisper to an intimate friend, the doors and windows being previously closed; but, in the public street! in a loud military voice! alleging his poverty as a reason for not taking a particular house. The ladies of Cranford were already rather moaning over the invasion of their territories by a man and a gentleman. He was a half-pay captain, and had obtained some situation on a neighbouring railroad, which had been vehemently petitioned against by the little town; and if, in addition to his masculine gender, and his connection with the obnoxious railroad, he was so brazen as to talk of being poor—why! then, indeed, he must be sent to Coventry. Death was as true and as common as poverty; yet people never spoke about that, loud out in the streets. It was a word not to be mentioned to ears polite. We had tacitly agreed to ignore that any with whom we associated on terms of visiting equality could ever be prevented by poverty from doing anything that they wished. If we walked to or from a party, it was because the night was so fine, or the air *so* refreshing; not because sedan-chairs were expensive. If we wore prints instead of summer silks, it was because we preferred a washing material; and so on, till we blinded ourselves to the vulgar fact that we were, all of us, people of very moderate means.

Sally tells of her Sweethearts

From *Ruth*, 1853

Mrs. Gaskell was noted as a kind mistress, and her servants stayed with her for years; one established a record and was in Mrs. Gaskell's service for over fifty years.

BUT Ruth said she would rather hear about Sally's sweethearts, much to the disappointment of the latter, who considered the dinner by far the greatest achievement.

"Well, you see, I don't know as I should call them sweethearts; for excepting John Rawson, who was shut up in the mad-house the next week, I never had what you may call a downright offer of marriage but once. But I had once; and so I may say I had a sweetheart. I was beginning to be afeared though, for one likes to be axed; that's but civility; and I remember, after I had turned forty, and afore Jeremiah Dickson had spoken, I began to think John Rawson had perhaps not been so very mad, and that I'd done ill to lightly his offer, as a madman's, if it was to be the only one I was ever to have; I don't mean as I'd have had him, but I thought, if it was to come o'er again, I'd speak respectful of him to folk, and say it were only his way to go about on all fours, but that he was a sensible man in most things. However, I'd had my laugh, and so had others, at my crazy lover, and it was late now to set him up as a Solomon. However, I thought it would be no bad thing to be tried again; but I little thought the trial would come when it did. You see, Saturday night is a leisure night in counting-houses and such-like places, while it's the busiest of all for servants. Well! it was a Saturday night, and I'd my baize apron on, and the tails of my bed-gown pinned together behind, down on my knees, pipeclaying the kitchen, when a knock comes to the back door. 'Come in!' says I; but it knocked again, as if it were too stately to open the door for itself; so I got up, rather cross, and opened the door; and there stood Jerry Dixon, Mr. Holt's head clerk; only he was not head clerk then. So I stood, stopping up the door, fancying he wanted to speak to master; but he kind of pushed past me, and telling me summut about the weather (as if I could not see it for myself), he took a chair, and sat down by the oven. 'Cool and easy!' thought I; meaning hisself, not his place, which I knew must be pretty hot. Well! it seemed no use standing waiting for my gentleman to go; not that he had much to say either; but he kept twirling his hat round and round, and smoothing the nap on't with the back of his hand. So at last I squatted down to my work, and thinks I, I shall be on my knees all ready if he puts up a prayer, for I knew he was a Methodee by bringing-up, and had only lately turned to master's way of thinking; and them Methodees are terrible hands at unexpected prayers when one least looks for 'em. I can't say I like their way of taking one by surprise, as it were; but then I'm a parish clerk's daughter, and could never demean myself to dissenting fashions, always save and except Master Thurstan's, bless him. However, I'd been caught once or twice unawares, so this time I thought I'd be up to it, and I moved a dry duster wherever I went, to kneel upon in case he began when I were in a wet place. By and by I thought, if the man would pray it would be a blessing, for it would prevent his sending his eyes after me wherever I went; for when they takes to praying they shuts their eyes, and quivers th' lids in a queer kind o' way—them Dissenters does. I can speak pretty plain to you, for you're bred in the Church like mysel', and must find it as out o' the way as I do to be among dissenting folk. God forbid I should speak disrespectful of Master Thurstan and Miss Faith, though; I never think on them as Church or Dissenters, but just as Christians. But to come back to Jerry. First, I tried always to be cleaning at his back; but when he wheeled round, so as always to face me, I thought I'd try a different game. So, says I, 'Master Dixon, I ax your pardon, but I must pipeclay under your chair. Will you please to move?' Well, he moved; and by and by I was at him again with the same words; and at after that, again and again, till he were always moving about wi' his chair behind him, like a snail as carries its house on its back. And the great gaupus never seed that I were pipeclaying the same places twice over. At last I got desperate cross, he were so in my way; so I made two big crosses on the tails of his brown coat; for you see, whenever he went, up or down, he drew out the tails of his coat from under him, and stuck them through the bars of the chair; and flesh and blood could not resist pipeclaying them for him; and a pretty brushing he'd have, I reckon, to get it off again. Well! at length he clears his throat uncommon loud; so I spreads my duster, and shuts my eyes all ready; but when nought comed of it, I opened my eyes a little bit to see what he were about. My word! if there he wasn't down on his knees right facing me, staring as hard as he could. Well! I thought it would be hard work to stand that, if he made a long ado; so I shut my eyes again, and tried to think serious, as became what I fancied were coming; but, forgive me! but I thought why couldn't the fellow go in and pray wi' Master Thurstan, as had always a calm spirit ready for prayer, instead o' me, who had my dresser to scour, let alone an apron to iron. At last he says, says he, 'Sally! will you oblige me with your hand?' So I thought it were, maybe, Methodee fashion to pray hand in hand; and I'll not deny but I wished I'd washed it better after blackleading the kitchen fire. I thought I'd better tell him it were not so clean as I could wish, so says I, 'Master Dixon, you shall have it, and welcome, if I may just go and wash 'em first.' But, says he, 'My dear Sally, dirty or clean it's all the same to me, seeing I'm only speaking in a figuring way. What I'm asking on my bended knees is, that you'd please to be so kind as to be my wedded wife; week after next will suit me, if it's agreeable to you!' My word!

I were up on my feet in an instant! It were odd now, weren't it? I never thought of taking the fellow, and getting married; for all, I'll not deny, I had been thinking it would be agreeable to be axed. But all at once, I couldn't abide the chap. 'Sir,' says I, trying to look shamefaced as became the occasion, but for all that, feeling a twittering round my mouth that I were afeared might end in a laugh.—'Master Dixon, I'm obleeged to you for the compliment, and thank ye all the same, but I think I'd prefer a single life.' He looked mighty taken aback; but in a minute he cleared up, and was as sweet as ever. He still kept on his knees, and I wished he'd take himself up; but, I reckon, he thought it would give force to his words; says he, 'Think again, my dear Sally. I've a four-roomed house, and furniture conformable; and eighty pound a year. You may never have such a chance again.' There were truth enough in that, but it was not pretty in the man to say it; and it put me up a bit. 'As for that, neither you nor I can tell, Master Dixon. You're not the first chap as I've had down on his knees afore me, axing me to marry him (you see I were thinking of John Rawson, only I thought there were no need to say he were on all fours—it were truth he were on his knees, you know), and maybe you'll not be the last. Anyhow, I've no wish to change my condition just now.' 'I'll wait till Christmas,' says he. 'I've a pig as will be ready for killing then, so I must get married before that.' Well now! would you believe it? the pig were a temptation. I'd a recipe for curing hams, as Miss Faith would never let me try, saying the old way were good enough. However, I resisted. Says I, very stern, because I felt I'd been wavering, 'Master Dixon, once for all, pig or no pig, I'll not marry you. And if you'll take my advice, you'll get up off your knees. The flags is but damp yet, and it would be an awkward thing to have rheumatiz just before winter.' With that he got up, stiff enough. He looked as sulky a chap as ever I clapped eyes on. And as he were so black and cross, I thought I'd done well (whatever came of the pig) to say 'No' to him. 'You may live to repent this,' says he, very red. 'But I'll not be too hard upon ye, I'll give you another chance. I'll let you have the night to think about it, and I'll just call in to hear your second thoughts, after chapel to-morrow.' Well now! did ever you hear the like? But that is the way with all of them men, thinking so much of theirselves, and that it's but ask and have. They've never had me, though; and I shall be sixty-one next Martinmas, so there's not much time left for them to try me, I reckon. Well! when Jeremiah said that, he put me up more than ever, and I says, 'My first thoughts, second thoughts, and third thoughts is all one and the same; you've but tempted me once, and that was when you spoke of your pig. But of yoursel' you're nothing to boast on, and so I'll bid you good-night, and I'll keep my manners, or else, if I told the truth, I should say it had been a great loss of time listening to you. But I'll be civil—so good-night.' He never said a word, but went off as black as thunder, slamming the door after him. The master called me in to prayers, but I can't say I could put my mind to them, for my heart was beating so. However, it was a comfort to have had an offer of holy matrimony; and though it flustered me, it made me think more of myself."

Sally Makes Her Will

From *Ruth*.

In one of her letters George Eliot mentions "the rich humour of Sally," and later goes on to say "Mrs. Gaskell has certainly a charming mind, and one cannot help loving her as one reads her books."

SALLY was, as usual, the talker; and, as usual, the subject was the family of whom for so many years she had formed a part.

"Aye! things was different when I was a girl," quoth she. "Eggs was thirty for a shilling, and butter only sixpence a pound. My wage when I came here was but three pound, and I did on it, and was always clean and tidy, which is more than many a lass can say now who gets her seven and eight pound a year; and tea was kept for an afternoon drink, and pudding was eaten afore meat in them days, and the upshot was, people paid their debts better; aye, aye! we'n gone backwards, and we thinken we'n gone forrards."

After shaking her head a little over the degeneracy of the times, Sally returned to a part of the subject on which she thought she had given Ruth a wrong idea.

"You'll not go for to think now that I've not more than three pound a year. I've a deal above that now. First of all, old missus gave me four pound, for she said I were worth it, and I thought in my heart that I were; so I took it without more ado; but after her death, Master Thurstan and Miss Faith took a fit of spending, and says they to me, one day as I carried tea in, 'Sally, we think your wages ought to be raised.' 'What matter what you think!' said I, pretty sharp, for I thought they'd ha' shown more respect to missus if they'd let things stand as they were in her time; and they'd gone and moved the sofa away from the wall to where it stands now, already that very day. So I speaks up sharp, and, says I, 'As long as I'm content, I think it's no business of yours to be meddling wi' me and my money matters.' 'But,' says Miss Faith (she's always the one to speak first if you'll notice, though it's master that comes in and clinches the matter with some reason she'd never ha' thought of—he were always a sensible lad), 'Sally, all the servants in the town have six pound and better, and you have as hard a place as any of 'em.' 'Did you ever hear me grumble about my work that you talk about it in that way? Wait till I grumble,' says I, 'but don't meddle wi' me till then.' So I flung off in a huff; but in the course of the evening, Master Thurstan came in and sat down in the kitchen, and he's such winning ways he wiles one over to anything; and besides, a notion had come into my head—now, you'll not tell" said she, glancing round the room, and hitching her chair nearer to Ruth in a confidential manner; Ruth promised, and Sally went on:

"I thought I should like to be an heiress wi' money, and leave it all to Master and Miss Faith; and I thought if I'd six pound a year I could, maybe, get to be an heiress; all I was feared on was that some chap or other might marry me for my money, but I've managed to keep the fellows off; so I looks mim and grateful, and I thanks Master Thurstan for his offer, and I takes the wages; and what do you think I've done?" asked Sally, with an exultant air.

"What have you done?" asked Ruth.

"Why," replied Sally slowly and emphatically, "I've saved thirty pound! But that's not it. I've getten a lawyer to make me a will; that's it, wench!" said she, slapping Ruth on the back.

"How did you manage it?" asked Ruth.

"Aye, that was it," said Sally; "I thowt about it many a night before I hit on the right way. I was afeared the money might be thrown into Chancery, if I didn't make it all safe, and yet I could na' ask Master Thurstan. At last and at length John Jackson, the grocer, had a nephew come to stay a week with him, as was 'prentice to a lawyer in Liverpool; so now was my time, and here was my lawyer. Wait a minute! I could tell you my story better if I had my will in my hand; and I'll scomfish you if ever you go for to tell."

She held up her hand, and threatened Ruth as she left the kitchen to fetch the will.

When she came back, she brought a parcel tied up in a blue pocket-handkerchief; she sat down, squared her knees, untied the handkerchief, and displayed a small piece of parchment.

"Now, do you know what this is?" said she, holding it up. "It's parchment, and it's the right stuff to make wills on. People gets into Chancery if they don't make them o' this stuff, and I reckon Tom Jackson thowt he'd have a fresh job on it if he could get it into Chancery; for the rascal went and wrote it on a piece of paper at first, and came and read it me out loud off a piece of paper no better than what one writes letters upon. I were up to him; and, thinks I, come, come, my lad, I'm not a fool, though you may think so; I know a paper will won't stand, but I'll let you run your rig. So I sits and I listens. And would you belie' me, he read it out as if it were as clear a business as your giving me that thimble—no more ado, though it were thirty pound! I could understand it mysel'—that were no law for me. I wanted summat to consider about, and for th' meaning to be wrapped up as I wrap up my best gown. So says I, 'Tom! it's not on parchment. I mun have it on parchment.' 'This 'ill do as well,' says he. 'We'll get it witnessed, and it will stand good.' Well! I liked the notion of having it witnessed, and for a while that soothed me; but after a bit, I felt I should like it done according to law, and not plain out as anybody might ha' done it; I mysel', if I could have written. So says I, 'Tom! I mun have it on parchment.' 'Parchment costs money,' says he very grave. 'Oh, oh, my lad! are ye there?' thinks I. 'That's the reason I'm clipped of law.' So says I, 'Tom! I mun have it on parchment. I'll pay the money and welcome. It's thirty pound, and what I can lay to it. I'll make it safe. It shall be on parchment, and I'll tell thee what, lad! I'll gie ye sixpence for every good law-word you put in it, sounding like, and not to be caught up as a person runs. Your master had need to be ashamed of you as a 'prentice if you can't do a thing more tradesman-like than this!' Well! he laughed above a bit, but I were firm, and stood to it. So he made it out on parchment. Now, woman, try and read it!" said she, giving it to Ruth.

Ruth smiled, and began to read, Sally listening with rapt attention. When Ruth came to the word "testatrix" Sally stopped her.

"That was the first sixpence," said she. "I thowt he was going to fob me off again wi' plain language; but when that word came, I out wi' my sixpence, and gave it to him on the spot. Now go on."

Presently Ruth read "accruing."

"That was the second sixpence. Four sixpences it were in all, besides six-and-eightpence as we bargained at first, and three-and-fourpence parchment. There! that's what I call a will; witnessed according to law, and all. Master Thurstan will be prettily taken in when I die, and he finds all his extra wage left back to him. But it will teach him it's not so easy as he thinks for, to make a woman give up her way."

Betty's Advice to Phillis

From Cousin Phillis, 1865

PHILLIS was carried downstairs, and lay for hour after hour quite silent on the great sofa, drawn up under the windows of the house-place. She seemed always the same, gentle, quiet and sad. Her energy did not return with her bodily strength. It was sometimes pitiful to see her parents' vain endeavours to rouse her to interest. One day the minister brought her a set of blue ribbons, reminding her with a tender smile of a former conversation in which she had owned to a love of such feminine vanities. She spoke gratefully to him, but when he was gone she laid them on one side, and languidly shut her eyes. Another time I saw her mother bring her the Latin and Italian books that she had been so fond of before her illness—or rather, before Holdsworth had gone away. That was worst of all. She turned her face to the wall, and cried as soon as her mother's back was turned. Betty was laying the cloth for the early dinner. Her sharp eyes saw the state of the case.

"Now, Phillis!" said she, coming up to the sofa; "we ha' done a' we can for you, and th' doctors has done a' they can for you, and I think the Lord has done a' He can for you, and more than you deserve, too, if you don't do something for yourself. If I were you, I'd rise up and snuff the moon, sooner than break your father's and your mother's hearts wi' watching and waiting till it pleases you to fight your own way back to cheerfulness. There, I never favoured long preachings, and I've said my say."

A day or two after Phillis asked me, when we were alone, if I thought my father and mother would allow her to go and stay with them for a couple of months. She blushed a little as she faltered out her wish for change of thought and scene.

"Only for a short time, Paul. Then—we will go back to the peace of the old days. I know we shall; I can, and I will!"

Practical Christianity

From My Lady Ludlow, 1859

"THERE has Mr. Gray been twice at my house, while I have been away in the mornings, talking to Sally about the state of her soul and that sort of thing. But when I found the meat all roasted to a cinder, I said, 'Come, Sally, let's have no more praying when beef is down at the fire. Pray at six o'clock in the morning and nine at night, and I won't hinder you.' So she sauced me, and said something about Martha and Mary, implying that, because she had let the beef get so overdone that I declare I could hardly find a bit for Nancy Pole's sick grandchild, she had chosen the better part. I was very much put about, I own, and perhaps, you'll be shocked at what I said—indeed, I don't know if it was right myself—but I told her I had a soul as well as she, and, if it was to be saved by my sitting still and thinking about salvation and never doing my duty, I thought I had as good a right as she had to be Mary, and save my soul. So, that afternoon, I sat quite still, and it was really a comfort, for I am often too busy, I know, to pray as I ought. There is first one person wanting me, and then another, and the house and the food and the neighbours to see after. So, when tea-time comes, there enters my maid with her hump on her back, and her soul to be saved. 'Please, ma'am, did you order the pound of butter?' 'No, Sally,' I said, shaking my head, 'this morning I did not go round by Hale's farm, and this afternoon I have been employed in spiritual things.'

"Now, our Sally likes tea and bread-and-butter above everything, and dry bread was not to her taste.

"'I'm thankful,' said the impudent hussy, 'that you have taken a turn towards godliness. It will be my prayers, I trust, that's given it you.'

"I was determined not to give her an opening towards the carnal subject of butter; so she lingered still, longing to ask leave to run for it. But I gave her none, and munched my dry bread myself, thinking what a famous cake I could make for little Ben Pole with a bit of butter we were saving; and, when Sally had had her butterless tea, and was in none of the best of tempers because Martha had not bethought herself of the butter, I just quietly said:

"'Now, Sally, to-morrow we'll try to hash that beef well, and to remember the butter, and to work out our salvation all at the same time, for I don't see why it can't all be done, as God has set us to do it all.' But I heard her at it again about Mary and Martha, and I have no doubt that Mr. Gray will teach her to consider me as a lost sheep."

Betty Gives Paul Manning a Lecture

From Cousin Phillis, 1865

I REMEMBER one thing more—an attack which Betty the servant made upon me one day as I came in through the kitchen where she was churning, and stopped to ask her for a drink of buttermilk.

"I say, cousin Paul" (she had adopted the family habit of addressing me generally as Cousin Paul, and always speaking of me in that form), "something's amiss with our Phillis, and I reckon you've a good guess what it is. She's not one to take up wi' such as you" (not complimentary, but that Betty never was, even to those for whom she felt the highest respect), "but I'd as lief yon Holdsworth had never come near us. So there you've a bit o' my mind."

And a very unsatisfactory bit it was. I did not know what to answer to the glimpse at the real state of the case implied in the shrewd woman's speech; so I tried to put her off by assuming surprise at her first assertion.

"Amiss with Phillis! I should like to know why you think anything is wrong with her. She looks as blooming as anyone can do."

"Poor lad! you're but a big child after all; and you've likely never heared of fever-flush. But you know better nor that, my fine fellow! So don't think for to put me off wi' blooms and blossoms and suchlike talk. What makes her walk about for hours and hours o' nights when she used to be abed and asleep? I sleep next room to her, and hear her plain as can be. What makes her come in panting and ready to drop into that chair"—nodding to one close to the door—"and it's 'Oh! Betty, some water, please?' That's the way she comes in now, when she used to come back as fresh and bright as she went out. If yon friend o' yours has played her false, he's a deal for t' answer for; she's a lass who's as sweet and as sound as a nut, and the very apple of her father's eye, and of her mother's too, only wi' her she ranks second to th' minister. You'll have to look after yon chap, for I, for one, will stand no wrong to our Phillis."

What was I to do or to say? I wanted to justify Holdsworth, to keep Phillis's secret, and to pacify the woman all in the same breath. I did not take the best course, I'm afraid.

"I don't believe Holdsworth ever spoke a word of—of love to her in all his life. I'm sure he didn't."

"Ay, ay! but there's eyes, and there's hands, as well as tongues; and a man has two o' th' one and but one o' t'other."

"And she's so young; do you suppose her parents would not have seen it?"

"Well! if you ax me that, I'll say out boldly, 'No.' They've called her 'the child' so long—'the child' is always their name for her when they talk on her between themselves, as if never anybody else had a ewe-lamb before them— that she's grown up to be a woman under their very eyes, and they look on her still as if she were in her long clothes. And you ne'er heard on a man falling in love wi' a babby in long clothes.

"No!" said I, half laughing. But she went on as grave as a judge.

"Ay! you see you'll laugh at the bare thought on it—and I'll be bound th' minister, though he's not a laughing man, would ha' sniggled at th' notion of falling in love wi' the child. Where's Holdsworth off to?"

"Canada," said I shortly.

"Canada here, Canada there," she replied testily. "Tell me how far he's off, instead of giving me your gibberish. Is he a two day's journey away, or a three, or a week?"

"He's ever so far off—three weeks at the least," cried I in despair. "And he's either married, or just going to be. So there!" I expected a fresh burst of anger. But no; the matter was too serious. Betty sate down, and kept silence for a minute or two. She looked so miserable and downcast, that I could not help going on and taking her a little into my confidence.

"It is quite true what I said. I know he never spoke a word to her. I think he liked her, but it's all over now. The best thing we can do—the best and kindest for her—and I know you love her, Betty——"

"I nursed her in my arms; I gave her little brother his last taste o' earthly food," said Betty, putting her apron up to her eyes.

"Well! don't let us show her we guess that she is grieving; she'll get over it the sooner. Her father and mother don't even guess at it, and we must make as if we didn't. It's too late now to do anything else."

"I'll never let on; I know nought. I've known true love mysel', in my day. But I wish he'd been farred before he ever came near this house, with his 'Please Betty' this, and 'Please Betty' that, and drinking up our new milk as if he'd been a cat. I hate such beguiling ways."

I thought it was as well to let her exhaust herself in abusing the absent Holdsworth; if it was shabby and treacherous in me, I came in for my punishment directly.

"It's a caution to a man how he goes about beguiling. Some men do it as easily and innocent as cooing doves. Don't you be none of 'em, my lad. Not that you've got the gifts to do it, either; you're no great shakes to look at, neither for figure, nor yet for face, and it would need be a deaf adder to be taken in wi' your words, though there may be no great harm in 'em." A lad of nineteen or twenty is not flattered by such an outspoken opinion even from the eldest and ugliest of her sex; and I was only too glad to change the subject by my repeated injunctions to keep Phillis's secret. The end of our conversation was this speech of hers:

"You great gaupus, for all you're called cousin o' th' minister—many a one is cursed wi' fools for cousins—d'ye think I can't see sense except through your spectacles? I give you leave to cut out my tongue, and nail it up on th' barn door for a caution to magpies, if I let out on that poor wench, either to herself, or anyone that is hers, as the Bible says. Now you've heard me speak Scripture language perhaps you'll be content, and leave me my kitchen to mysel'."

Descriptive

Green Heys Fields

From *Mary Barton*, 1848

This is a description of the neighbourhood near Mrs. Gaskell's home at the time of writing *Mary Barton*, and it was the accuracy with which she described

Manchester and its surroundings that led her readers to the conclusion that "Cotton Malther Mills, Esq.," the *nom de guerre* under which she hid her identity, was none other than Mrs. Gaskell. Writing of *Mary Barton* a few weeks after it was published, Miss Winkworth said, "I knew by the first few words it was hers (Mrs. Gaskell's)—about Green Heys Fields, and the stile she was describing to me."

THERE are some fields near Manchester, well known to the inhabitants as "Green Heys Fields," through which runs a public footpath to a little village about two miles distant. In spite of these fields being flat and low, nay, in spite of the want of wood (the great and usual recommendation of level tracts of land), there is a charm about them which strikes even the inhabitant of a mountainous district, who sees and feels the effect of contrast in these commonplace but thoroughly rural fields, with the busy, bustling manufacturing town he left but half an hour ago. Here and there an old black and white farm-house, with its rambling outbuildings, speaks of other times and other occupations than those which now absorb the population of the neighbourhood. Here in their seasons may be seen the country business of haymaking, ploughing, etc., which are such pleasant mysteries for townspeople to watch; and here the artisan, deafened with noise of tongues and engines, may come to listen awhile to the delicious sounds of rural life: the lowing of cattle, the milkmaid's call, the clatter and cackle of poultry in the old farmyards. You cannot wonder, then, that these fields are popular places of resort at every holiday time; and you would not wonder, if you could see, or I properly describe, the charm of one particular stile, that it should be, on such occasions, a crowded halting-place. Close by it is a deep, clear pond, reflecting in its dark green depths the shadowy trees that bend over it to exclude the sun. The only place where its banks are shelving is on the side next to a rambling farmyard, belonging to one of those old-world gabled black and white houses I named above, overlooking the field through which the public footpath leads. The porch of this farm-house is covered by a rose tree; and the little garden surrounding it is crowded with a medley of old-fashioned herbs and flowers, planted long ago, when the garden was the only druggist's shop within reach, and allowed to grow in scrambling and wild luxuriance—roses, lavender, sage, balm (for tea), rosemary, pinks and wallflowers, onions and jessamine, in most republican and indiscriminate order. This farm-house and garden are within a hundred yards of the stile of which I spoke, leading from the large pasture field into a smaller one, divided by a hedge of hawthorn and blackthorn; and near this stile, on the farther side, there runs a tale that primroses may often be found, and occasionally the blue sweet violet on the grassy hedge bank.

I do not know whether it was on a holiday granted by the masters, or a holiday seized in right of Nature and her beautiful spring-time by the workmen, but one afternoon (now ten or a dozen years ago) these fields were much thronged. It was an early May evening—the April of the poets; for heavy showers had fallen all the morning, and the round, soft, white clouds which were blown by a west wind over the dark blue sky, were sometimes varied by one blacker and more threatening. The softness of the day tempted forth the young green leaves, which almost visibly fluttered into life; and the willows, which that morning had had only a brown reflection in the water below, were now of that tender grey-green which blends so delicately with the spring harmony of colours.

Groups of merry and somewhat loud-talking girls, whose ages might range from twelve to twenty, came by with a buoyant step. They were most of them factory girls, and wore the usual out-of-doors dress of that particular class of maidens: namely, a shawl, which at midday or in fine weather was allowed to be merely a shawl, but towards evening, or if the day were chilly, became a sort of Spanish mantilla or Scotch plaid, and was brought over the head and hung loosely down, or was pinned under the chin in no unpicturesque fashion.

Their faces were not remarkable for beauty; indeed, they were below the average, with one or two exceptions; they had dark hair, neatly and classically arranged, dark eyes, but sallow complexions and irregular features. The only thing to strike a passer-by was an acuteness and intelligence of countenance, which has often been noticed in a manufacturing population.

There were also numbers of boys, or rather young men, rambling among these fields, ready to bandy jokes with any one, and particularly ready to enter into conversation with the girls, who, however, held themselves aloof, not in a shy, but rather in an independent way, assuming an indifferent manner, to the noisy wit or obstreperous compliments of the lads. Here and there came a sober, quiet couple, either whispering lovers or husband and wife, as the case might be; and if the latter, they were seldom unencumbered by an infant, carried for the most part by the father, while occasionally even three or four little toddlers had been carried or dragged thus far, in order that the whole family might enjoy the delicious May afternoon together.

A Lancashire Tea-party in the Early Forties

From Mary Barton.

MRS. BARTON produced the key of the door from her pocket; and on entering the house-place it seemed as if they were in total darkness, except one bright spot, which might be a cat's eye, or might be, what it was, a red-hot fire, smouldering under a large piece of coal, which John Barton immediately applied himself to break up, and the effect instantly produced was warm and glowing light in every corner of the room. To add to this (although the coarse yellow glare seemed lost in the ruddy glow from the fire), Mrs. Barton lighted a dip by sticking it in the fire, and having placed it satisfactorily in a tin candlestick, began to look further about her, on hospitable thoughts intent. The room was tolerably large, and possessed many conveniences. On the right of the door, as you entered, was a longish window, with a broad ledge. On each side of this hung blue-and-white check curtains, which were now drawn, to shut in the friends met to enjoy themselves. Two geraniums, unpruned and leafy, which stood on the sill, formed a further defence from out-door pryers. In the corner between the window and the fireside was a cupboard, apparently full of plates and dishes, cups and saucers, and some more nondescript articles, for which one would have fancied their possessors could find no use—such as triangular pieces of glass to save carving knives and forks from dirtying table-cloths. However, it was evident Mrs. Barton was proud of her crockery and glass, for she left her cupboard door open, with a glance round of satisfaction and pleasure. On the opposite side to the door and window was the staircase and two doors, one of which (the nearest to the fire) led into a sort of little back kitchen, where dirty work, such as washing up dishes, might be done, and whose shelves served as larder and pantry and store-room and all. The other door, which was considerably lower, opened into the coal-hole—the slanting closet under the stairs, from which to the fire-place there was a gay-coloured piece of oil-cloth laid. The place seemed almost crammed with furniture (sure sign of good times among the mills). Beneath the window was a dresser, with three deep drawers. Opposite the fire-place was a table, which I should call a Pembroke, only that it was made of deal, and I cannot tell how far such a name may be applied to such humble material. On it, resting against the wall, was a bright green japanned tea-tray, having a couple of scarlet lovers embracing in the middle. The fire-light danced merrily on this, and really (setting all taste but that of a child's aside) it gave a richness of colouring to that side of the room. It was in some measure propped up by a crimson tea-caddy, also of japan ware. A round table on one branching leg, really for use, stood in the corresponding corner to the cupboard; and, if you can picture all this, with a washy, but clean stencilled pattern on the walls, you can form some idea of John Barton's home.

The tray was soon hoisted down, and before the merry clatter of cups and saucers began, the women disburdened themselves of their out-of-door things, and sent Mary upstairs with them. Then came a long whispering, and chinking of money, to which Mr. and Mrs. Wilson were too polite to attend; knowing, as they did full well, that it all related to the preparations for hospitality: hospitality that, in their turn, they should have such pleasure in offering. So they tried to be busily occupied with the children, and not to hear Mrs. Barton's directions to Mary.

"Run, Mary dear, just round the corner, and get some fresh eggs at Tipping's (you may get one apiece, that will be fivepence), and see if he has any nice ham cut, that he would let us have a pound of."

"Say two pounds, missis, and don't be stingy," chimed in the husband.

"Well, a pound and a half, Mary. And get it Cumberland ham, for Wilson comes from there-away, and it will have a sort of relish of home with it he'll like—and Mary" (seeing the lassie fain to be off), "you must get a pennyworth of milk and a loaf of bread—mind you get it fresh and new—and, and—that's all, Mary."

"No, it's not all," said her husband. "Thou must get sixpennyworth of rum to warm the tea; thou'll get it at the 'Grapes.' And thou just go to Alice Wilson; he says she lives just right round the corner, under 14, Barber Street" (this was addressed to his wife); "and tell her to come and take her tea with us; she'll like to see her brother I'll be bound, let alone Jane and the twins."

"If she comes she must bring a tea-cup and saucer, for we have but half a dozen, and here's six of us," said Mrs. Barton.

"Pooh, pooh! Jem and Mary can drink out of one, surely."

But Mary secretly determined to take care that Alice brought her tea-cup and saucer, if the alternative was to be her sharing anything with Jem.

Alice Wilson had but just come in. She had been out all day in the fields, gathering wild herbs for drinks and medicine, for, in addition to her invaluable qualities as a sick nurse and her worldly occupations as a washerwoman, she added a considerable knowledge of hedge and field simples; and on fine days, when no more profitable occupation offered itself, she used to ramble off into the lanes and meadows as far as her legs could carry her. This evening she had returned loaded with nettles, and her first object was to light a candle, and see to hang them up in bunches in every available place in her cellar room. It was the perfection of cleanliness; in one corner stood the modest-looking bed, with a check curtain at the head, the whitewashed wall filling up the place where the corresponding one should have been. The floor was bricked, and scrupulously clean, although so damp that it seemed as if the last washing would never dry up. As the cellar window looked into an area in the street, down which boys might throw stones, it was protected by an outside shutter, and was oddly festooned with all manner of hedgerow, ditch, and field plants, which we are accustomed to call valueless, but which have a powerful effect either for good or for evil, and are consequently much used among the poor. The room was strewn, hung, and darkened with these bunches, which emitted no very fragrant odour in their process of drying. In one corner was a sort of broad hanging shelf, made of old planks, where some old hoards of Alice's were kept. Her little bit of crockery-ware was ranged on the mantelpiece, where also stood her candlestick and box of matches. A small cupboard contained at the bottom coals, and at the top her bread and basin of oatmeal, her frying-pan, teapot, and a small tin saucepan, which served as a kettle, as well as for cooking the delicate little messes of broth which Alice was sometimes able to manufacture for a sick neighbour.

After her walk she felt chilly and weary, and was busy trying to light her fire with the damp coals and half-green sticks, when Mary knocked.

"Come in," said Alice, remembering, however, that she had barred the door for the night, and hastening to make it possible for anyone to come in.

"Is that you, Mary Barton?" exclaimed she, as the light from the candle streamed on the girl's face. "How you are grown since I used to see you at my brother's! Come in, lass, come in."

"Please," said Mary, almost breathless, "mother says you're to come to tea, and bring your cup and saucer, for George and Jane Wilson is with us, and the twins, and Jem. And you're to make haste, please."

"I'm sure it's very neighbourly and kind in your mother, and I'll come, with many thanks. Stay, Mary; has your mother got any nettles for spring drink? If she hasn't, I'll take her some."

"No, I don't think she has."

Mary ran off like a hare to fulfil what, to a girl of thirteen, fond of power, was the more interesting part of her errand—the money-spending part. And well and ably did she perform her business, returning home with a little bottle of rum and the eggs in one hand, while her other was filled with some excellent red-and-white, smoke-flavoured, Cumberland ham, wrapped up in paper.

She was at home, and frying ham, before Alice had chosen her nettles, put out her candle, locked the door, and walked in a very footsore manner as far as John Barton's. What an aspect of comfort did his house-place present, after her humble cellar! She did not think of comparing; but for all that she felt the delicious glow of the fire, the bright light that revelled in every corner of the room, the savoury smells, the comfortable sounds of a boiling kettle, and the hissing, frizzling ham. With a little old-fashioned curtsey she shut the door, and replied with a loving heart to the boisterous and surprised greeting of her brother.

And now, all preparations being made, the party sat down; Mrs. Wilson in the post of honour, the rocking-chair, on the right-hand side of the fire, nursing her baby, while its father, in an opposite arm-chair, tried vainly to quieten the other with bread soaked in milk.

Mrs. Barton knew manners too well to do anything but sit at the tea-table and make tea, though in her heart she longed to be able to superintend the frying of the ham, and cast many an anxious look at Mary as she broke the eggs and turned the ham, with a very comfortable portion of confidence in her own culinary powers. Jem stood awkwardly leaning against the dresser, replying rather gruffly to his aunt's speeches, which gave him, he thought, the air of being a little boy; whereas he considered himself as a young man, and not so very young neither, as in two months he would be eighteen. Barton vibrated between the fire and the tea-table, his only drawback being a fancy that every now and then his wife's face flushed and contracted as if in pain.

At length the business actually began. Knives and forks, cups and saucers, made a noise, but human voices were still, for human beings were hungry and had no time to speak. Alice first broke silence; holding the tea-cup with the manner of one proposing a toast, she said, "Here's to absent friends. Friends may meet, but mountains never."

It was an unlucky toast or sentiment, as she instantly felt. Everyone thought of Esther, the absent Esther; and Mrs. Barton put down her food, and could not hide the fast-dropping tears. Alice could have bitten her tongue out.

It was a wet blanket to the evening; for though all had been said and suggested in the fields that could be said or suggested, everyone had a wish to say something in the way of comfort to poor Mrs. Barton, and a dislike to talk about anything else, while her tears fell fast and scalding. So George Wilson, his wife, and children set off early home, not before (in spite of *mal-à-propos* speeches) they had expressed a wish that such meetings might often take place, and not before John Barton had given his hearty consent, and declared that as soon as ever his wife was well again they would have just such another evening.

"I will take care not to come and spoil it," thought poor Alice; and going up to Mrs. Barton, she took her hand almost humbly, and said, "You don't know how sorry I am I said it."

To her surprise, a surprise that brought tears of joy into her eyes, Mary Barton put her arms round her neck, and kissed the self-reproaching Alice. "You didn't mean any harm, and it was me as was foolish; only this work about Esther, and not knowing where she is, lies so heavy on my heart. Good-night, and never think no more about it. God bless you, Alice."

Many and many a time, as Alice reviewed that evening in her after life, did she bless Mary Barton for these kind and thoughtful words. But just then all she could say was, "Good night, Mary, and may God bless *you.*"

Babby's Journey from London to Manchester

From *Mary Barton.*

"THEN we'd the stout little babby to bring home. We'd not overmuch money left; but it were fine weather, and we thought we'd take th' coach to Brummagem, and walk on. It were a bright May morning when I last saw London town, looking back from a big hill a mile or two off. And in that big mass o' a place I were leaving my blessed child asleep—in her last sleep. Well, God's will be done! She's gotten to heaven afore me; but I shall get there at last, please God, though it's a long while first.

"The babby had been fed afore we set out, and th' coach moving kept it asleep, bless its little heart! But when th' coach stopped for dinner it were awake, and crying for its pobbies. So we asked for some bread and milk, and Jennings took it first for to feed it; but it made its mouth like a square, and let it run out at each o' the four corners. 'Shake it, Jennings,' says I; 'that's the way they make water run through a funnel, when it's o'er full; and a child's mouth is broad end o' th' funnel, and th' gullet the narrow one.' So he shook it, but it only cried th' more. 'Let me have it,' says I, thinking he were an awkward oud chap. But it were just as bad wi' me. By shaking the babby we got better nor a gill into its mouth, but more nor that came up again, wetting a' th' nice dry clothes landlady had put on. Well, just as we'd gotten to th' dinner-table, and help oursels, and eaten two mouthfuls, came in th' guard, and a fine chap wi' a sample o' calico flourishing in his hand. 'Coach is ready!' says one; 'Half a crown your dinner!' says the other. Well, we thought it a deal for both our dinners, when we'd hardly tasted 'em; but, bless your life, it were half a crown apiece and a shilling for th' bread and milk as were posseted all over babby's clothes. We spoke up again it; but everybody said it were the rule, so what could two poor oud chaps like us do again' it? Well, poor babby cried without stopping to take breath, fra' that time till we got to Brummagem for the night. My heart ached for the little thing. It caught wi' its wee mouth at our coat sleeves and at our mouths, when we tried t' comfort it by talking to it. Poor little wench; it wanted its mammy, as were lying cold in th' grave. 'Well,' says I, 'it'll be clemmed to death, if it lets out its supper as it did its dinner. Let's get some woman to feed it; it comes natural to women to do for babbies.' So we asked for the chambermaid at the inn, and she took quite kindly to it; and we got a good supper, and grew rare and sleepy, what wi' th' warmth and wi' our long ride i' the open air. Th' chambermaid said she would like t' have it t' sleep wi' her, only missis would scold so; but it looked so quiet and smiling like, as it lay in her arms, that we thought 'twould be no trouble to have it wi' us. I says, 'See, Jennings, how women folk do quieten babbies; it's just as I said.' He looked grave; he were always thoughtful-looking, though I never heard him say anything very deep. At last says he:

"'Young woman! have you gotten a spare nightcap?'

"'Missis always keeps nightcaps for gentlemen as does not like to unpack,' says she, rather quick.

"'Aye, but, young woman, it's one of your nightcaps I want. Th' babby seems to have taken a mind to yo; and maybe in the dark it might take me for yo if I'd getten your nightcap on.'

"The chambermaid smirked and went for a cap, but I laughed outright at th' oud bearded chap thinking he'd make hissel like a woman just by putting on a woman's cap. Howe'er, he'd not be laughed out on't, so I held th' babby till he were in bed. Such a night as we had on it! Babby began to scream o' th' oud fashion, and we took it turn and turn about to sit up and rock it. My heart were very sore for the little one, as it groped about wi' its mouth; but for a' that I could scarce keep fra' smiling at th' thought o' us two oud chaps, th' one wi' a woman's nightcap on sitting on our hinder ends for half the night, hushabying a babby as wouldn't be hushabied. Toward morning, poor little wench! it fell asleep, fairly tired out wi' crying, but even in its sleep it gave such pitiful sobs, quivering up fra' the very bottom of its little heart, that once or twice I almost wished it lay on its mother's breast, at peace for ever. Jennings fell asleep too; but I began for to reckon up our money. It were little enough we had left, our dinner the day afore had ta'en so much. I didn't know what our reckoning would be for that night lodging, and supper, and breakfast. Doing a sum always sent me asleep ever sin' I were a lad; so I fell sound in a short time, and were only awakened by chambermaid tapping at th' door, to say she'd dress the babby before her missis were up if we liked. But bless yo' we'd never thought o' undressing it the night afore, and now it were sleeping so sound, and we were so glad o' the peace and quietness, that we thought it were no good to waken it up to screech again.

"Well! (there's Mary asleep for a good listener!) I suppose you're getting weary of my tale, so I'll not be long over ending it. Th' reckoning left us very bare, and we thought we'd best walk home, for it were only sixty mile, they telled us, and not stop again for nought save victuals. So we left Brummagem (which is as black a place as Manchester, without looking so like home), and walked a' that day, carrying babby turn and turn about. It were well fed by chambermaid afore we left, and th' day were fine, and folk began to have some knowledge o' th' proper way o' speaking, and we were more cheery at thought o' home (though mine, God knows, were lonesome enough). We stopped none for dinner, but at baggin-time we getten a good meal at a public-house, an' fed th' babby as well as we could, but that were but poorly. We got a crust too for it to suck—chambermaid put us up to that. That night, whether we were tired or whatten, I don't know, but it were dree work, and th' poor little wench had slept out her sleep, and began th' cry as wore my heart out again. Says Jennings, says he:

"'We should na ha' set out so like gentlefolk a top o' the coach yesterday.'

"'Nay, lad! We should ha' had more to walk if we had na ridden, and I'm sure both you and I'se weary of tramping.'

"So he were quiet a bit. But he were one o' them as were sure to find out somewhat had been done amiss when there were no going back to undo it. So presently he coughs, as if he were going to speak, and I says to myself, 'At it again, my lad.' Says he:

"'I ax pardon, neighbour, but it strikes me it would ha' been better for my son if he had never begun to keep company wi' your daughter.'

"Well! that put me up, and my heart got very full, and but that I were carrying *her* babby, I think I should ha' struck him. At last I could hold in no longer, and says I:

"'Better say at once it would ha' been better for God never to ha' made th' world, for then we'd never ha' been in it, to have had th' weary hearts we have now.'

"Well! he said that were rank blasphemy; but I thought his way of casting up again' th' events God had pleased to send, were worse blasphemy. Howe'er, I said nought more angry, for th' little babby's sake, as were th' child o' his dead son, as well as o' my dead daughter.

"Th' longest lane will have a turning, and that night came to an end at last; and we were footsore and tired enough, and to my mind the babby were getting weaker and weaker, and it wrung my heart to hear its little wail! I'd ha' given my right hand for one of yesterday's hearty cries. We were wanting our breakfasts, and so were it too, motherless babby! We could see no public-houses, so about six o'clock (only we thought it were later) we stopped at a cottage where a woman were moving about near th' open door. Says I, 'Good woman, may we rest us a bit?' 'Come in,' says she, wiping a chair, as looked bright enough afore, wi' her apron. It were a cheery, clean room; and we were glad to sit down again, though I thought my legs would never bend at th' knees. In a minute she fell a noticin' the babby, and took it in her arms, and kissed it again and again. 'Missis,' says I, 'we're not without money, and if yo'd give us somewhat for breakfast, we'd pay yo honest, and if yo would wash and dress that poor babby, and get some pobbies down its throat, for it's wellnigh clemmed, I'd pray for you till my dying day.' So she said nought, but gived me th' babby back, and afore you could say Jack Robinson, she'd a pan on th' fire, and bread and cheese on th' table. When she turned round, her face looked red, and her lips were tight pressed together. Well! we were right down glad on our breakfast, and God bless and reward that woman for her kindness that day! She fed th' poor babby as gently and softly, and spoke to it as tenderly as its own poor mother could ha' done. It seemed as if that stranger and it had known each other afore, maybe in heaven, where folks' spirits come from, they say; th' babby looked up so lovingly in her eyes, and made little noises more like a dove than aught else. Then she undressed it (poor darling! it were time), touching it so softly, and washed it from head to foot; and as many on its clothes were dirty, and what bits o' things its mother had gotten ready for it had been sent by th' carrier fra' London, she put 'em aside; and wrapping little naked babby in her apron, she pulled out a key, as were fastened to a black ribbon, and hung down her breast, and unlocked a drawer in th' dresser. I were sorry to be prying, but I could na' help seeing in that drawer some little child's clothes, all strewed wi' lavender, and lying by 'em a little whip an' a broken rattle. I began to have an insight into that woman's heart then. She took out a thing or two, and locked the drawer, and went on dressing babby. Just about then come her husband down, a great big fellow as didn't look half awake, though it were getting late; but he'd heard all as had been said downstairs, as were plain to be seen; but he were a gruff chap. We'd finished our breakfast, and Jennings were looking hard at th' woman as she were getting the babby to sleep wi' a sort of rocking way. At length says he, 'I ha' learnt the way now; it's two jiggits and a shake, two jiggits and a shake. I can get that babby asleep now myself.'

"The man had nodded cross enough to us, and had gone to th' door, and stood there whistling wi' his hands in his breeches pockets, looking abroad. But at last turns and says, quite sharp—

"'I say, missis, I'm to have no breakfast to-day, I s'pose.'

"So wi' that she kissed th' child, a long, soft kiss; and looking in my face to see if I could take her meaning, gave me th' babby without a word. I were loath to stir, but I saw it were better to go. So giving Jennings a sharp nudge (for he'd fallen asleep), I says, 'Missis, what's to pay?' pulling out my money wi' a jingle that she might na guess we were at all bare o' cash. So she looks at her husband, who said ne'er a word, but were listening with all his ears nevertheless; and when she saw he would na say, she said, hesitatingly, as if pulled two ways, by her fear o' him,' Should you think sixpence over much?' It were so different to public-house reckoning, for we'd eaten a main deal afore the chap came down. So says I, 'And, missis, what should we gi' you for the babby's bread and milk?' (I had it once in my mind to say 'and for a' your trouble with it,' but my heart would na let me say it, for I could read in her ways how it had been a work o' love.) So says she, quite quick, and stealing a look at her husband's back, as looked all ear, if ever a back did, 'Oh, we could take naught for the little babby's food, if it had eaten twice as much, bless it.' Wi' that he looked at her; such a scowling look! She knew what he meant, and stepped softly across the floor to him, and put her hand on his arm. He seemed as though he'd shake it off by a jerk on his elbow, but she said quite low, 'For poor little Johnnie's sake, Richard.' He did not move or speak again, and after looking in his face for a minute, she turned away, swallowing deep in her throat. She kissed the sleeping babby as she passed, when I paid her. To quieten th' gruff husband, and stop him if he rated her, I could na help slipping another sixpence under th' loaf, and then we set off again. Last look I had o' that woman she were quietly wiping her eyes wi' the corner of her apron, as she went about her husband's breakfast. But I shall know her in heaven."

A Dissenting Minister's Household

From *Ruth*, 1853

George Eliot, writing of *Ruth* just after it was published, said, "Of course, you have read *Ruth* by this time. Its style was a great refreshment to me from its finish and fullness. How pretty and graphic are the touches of description.... That little attic in the minister's vestry, for example, which, with its pure white dimity bed-curtains, its bright green walls, and the rich brown of its stained floor, reminded me of a snowdrop springing out of the soil."—*Life of George Eliot.*

AFTER tea Miss Benson took her upstairs to her room. The white dimity bed, and the walls, stained green, had something of the colouring and purity of effect of a snowdrop; while the floor, rubbed with a mixture that turned it into a rich dark brown, suggested the idea of the garden-mould out of which the snowdrop grows. As Miss Benson helped the pale Ruth to undress, her voice became less full-toned and hurried; the hush of approaching night subdued her into a softened, solemn kind of tenderness, and the murmured blessing sounded like granted prayer.

In the Bensons' house there was the same unconsciousness of individual merit, the same absence of introspection and analysis of motive, as there had been in her mother; but it seemed that their lives were pure and good, not merely from a lovely and beautiful nature, but from some law, the obedience to which was, of itself, harmonious peace, and which governed them almost implicitly, and with as little questioning on their part, as the glorious stars which haste not, rest not, in their eternal obedience. This household had many failings: they were but human, and, with all their loving desire to bring their lives into harmony with the will of God, they often erred and fell short;

but, somehow, the very errors and faults of one individual served to call out higher excellences in another, and so they re-acted upon each other, and the result of short discords was exceeding harmony and peace. But they had themselves no idea of the real state of things; they did not trouble themselves with marking their progress by self-examination; if Mr. Benson did sometimes, in hours of sick incapacity for exertion, turn inwards, it was to cry aloud with almost morbid despair, "God be merciful to me a sinner!" But he strove to leave his life in the hands of God, and to forget himself.

Ruth sat still and quiet through the long first day. She was languid and weary from her journey; she was uncertain what help she might offer to give in the household duties, and what she might not. And, in her languor and in her uncertainty, it was pleasant to watch the new ways of the people among whom she was placed. After breakfast, Mr. Benson withdrew to his study, Miss Benson took away the cups and saucers, and, leaving the kitchen door open, talked sometimes to Ruth, sometimes to Sally, while she washed them up. Sally had upstairs duties to perform, for which Ruth was thankful, as she kept receiving rather angry glances for her unpunctuality as long as Sally remained downstairs. Miss Benson assisted in the preparation for the early dinner, and brought some kidney-beans to shred into a basin of bright, pure spring-water, which caught and danced in the sunbeams as she sat near the open casement of the parlour, talking to Ruth of things and people which as yet the latter did not understand, and could not arrange and comprehend. She was like a child who gets a few pieces of a dissected map, and is confused until a glimpse of the whole unity is shown him.

The Chapel at Eccleston

From *Ruth*.

This is a beautiful description of the old Unitarian chapel at Knutsford as it is to-day. In the burial-ground is the grave of Mrs. Gaskell.

THE chapel was up a narrow street, or rather *cul-de-sac*, close by. It stood on the outskirts of the town, almost in fields. It was built about the time of Matthew and Philip Henry, when the Dissenters were afraid of attracting attention or observation and hid their places of worship in obscure and out-of-the-way parts of the towns in which they were built. Accordingly, it often happened, as in the present case, that the buildings immediately surrounding, as well as the chapels themselves, looked as if they carried you back to a period a hundred and fifty years ago. The chapel had a picturesque and old-world look, for luckily the congregation had been too poor to rebuild it, or new face it in George the Third's time. The staircases which led to the galleries were outside, at each end of the building, and the irregular roof and worn stone steps looked grey and stained by time and weather. The grassy hillock, each with a little upright headstone, were shaded by a grand old wych-elm. A lilac bush or two, a white rose tree, and a few laburnums, all old and gnarled enough, were planted round the chapel yard; and the casement windows of the chapel were made of heavy-leaded, diamond-shaped panes, almost covered with ivy, producing a green gloom, not without its solemnity, within. This ivy was the home of an infinite number of little birds, which twittered and warbled, till it might have been thought that they were emulous of the power of praise possessed by the human creatures within, with such earnest, long-drawn strains did this crowd of winged songsters rejoice and be glad in their beautiful gift of life. The interior of the building was plain and simple as plain and simple could be. When it was fitted up, oak timber was much cheaper than it is now, so the woodwork was all of that description; but roughly hewed, for the early builders had not much wealth to spare. The walls were whitewashed, and were recipients of the shadows of the beauty without; on their "white plains" the tracery of the ivy might be seen, now still, now stirred by the sudden flight of some little bird. The congregation consisted of here and there a farmer with his labourers, who came down from the uplands beyond the town to worship where their fathers worshipped, and who loved the place because they knew how much those fathers had suffered for it, although they never troubled themselves with the reason why they left the parish church; of a few shopkeepers, far more thoughtful and reasoning, who were Dissenters from conviction, unmixed with old ancestral association; and of one or two families of still higher worldly station. With many poor, who were drawn there by love for Mr. Benson's character, and by a feeling that the faith which made him what he was could not be far wrong, for the base of the pyramid, and with Mr. Bradshaw for its apex, the congregation stood complete.

The country people came in sleeking down their hair, and treading with earnest attempts at noiseless lightness of step over the floor of the aisle; and by and by, when all were assembled, Mr. Benson followed unmarshalled and unattended. When he had closed the pulpit door, and knelt in prayer for an instant or two, he gave out a psalm from the dear old Scottish paraphrase, with its primitive inversion of the simple perfect Bible words; and a kind of precentor stood up, and, having sounded the note on a pitch-pipe, sang a couple of lines by way of indicating the tune; then all the congregation stood up, and sang aloud.

The Dawn of a Gala Day

From *Wives and Daughters*, 1866

TO begin with the old rigmarole of childhood. In a country there was a shire, and in that shire there was a town, and in that town there was a house, and in that house there was a room, and in that room there was a bed, and in that bed there lay a little girl; wide awake and longing to get up, but not daring to do so for fear of the unseen power in the next room—a certain Betty, whose slumbers must not be disturbed until six o'clock struck, when she wakened of herself "as sure as clockwork," and left the household very little peace afterwards. It was a June morning, and early as it was, the room was full of sunny warmth and light.

On the drawers opposite to the little white dimity bed in which Molly Gibson lay, was a primitive kind of bonnet stand, on which was hung a bonnet, carefully covered over from any chance of dust, with a large cotton handkerchief; of so heavy and serviceable a texture that, if the thing underneath it had been a flimsy fabric of gauze and lace and flowers, it would have been altogether "scomfished" (again to quote from Betty's vocabulary). But the bonnet was made of solid straw, and its only trimming was a plain white ribbon put over the crown, and forming the strings. Still, there was a neat little quilling inside, every plait of which Molly knew, for had she not made it herself the evening before, with infinite pains? and was there not a little blue bow in this quilling, the very first bit of such finery Molly had ever had the prospect of wearing?

Six o'clock now! the pleasant, brisk ringing of the church bells told that; calling everyone to their daily work, as they had done for hundreds of years. Up jumped Molly, and ran with her bare little feet across the room, and lifted off the handkerchief and saw once again the bonnet—the pledge of the gay bright day to come. Then to the window, and after some tugging she opened the casement, and let in the sweet morning air. The dew was already off the flowers in the garden below, but still rising from the long hay-grass in the meadows directly beyond. At one side lay the little town of Hollingford, into a street of which Mr. Gibson's front door opened; and delicate columns and little puffs of smoke were already beginning to rise from many a cottage chimney, where some housewife was already up, and preparing breakfast for the bread-winner of the family.

Molly Gibson saw all this, but all she thought about it was, "Oh! it will be a fine day! I was afraid it never, never would come; or that, if it ever came, it would be a rainy day!" Five-and-forty years ago, children's pleasures in a country town were very simple, and Molly had lived for twelve long years without the occurrence of any event so great as that which was now impending. Poor child! it is true that she had lost her mother, which was a jar to the whole tenour of her life; but that was hardly an event in the sense referred to; and besides, she had been too young to be conscious of it at the time. The pleasure she was looking forward to to-day was her first share in a kind of annual festival in Hollingford.

The little straggling town faded away into country on one side, close to the entrance-lodge of a great park, where lived my Lord and Lady Cumnor: "the earl" and "the countess," as they were always called by the inhabitants of the town, where a very pretty amount of feudal feeling still lingered, and showed itself in a number of simple ways, droll enough to look back upon, but serious matters of importance at the time. It was before the passing of the Reform Bill, but a good deal of liberal talk took place occasionally between two or three of the more enlightened freeholders living in Hollingford; and there was a great Whig family in the county who, from time to time, came forward and contested the election with the rival Tory family of Cumnor. One would have thought that the above-mentioned liberal-talking inhabitants of Hollingford would have, at least, admitted the possibility of their voting for the Hely-Harrison who represented their own opinions. But no such thing. "The earl" was lord of the manor, and owner of much of the land on which Hollingford was built; he and his household were fed, and doctored, and, to a certain measure, clothed by the good people of the town; their fathers' grandfathers had always voted for the eldest son of Cumnor Towers, and following in the ancestral track, every man-jack in the place gave his vote to the liege lord, totally irrespective of such chimeras as political opinion.

This was no unusual instance of the influence of the great landowners over humbler neighbours in those days before railways, and it was well for a place where the powerful family, who thus overshadowed it, were of so respectable a character as the Cumnors. They expected to be submitted to, and obeyed; the simple worship of the townspeople was accepted by the earl and countess as a right; and they would have stood still in amazement and with a horrid memory of the French sansculottes who were the bugbears of their youth, had any inhabitant of Hollingford ventured to set his will or opinions in opposition to those of the earl. But, yielded all that obeisance, they did a good deal for the town, and were generally condescending, and often thoughtful and kind, in their treatment of their vassals. Lord Cumnor was a forbearing landlord, putting his steward a little on one side sometimes, and taking the reins into his own hands now and then, much to the annoyance of the agent, who was, in fact, too rich and independent to care greatly for preserving a post where his decisions might any day be overturned by my lord's taking a fancy to go "pottering" (as the agent irreverently expressed it in the sanctuary of his own home), which, being interpreted, meant that occasionally the earl asked his own questions of his own tenants, and used his own eyes and ears in the management of the smaller details of his property. But his tenants liked my lord all the better for this habit of his. Lord Cumnor had certainly a little time for gossip, which he contrived to combine with the failing of personal intervention between the old land steward and the tenantry. But, then, the countess made up by her unapproachable dignity for this weakness of the earl's. Once a year she was condescending. She and the ladies, her daughters, had set up a school; not a school after the manner of schools nowadays, where far better intellectual teaching is given to the boys and girls of labourers and work-people than often falls to the lot of their betters in worldly estate; but a school of the kind we should call "industrial," where girls are taught to sew beautifully, to be capital housemaids, and pretty fair cooks, and, above all, to dress neatly in a kind of charity uniform devised by the ladies of Cumnor Towers—white caps, white tippets, check aprons, blue gowns, and ready curtsies, and "please ma'ams" being *de rigueur*.

Now, as the countess was absent from the Towers for a considerable part of the year, she was glad to enlist the sympathy of the Hollingford ladies in this school, with a view to obtaining their aid as visitors during the many months that she and her daughters were away. And the various unoccupied gentlewomen of the town responded to the call of their liege lady, and gave her their service as required; and along with it, a great deal of whispered and fussy admiration. "How good of the countess! So like the dear countess—always thinking of others!" and so on; while it was always supposed that no strangers had seen Hollingford properly, unless they had been taken to the countess's school, and been duly impressed by the neat little pupils, and the still neater needlework there to be inspected. In return, there was a day of honour set apart every summer, when, with much gracious and stately hospitality, Lady Cumnor and her daughters received all the school visitors at the Towers, the great family mansion standing in aristocratic seclusion in the centre of the large park, of which one of the lodges was close to the little town. The order of this annual festivity was this. About ten o'clock one of the Towers' carriages rolled through the lodge, and drove to different houses, wherein dwelt a woman to be honoured; picking them up by ones or twos, till the loaded carriage drove back again through the ready portals, bowled along the smooth tree-shaded road, and deposited its covey of smartly dressed ladies on the great flight of steps leading to the ponderous doors of Cumnor Towers. Back again to the town; another picking up of womankind in their best clothes, and another return, and so on till the whole party were assembled either in the house or in the really beautiful gardens. After the proper amount of exhibition on the one part, and admiration on the other, had been done, there was a collation for the visitors, and some more display and admiration of the treasures inside the house. Towards four o'clock coffee was brought round; and this was a signal of the approaching carriage that was to take them back to their own homes; whither they returned with the happy consciousness of a well-spent day, but with some fatigue at the long-continued exertion of behaving their best, and talking on stilts for so many hours. Nor were Lady Cumnor and her daughters free from something of the same self-approbation, and something, too, of the same fatigue; the fatigue that always follows on conscious efforts to behave as will best please the society you are in.

For the first time in her life, Molly Gibson was to be included among the guests at the Towers.

A Manchester Mill on Fire

From *Mary Barton*, 1848

SUDDENLY there were steps heard in the little paved court; person after person ran past the curtained window.

"Something's up," said Mary. She went to the door, and stopped the first person she saw, inquiring the cause of the commotion.

"Eh, wench! donna ye see the fire-light? Carsons' mill is a blazing away like fun"; and away her informant ran.

"Come, Margaret, on wi' your bonnet, and let's go to see Carsons' mill; it's afire, and they say a burning mill is such a grand sight. I never saw one."

"Well, I think it's a fearful sight. Besides, I've all this work to do."

But Mary coaxed in her sweet manner, and with her gentle caresses, promising to help with the gowns all night long, if necessary—nay, saying she should quite enjoy it.

The truth was, Margaret's secret weighed heavily and painfully on her mind, and she felt her inability to comfort; besides, she wanted to change the current of Margaret's thoughts; and in addition to these unselfish feelings, came the desire she had honestly expressed, of seeing a factory on fire.

So in two minutes they were ready. At the threshold of the house they met John Barton, to whom they told their errand.

"Carsons' mill! Ay, there is a mill on fire somewhere, sure enough by the light, and it will be a rare blaze, for there's not a drop o' water to be got. And much Carsons will care, for they're well insured, and the machines are a' th' oud-fashioned kind. See if they don't think it a fine thing for themselves. They'll not thank them as tries to put it out."

He gave way for the impatient girls to pass. Guided by the ruddy light more than by any exact knowledge of the streets that led to the mill, they scampered along with bent heads, facing the terrible east wind as best they might.

Carsons' mill ran lengthways from east to west. Along it went one of the oldest thoroughfares in Manchester. Indeed, all that part of the town was comparatively old; it was there that the first cotton mills were built, and the crowded alleys and back streets of the neighbourhood made a fire there particularly to be dreaded. The staircase of the mill ascended from the entrance at the western end, which faced into a wide, dingy-looking street, consisting principally of public-houses, pawnbrokers' shops, rag and bone warehouses, and dirty provision shops. The other, the east end of the factory, fronted into a very narrow back street, not twenty feet wide, and miserably lighted and paved. Right against this end of the factory were the gable ends of the last house in the principal street—a house which from its size, its handsome stone facings, and the attempt at ornament in the front, had probably been once a gentleman's house; but now the light which streamed from its enlarged front windows made clear the interior of the splendidly fitted up room, with its painted walls, its pillared recesses, its gilded and gorgeous fittings-up, its miserable, squalid inmates. It was a gin-palace.

Mary almost wished herself away, so fearful (as Margaret had said) was the sight when they joined the crowd assembled to witness the fire. There was a murmur of many voices whenever the roaring of the flames ceased for an instant. It was easy to perceive the mass were deeply interested.

"What do they say?" asked Margaret of a neighbour in the crowd, as she caught a few words, clear and distinct from the general murmur.

"There never is anyone in the mill, surely!" exclaimed Mary, as the sea of upward-turned faces moved with one accord to the eastern end, looking into Dunham Street, the narrow back lane already mentioned.

The western end of the mill, whither the raging flames were driven by the wind, was crowned and turreted with triumphant fire. It sent forth its infernal tongues from every window hole, licking the black walls with amorous fierceness; it was swayed or fell before the mighty gale, only to rise higher and yet higher, to ravage and roar yet more wildly. This part of the roof fell in with an astounding crash, while the crowd struggled more and more to press into Dunham Street; for what were magnificent, terrible flames—what were falling timbers or tottering walls, in comparison with human life?

There, where the devouring flames had been repelled by the yet more powerful wind, but where yet black smoke gushed out from every aperture— there, at one of the windows on the fourth storey—or, rather, a doorway where a crane was fixed to hoist up goods, might occasionally be seen, when the thick gusts of smoke cleared partially away for an instant, the imploring figures of two men. They had remained after the rest of the workmen for some reason or other, and, owing to the wind having driven the fire in the opposite direction, had perceived no sight or sound of alarm, till long after (if anything could be called long in that throng of terrors which passed by in less than half an hour) the fire had consumed the old wooden staircase at the other end of the building. I am not sure whether it was not the first sound of the rushing crowd below that made them fully aware of their awful position.

"Where are the engines?" asked Margaret of her neighbour.

"They're coming, no doubt; but bless you, I think it's bare ten minutes since we first found out th' fire; it rages so wi' this wind, and all so dry-like."

"Is no one gone for a ladder?" gasped Mary, as the men were perceptibly, though not audibly, praying the great multitude below for help.

"Ay, Wilson's son and another man were off like a shot, wellnigh five minutes ago. But th' masons and slaters, and such-like, have left their work, and locked up the yards."

Wilson, then, was that man whose figure loomed out against the ever-increasing dull hot light behind, whenever the smoke was clear—was that George Wilson? Mary sickened with terror. She knew he worked for Carsons; but at first she had had no idea that any lives were in danger; and since she had become aware of this, the heated air, the roaring flames, the dizzy light, and the agitated and murmuring crowd, had bewildered her thoughts.

"Oh! let us go home, Margaret; I cannot stay."

"We cannot go! See how we are wedged in by folks. Poor Mary! ye won't hanker after a fire again. Hark! listen!"

For through the hushed crowd pressing round the angle of the mill, and filling up Dunham Street, might be heard the rattle of the engine, the heavy, quick tread of loaded horses.

"Thank God!" said Margaret's neighbour, "the engine's come."

Another pause; the plugs were stiff, and water could not be got.

Then there was a pressure through the crowd, the front rows bearing back on those behind, till the girls were sick with the close, ramming confinement. Then a relaxation, and a breathing freely once more.

"'Twas young Wilson and a fireman wi' a ladder," said Margaret's neighbour, a tall man who could overlook the crowd.

"Oh, tell us what you see?" begged Mary.

"They've getten it fixed against the gin-shop wall. One o' the men i' the factory has fell back; dazed wi' the smoke, I'll warrant. The floor's not given way there. God!" said he, bringing his eye lower down, "the ladder's too short! It's a' over wi' them, poor chaps! Th' fire's coming slow and sure to that end, and afore they've either getten water, or another ladder, they'll be dead out and out. Lord have mercy on them."

A sob, as if of excited women, was heard in the hush of the crowd. Another pressure like the former! Mary clung to Margaret's arm with a pinching grasp, and longed to faint, and be insensible, to escape from the oppressing misery of her sensations. A minute or two.

"They've taken th' ladder into th' Temple of Apollor. Can't press back with it to the yard it came from."

A mighty shout arose; a sound to wake the dead. Up on high, quivering in the air, was seen the end of the ladder, protruding out of the garret window, in the gable end of the gin palace, nearly opposite to the doorway where the men had been seen. Those in the crowd nearest the factory, and consequently best able to see up to the garret window, said that several men were holding one end, and guiding by their weight its passage to the doorway. The garret window-frame had been taken out before the crowd below were aware of the attempt.

At length—for it seemed long, measured by beating hearts, though scarce two minutes had elapsed—the ladder was fixed, an aerial bridge at a dizzy height, across the narrow street.

Every eye was fixed in unwinking anxiety, and people's very breathing seemed stilled in suspense. The men were nowhere to be seen, but the wind appeared, for the moment, higher than ever, and drove back the invading flames to the other end.

Mary and Margaret could see now; right above them danced the ladder in the wind. The crowd pressed back from under; firemen's helmets appeared at the window, holding the ladder firm, when a man, with quick, steady tread, and unmoving head, passed from one side to the other. The multitude did not even whisper while he crossed the perilous bridge, which quivered under him; but when he was across, safe comparatively in the factory, a cheer arose for an instant, checked, however, almost immediately, by the uncertainty of the result, and the desire not in any way to shake the nerves of the brave fellow who had cast his life on such a die.

"There he is again!" sprang to the lips of many, as they saw him at the doorway, standing as if for an instant to breathe a mouthful of the fresher air, before he trusted himself to cross. On his shoulders he bore an insensible body.

"It's Jem Wilson and his father," whispered Margaret; but Mary knew it before.

The people were sick with anxious terror. He could no longer balance himself with his arms; everything must depend on nerve and eye. They saw the latter was fixed, by the position of the head, which never wavered; the ladder shook under the double weight; but still he never moved his head—he dared not look below. It seemed an age before the crossing was accomplished. At last the window was gained; the bearer relieved from his burden; both had disappeared.

Then the multitude might shout; and above the roaring flames, louder than the blowing of the mighty wind, arose that tremendous burst of applause at the success of the daring enterprise. Then a shrill cry was heard, asking—

"Is the oud man alive, and likely to do?"

"Ay," answered one of the firemen to the hushed crowd below. "He's coming round finely, now he's had a dash of cowd water."

He drew back his head; and the eager inquiries, the shouts, the sea-like murmurs of the moving rolling mass began again to be heard—but only for an instant. In far less time than even that in which I have endeavoured briefly to describe the pause of events, the same bold hero stepped again upon the ladder, with evident purpose to rescue the man yet remaining in the burning mill.

He went across in the same quick, steady manner as before, and the people below, made less acutely anxious by his previous success, were talking to each other, shouting out intelligence of the progress of the fire at the other end of the factory, telling of the endeavours of the firemen at that part to obtain water, while the closely-packed body of men heaved and rolled from side to side. It was different from the former silent breathless hush. I do not know if it were from this cause, or from the recollection of peril past, or that he looked below in the breathing moment before returning with the remaining person (a slight little man) slung across his shoulders, but Jem Wilson's step was less steady, his tread more uncertain; he seemed to feel with his foot for the next round of the ladder, to waver, and finally to stop half-way. By this time the crowd was still enough; in the awful instant that intervened no one durst speak, even to encourage. Many turned sick with terror, and shut their eyes to avoid seeing the catastrophe they dreaded. It came. The brave man swayed from side to side, at first as slightly as if only balancing himself; but he was evidently losing nerve, and even sense; it was only wonderful how the animal instinct of self-preservation did not overcome every generous feeling, and impel him at once to drop the helpless, inanimate body he carried;

perhaps the same instinct told him, that the sudden loss of so heavy a weight would of itself be a great and imminent danger.

"Help me; she's fainted," cried Margaret. But no one heeded. All eyes were directed upwards. At this point of time a rope, with a running noose, was dexterously thrown by one of the firemen, after the manner of a lasso, over the head and round the bodies of the two men. True, it was with rude and slight adjustment; but slight as it was, it served as a steadying guide; it encouraged the sinking heart, the dizzy head. Once more Jem stepped onwards. He was not hurried by any jerk or pull. Slowly and gradually the rope was hauled in, slowly and gradually did he make the four or five paces between him and safety. The window was gained, and all were saved. The multitude in the street absolutely danced with triumph, and huzzaed, and yelled till you would have fancied their very throats would crack; and then, with all the fickleness of interest characteristic of a large body of people, pressed and stumbled, and cursed and swore, in the hurry to get out of Dunham Street, and back to the immediate scene of the fire, the mighty diapason of whose roaring flames formed an awful accompaniment to the screams, and yells, and imprecations, of the struggling crowd.

As they pressed away, Margaret was left, pale and almost sinking under the weight of Mary's body, which she had preserved in an upright position by keeping her arms tight round Mary's waist, dreading, with reason, the trampling of unheeding feet.

Now, however, she gently let her down on the cold, clean pavement; and the change of posture, and the difference in temperature, now that the people had withdrawn from their close neighbourhood, speedily restored her to consciousness.

Her first glance was bewildered and uncertain. She had forgotten where she was. Her cold, hard bed felt strange; the murky glare in the sky affrighted her. She shut her eyes to think, to recollect.

Her next look was upwards. The fearful bridge had been withdrawn; the window was unoccupied.

"They are safe," said Margaret.

"All? Are all safe, Margaret?" asked Mary.

"Ask yon fireman, and he'll tell you more about it than I can. But I know they're all safe."

The fireman hastily corroborated Margaret's words.

"Why did you let Jem Wilson go twice?" asked Margaret.

"Let!—why, we could not hinder him. As soon as ever he'd heard his father speak (which he was na long a-doing), Jem were off like a shot; only saying he knowed better nor us where to find t'other man. We'd all ha' gone, if he had na been in such a hurry, for no one can say as Manchester firemen is ever backward when there's danger."

So saying he ran off; and the two girls, without remark or discussion, turned homewards.

"In Pursuit of the *John Cropper*"

From *Mary Barton*, 1848

"OH, how much do you want? Only make haste—I've enough to pay you, but every moment is precious," said Mary.

"Ay, that it is. Less than an hour won't take us to the mouth of the river, and she'll be off by two o'clock!"

Poor Mary's ideas of "plenty of money," however, were different to those entertained by the boatmen. Only fourteen or fifteen shillings remained out of the sovereign Margaret had lent her, and the boatmen, imagining "plenty" to mean no less than several pounds, insisted upon receiving a sovereign (an exorbitant fare, by the bye, although reduced from their first demand of thirty shillings).

While Charley, with a boy's impatience, said:

"Give it 'em, Mary; they'll none of them take you for less. It's your only chance. There's St. Nicholas ringing one!"

"I've only got fourteen and ninepence," cried she in despair, after counting over her money; "but I'll give you my shawl, and you can sell it for four or five shillings—oh! won't that much do?" asked she, in such a tone of voice, that they must indeed have hard hearts who could refuse such agonised entreaty.

They took her on board.

And in less than five minutes she was rocking and tossing in a boat for the first time in her life, alone with two rough hard-looking men.

Mary had not understood that Charley was not coming with her. In fact, she had not thought about it, till she perceived his absence, as they pushed off from the landing-place, and remembered that she had never thanked him for all his kind interest in her behalf; and now his absence made her feel most lonely—even his, the little mushroom friend of an hour's growth.

The boat threaded her way through the maze of larger vessels which surrounded the shore, bumping against one, kept off by the oars from going right against another, overshadowed by a third, until at length they were fairly out on the broad river, away from either shore; the sights and sounds of land being heard in the distance.

And then came a sort of pause.

Both wind and tide were against the two men, and labour as they would they made but little way. Once Mary in her impatience had risen up to obtain a better view of the progress they had made; but the men had roughly told her to sit down immediately, and she had dropped on her seat like a chidden child, although the impatience was still at her heart.

But now she grew sure they were turning off from the straight course which they had hitherto kept on the Cheshire side of the river, whither they had gone to avoid the force of the current, and after a short time she could not help naming her conviction, as a kind of nightmare dread and belief came over her, that everything animate and inanimate was in league against her one sole aim and object of overtaking Will.

They answered gruffly. They saw a boatman whom they knew, and were desirous of obtaining his services as a steersman, so that both might row with greater effect. They knew what they were about. So she sat silent with clenched hands while the parley went on, the explanation was given, the favour asked and granted. But she was sickening all the time with nervous fear.

They had been rowing a long, long time—half a day it seemed, at least—yet Liverpool appeared still close at hand, and Mary began almost to wonder that the men were not as much disheartened as she was, when the wind, which had been hitherto against them, dropped, and thin clouds began to gather over the sky, shutting out the sun, and casting a chilly gloom over everything.

There was not a breath of air, and yet it was colder than when the soft violence of the westerly wind had been felt.

The men renewed their efforts. The boat gave a bound forwards at every pull of the oars. The water was glassy and motionless, reflecting tint by tint of the Indian-ink sky above. Mary shivered, and her heart sank within her. Still, now they evidently were making progress. Then the steersman pointed to a rippling line on the river only a little way off, and the men disturbed Mary, who was watching the ships that lay in what appeared to her the open sea, to get at their sails.

She gave a little start and rose. Her patience, her grief, and perhaps her silence, had begun to win upon the men.

"Yon second to the norrard is the *John Cropper*. Wind's right now, and sails will soon carry us alongside of her."

He had forgotten (or perhaps he did not like to remind Mary) that the same wind which now bore their little craft along with easy, rapid motion, would also be favourable to the *John Cropper*.

But as they looked with straining eyes, as if to measure the decreasing distance that separated them from her, they saw her sails unfurled and flap in the breeze, till, catching the right point, they bellied forth into white roundness, and the ship began to plunge and heave, as if she were a living creature, impatient to be off.

"They're heaving anchor!" said one of the boatmen to the other, as the faint musical cry of the sailors came floating over the waters that still separated them.

Full of the spirit of the chase, though as yet ignorant of Mary's motives, the men sprang to hoist another sail. It was fully as much as the boat could bear, in the keen, gusty east wind which was now blowing, and she bent, and laboured, and ploughed, and creaked upbraidingly as if tasked beyond her strength; but she sped along with a gallant swiftness.

They drew nearer, and they heard the distant "ahoy" more clearly. It ceased. The anchor was up, and the ship was away.

Mary stood up, steadying herself by the mast, and stretching out her arms, imploring the flying vessel to stay its course, by that mute action, while the tears streamed down her cheeks. The men caught up their oars, and hoisted them in the air, and shouted to arrest attention.

They were seen by the men aboard the larger craft; but they were too busy with all the confusion prevalent in an outward-bound vessel to pay much attention. There were coils of ropes and seamen's chests to be stumbled over at every turn; there were animals not properly secured, roaming bewildered about the deck, adding their pitiful lowings and bleatings to the aggregate of noises. There were carcases not cut up, looking like corpses of sheep and pigs rather than like mutton and pork; there were sailors running here and there and everywhere, having had no time to fall into method, and with their minds divided between thoughts of the land and the people they had left, and the present duties on board ship; while the captain strove hard to procure some kind of order by hasty commands given, in a loud, impatient voice, to right and left, starboard and larboard, cabin and steerage.

As he paced the deck with a chafed step, vexed at one or two little mistakes on the part of the mate, and suffering himself from the pain of separation from wife and children, but showing his suffering only by his outward irritation, he heard a hail from the shabby little river boat that was striving to overtake his winged ship. For the men fearing that, as the ship was now fairly over the bar, they should only increase the distance between them, and being now within shouting range, had asked of Mary her more particular desire.

Her throat was dry, all musical sound had gone out of her voice; but in a loud harsh whisper she told the men her errand of life and death, and they hailed the ship.

"We're come for one William Wilson, who is wanted to prove an *alibi* in Liverpool Assize Courts to-morrow. James Wilson is to be tried for a murder done on Thursday night when he was with William Wilson. Anything more, missis?" asked the boatman of Mary, in a lower voice, and taking his hands down from his mouth.

"Say I'm Mary Barton. Oh, the ship is going on! Oh, for the love of Heaven, ask them to stop."

The boatman was angry at the little regard paid to his summons, and called out again; repeating the message with the name of the young woman who sent it, and interlarding it with sailors' oaths.

The ship flew along—away—the boat struggled after.

They could see the captain take his speaking-trumpet. And oh! and alas! they heard his words.

He swore a dreadful oath; he called Mary a disgraceful name; and he said he would not stop his ship for anyone, nor could he part with a single hand, whoever swung for it.

The words came in unpitying clearness with their trumpet-sound. Mary sat down looking like one who prays in the death agony. For her eyes were turned up to that heaven where mercy dwelleth, while her blue lips quivered, though no sound came. Then she bowed her head and hid it in her hands.

"Hark! yon sailor hails us."

She looked up. And her heart stopped its beating to listen.

William Wilson stood as near the stern of the vessel as he could get; and unable to obtain the trumpet from the angry captain, made a tube of his own hands.

"So help me God, Mary Barton, I'll come back in the pilot-boat time enough to save the life of the innocent."

"What does he say?" asked Mary wildly, as the voice died away in the increasing distance, while the boatmen cheered, in their kindled sympathy with their passenger.

"What does he say?" repeated she. "Tell me. I could not hear."

She had heard with her ears, but her brain refused to recognise the sense.

They repeated his speech, all three speaking at once, with many comments; while Mary looked at them and then at the vessel far away.

"I don't rightly know about it," said she sorrowfully. "What is the pilot-boat?"

They told her, and she gathered the meaning out of the sailors' slang which enveloped it. There was a hope still, although so slight and faint.

Hobbies Among the Lancashire Poor

From *Mary Barton*, 1848

THERE is a class of men in Manchester, unknown even to many of the inhabitants, and whose existence will probably be doubted by many, who yet may claim kindred with all the noble names that science recognizes. I said in "Manchester," but they are scattered all over the manufacturing district of Lancashire. In the neighbourhood of Oldham there are weavers, common hand-loom weavers, who throw the shuttle with unceasing sound, though Newton's *Principia* lies open on the loom, to be snatched at in work hours, but revelled over in meal times, or at night. Mathematical problems are received with interest, and studied with absorbing attention by many a broad-spoken, common-looking factory-hand. It is perhaps less astonishing that the more popularly interesting branches of natural history have their warm and devoted followers among this class. There are botanists among them, equally familiar with either the Linnæan or the Natural system, who know the name and habitat of every plant within a day's walk from their dwellings; who steal the holiday of a day or two when any particular plant should be in flower, and tying up their simple food in their pocket-handkerchiefs, set off with single purpose to fetch home the humble-looking weed. There are entomologists, who may be seen with a rude-looking net, ready to catch any winged insect, or a kind of dredge, with which they rake the green and slimy pools; practical, shrewd, hard-working men, who pore over every new specimen with real scientific delight. Nor is it the common and more obvious divisions of Entomology and Botany that alone attract these earnest seekers after knowledge. Perhaps it may be owing to the great annual town-holiday of Whitsun-week so often falling in May or June, that the two great, beautiful families of Ephemeridæ and Phryganidæ have been so much and so closely studied by Manchester workmen, while they have in a great measure escaped general observation. If you will refer to the preface to Sir J. E. Smith's Life (I have it not by me, or I would copy you the exact passage), you will find that he names a little circumstance corroborative of what I have said. Being on a visit to Roscoe, of Liverpool, he made some inquiries from him as to the habitat of a very rare plant, said to be found in certain places in Lancashire. Mr. Roscoe knew nothing of the plant; but stated that if anyone could give him the desired information, it would be a hand-loom weaver in Manchester, whom he named. Sir J. E. Smith proceeded by boat to Manchester, and on arriving at that town he inquired of the porter who was carrying his luggage if he could direct him to So-and-So.

"Oh, yes," replied the man. "He does a bit in my way"; and on further investigation it turned out that both the porter and his friend the weaver were both skilful botanists, and able to give Sir J. E. Smith the very information which he wanted.

Such are the tastes and pursuits of some of the thoughtful, little-understood working-men of Manchester.

And Margaret's grandfather was one of these. He was a little, wiry-looking old man, who moved with a jerking motion, as if his limbs were worked by a string, like a child's toy, with dun-coloured hair lying thin and soft at the back and sides of his head; his forehead was so large it seemed to overbalance the rest of his face, which had, indeed, lost its natural contour by the absence of all the teeth. The eyes absolutely gleamed with intelligence; so keen, so observant, you felt as if they were almost wizard-like. Indeed, the whole room looked not unlike a wizard's dwelling. Instead of pictures were hung rude wooden frames of impaled insects; the little table was covered with cabalistic books; and beside them lay a case of mysterious instruments, one of which Job Legh was using when his granddaughter entered.

On her appearance he pushed his spectacles up so as to rest midway on his forehead, and gave Mary a short, kind welcome. But Margaret he caressed as a mother caresses her first-born; stroking her with tenderness, and almost altering his voice as he spoke to her.

Mary looked round on the odd, strange things she had never seen at home, and which seemed to her to have a very uncanny look.

"Is your grandfather a fortune-teller?" whispered she to her new friend.

"No," replied Margaret in the same voice; "but you are not the first as has taken him for such. He is only fond of such things as most folks know nothing about."

"And do you know aught about them too?"

"I know a bit about some of the things grandfather is fond on; just because he's fond on 'em, I tried to learn about them."

"What things are these?" said Mary, struck with the weird-looking creatures that sprawled around the room in their roughly-made glass cases.

But she was not prepared for the technical names which Job Legh pattered down on her ear, on which they fell like hail on a skylight; and the strange language only bewildered her more than ever. Margaret saw the state of the case, and came to the rescue.

"Look, Mary, at this horrid scorpion. He gave me such a fright: I am all of a twitter yet when I think of it. Grandfather went to Liverpool one Whitsun-week to go strolling about the docks and pick up what he could from the sailors, who often bring some queer thing or another from the hot countries they go to; and so he sees a chap with a bottle in his hand, like a druggist's physic-bottle; and says grandfather, 'What have ye gotten there?' So the sailor holds it up, and grandfather knew it was a rare kind o' scorpion, not common even in the East Indies where the man came from; and says he, 'How did you catch this fine fellow, for he wouldn't be taken for nothing, I'm thinking?' And the man said as how when they were unloading the ship he'd found him lying behind a bag of rice, and he thought the cold had killed him, for he was not squashed nor injured a bit. He did not like to part with any of the spirit out of his grog to put the scorpion in, but slipped him into the bottle, knowing there were folks enow who would give him something for him. So grandfather gives him a shilling."

"Two shillings," interrupted Job Legh; "and a good bargain it was."

"Well, grandfather came home as proud as Punch, and pulled the bottle out of his pocket. But, you see, th' scorpion were doubled up, and grandfather thought I couldn't fairly see how big he was. So he shakes him out right before the fire; and a good warm one it was, for I was ironing, I remember. I left off ironing, and stooped down over him, to look at him better, and grandfather got a book, and began to read how this very kind were the most poisonous and vicious species, how their bite were often fatal, and then went on to read how people who were bitten got swelled, and screamed with pain. I was listening hard, but as it fell out, I never took my eyes off the creature, though I could not ha' told I was watching it. Suddenly it seemed to give a jerk, and before I could speak it gave another, and in a minute it was as wild as it could be, running at me just like a mad dog."

"What did you do?" asked Mary.

"Me! why, I jumped first on a chair, and then on all the things I'd been ironing on the dresser, and I screamed for grandfather to come up by me, but he did not hearken to me."

"Why, if I'd come up by thee, who'd ha' caught the creature, I should like to know?"

"Well, I begged grandfather to crush it, and I had the iron right over it once, ready to drop, but grandfather begged me not to hurt it in that way. So I couldn't think what he'd have, for he hopped round the room as if he were sore afraid, for all he begged me not to injure it. At last he goes to th' kettle, and lifts up the lid, and peeps in. 'What on earth is he doing that for?' thinks I; 'he'll never drink his tea with a scorpion running free and easy about the room!' Then he takes the tongs, and he settles his spectacles on his nose, and in a minute he had lifted the creature up by th' leg, and dropped him into the boiling water."

"And did that kill him?" said Mary.

"Ay, sure enough; he boiled for longer time than grandfather liked, though. But I was so afeared of his coming round again, I ran to the public-house for some gin, and grandfather filled the bottle, and then we poured off the water, and picked him out of the kettle, and dropped him into the bottle, and he were there above a twelvemonth."

"What brought him to life at first?" asked Mary.

"Why, you see, he were never really dead, only torpid—that is, dead asleep with the cold, and our good fire brought him round."

"I'm glad father does not care for such things," said Mary.

"Are you? Well, I'm often downright glad grandfather is so fond of his books, and his creatures, and his plants. It does my heart good to see him so happy, sorting them all at home, and so ready to go in search of more, whenever he's a spare day. Look at him now! he's gone back to his books, and he'll be as happy as a king, working away till I make him go to bed. It keeps him silent, to be sure; but so long as I see him earnest, and pleased, and eager, what does that matter? Then, when he has his talking bouts, you can't think how much he has to say. Dear grandfather! you don't know how happy we are!"

Mary wondered if the dear grandfather heard all this, for Margaret did not speak in an undertone; but no! he was far too deep and eager in solving a problem. He did not even notice Mary's leave-taking, and she went home with the feeling that she had that night made the acquaintance of two of the strangest people she ever saw in her life. Margaret so quiet, so commonplace, until her singing powers were called forth; so silent from home, so cheerful and agreeable at home; and her grandfather so very different to anyone Mary had ever seen. Margaret had said he was not a fortune-teller, but she did not know whether to believe her.

To resolve her doubts, she told the history of the evening to her father, who was interested by her account, and curious to see and judge for himself. Opportunities are not often wanting where inclination goes before, and ere the end of that winter Mary looked upon Margaret almost as an old friend. The latter would bring her work when Mary was likely to be at home in the evenings, and sit with her; and Job Legh would put a book and his pipe in his pocket, and just step round the corner to fetch his grandchild, ready for a talk if he found Barton in; ready to pull out pipe and book if the girls wanted him to wait, and John was still at his club. In short, ready to do whatever would give pleasure to his darling Margaret.

I do not know what points of resemblance or dissimilitude (for this joins people as often as that) attracted the girls to each other. Margaret had the great charm of possessing good strong common sense, and do you not perceive how involuntarily this is valued? It is so pleasant to have a friend who possesses the power of setting a difficult question in a clear light; whose judgment can tell what is best to be done; and who is so convinced of what is "wisest, best," that in consideration of the end, all difficulties in the way diminish. People admire talent, and talk about their admiration. But they value common sense without talking about it, and often without knowing it.

The Press-gang in Yorkshire during the latter part of the Eighteenth Century

From Sylvia's Lovers, 1863

SINCE the termination of the American war, there had been nothing to call for any unusual energy in manning the navy; and the grants required by Government for this purpose diminished with every year of peace. In 1792 this grant touched its minimum for many years. In 1793 the proceedings of the French had set Europe on fire, and the English were raging with anti-Gallican excitement, fomented into action by every expedient of the Crown and its Ministers. We had our ships; but where were our men? The Admiralty had, however, a ready remedy at hand, with ample precedent for its use, and with common (if not statute) law to sanction its application. They issued "press warrants," calling upon the civil power throughout the country to support their officers in the discharge of their duty. The sea-coast was divided into districts, under the charge of a captain in the navy, who again delegated sub-districts to lieutenants; and in this manner all homeward-bound vessels were watched and waited for, all ports were under supervision; and in a day, if need were, a large number of men could be added to the forces of his Majesty's navy. But if the Admiralty became urgent in their demands, they were also willing to be unscrupulous. Landsmen, if able-bodied, might soon be trained into good sailors; and once in the hold of the tender, which always awaited the success of the operation of the press-gang, it was difficult for such prisoners to bring evidence of the nature of their former occupations, especially when none had leisure to listen to such evidence, or were willing to believe it if they did listen, or would act upon it for the release of the captive if they had by possibility both listened and believed. Men were kidnapped, literally disappeared, and nothing was ever heard of them again. The street of a busy town was not safe from such press-gang captures, as Lord Thurlow could have told, after a certain walk he took about this time on Tower Hill, when he, the attorney-general of England, was impressed, when the Admiralty had its own peculiar ways of getting rid of tiresome besiegers and petitioners. Nor yet were lonely inland dwellers more secure; many a rustic went to a statute fair or "mop," and never came home to tell of his hiring; many a stout young farmer vanished from his place by the hearth of his father, and was no more heard of by mother or lover; so great was the press for men to serve in the navy during the early years of the war with France, and after every great naval victory of that war.

The servants of the Admiralty lay in wait for all merchant-men and traders; there were many instances of vessels returning home after long absence, and laden with rich cargo, being boarded within a day's distance of land, and so many men pressed and carried off, that the ship with her cargo became unmanageable from the loss of her crew, drifted out again into the wild wide ocean, and was sometimes found in the helpless guidance of one or two infirm or ignorant sailors; sometimes such vessels were never heard of more. The men thus pressed were taken from the near grasp of parent or wives, and were often deprived of the hard earnings of years, which remained in the hands of the masters of the merchantman in which they had served, subject to all the chances of honesty or dishonesty, life or death. Now all this tyranny (for I can use no other word) is marvellous to us; we cannot imagine how it is that a nation submitted to it for so long, even under any warlike enthusiasm, any panic of invasion, any amount of loyal subservience to the governing powers. When we read of the military being called in to assist the civil power in backing up the press-gang, of parties of soldiers patrolling the streets, and sentries with screwed bayonets placed at every door while the press-gang entered and searched each hole and corner of the dwelling; when we hear of churches being surrounded during divine service by troops, while the press-gang stood ready at the door to seize men as they came out from attending public worship, and take these instances as merely types of what was constantly going on in different forms, we do not wonder at Lord Mayors, and other civic authorities in large towns, complaining that a stop was put to business by the danger which the tradesmen and their servants incurred in leaving their houses and going into the streets, infested by press-gangs.

Whether it was that living in closer neighbourhood to the metropolis—the centre of politics and news—inspired the inhabitants of the southern counties with a strong feeling of that kind of patriotism which consists in hating all other nations; or whether it was that the chances of capture were so much greater at all the southern ports that the merchant sailors became inured to the danger; or whether it was that serving in the navy, to those familiar with such towns as Portsmouth and Plymouth, had an attraction to most men from the dash and brilliancy of the adventurous employment—it is certain that the southerners took the oppression of press-warrants more submissively than the wild north-eastern people. For with them the chances of profit beyond their wages in the whaling or Greenland trade extended to the lowest description of sailor. He might rise by daring and saving to be a ship-owner himself. Numbers around him had done so; and this very fact made the distinction between class and class less apparent; and the common ventures and dangers, the universal interest felt in one pursuit, bound the inhabitants of that line of coast together with a strong tie, the severance of which by any violent extraneous measure, gave rise to passionate anger and thirst for vengeance. A Yorkshire man once said to me, "My county folk are all alike. Their first thought is how to resist. Why! I myself, if I hear a man say it is a fine day, catch myself trying to find out that it is no such thing. It is so in thought; it is so in word; it is so in deed."

So you may imagine the press-gang had no easy time of it on the Yorkshire coast. In other places they inspired fear, but here rage and hatred. The Lord Mayor of York was warned on 20th January, 1777, by an anonymous letter, that "if those men were not sent from the city on or before the following Tuesday, his lordship's own dwelling, and the Mansion-house also, should be burned to the ground."

The Sailor's Funeral at Monkshaven

From *Sylvia's Lovers*, 1863

THE vicar of Monkshaven was a kindly, peaceable old man, hating strife and troubled waters above everything. He was a vehement Tory in theory, as became his cloth in those days. He had two bugbears to fear—the French and the Dissenters. It was difficult to say of which he had the worst opinion and the most intense dread. Perhaps he hated the Dissenters most, because they came nearer in contact with him than the French; besides, the French had the excuse of being Papists, while the Dissenters might have belonged to the Church of England if they had not been utterly depraved. Yet in practice Dr. Wilson did not object to dine with Mr. Fishburn, who was a personal friend and follower of Wesley; but then, as the doctor would say, "Wesley was an Oxford man, and that makes him a gentleman; and he was an ordained minister of the Church of England, so that grace can never depart from him." But I do not know what excuse he would have alleged for sending broth and vegetables to old Ralph Thompson, a rabid Independent, who had been given to abusing the church and the vicar, from a Dissenting pulpit, as long as ever he could mount the stairs. However, that inconsistency between Dr. Wilson's theories and practice was not generally known in Monkshaven, so we have nothing to do with it.

Dr. Wilson had had a very difficult part to play, and a still more difficult sermon to write, during this last week. The Darley who had been killed was the son of the vicar's gardener, and Dr. Wilson's sympathies as a man had been all on the bereaved father's side. But then he had received, as the oldest magistrate in the neighbourhood, a letter from the captain of the *Aurora*, explanatory and exculpatory. Darley had been resisting the orders of an officer in his Majesty's service. What would become of due subordination and loyalty, and the interests of the service, and the chances of beating those confounded French, if such conduct as Darley's was to be encouraged? (Poor Darley! he was past all evil effects of human encouragement now!)

So the vicar mumbled hastily over a sermon on the text, "In the midst of life we are in death"; which might have done as well for a baby cut off in a convulsion-fit as for the strong man shot down with all his eager blood hot within him, by men as hot-blooded as himself. But once, when the old doctor's eye caught the upturned, straining gaze of the father Darley, seeking with all his soul to find a grain of holy comfort in the chaff of words, his conscience smote him. Had he nothing to say that should calm anger and revenge with spiritual power? no breath of the comforter to soothe repining into resignation? But again the discord between the laws of man and the laws of Christ stood before him; and he gave up the attempt to do more than he was doing, as beyond his power. Though the hearers went away as full of anger as they had entered the church, and some with a dull feeling of disappointment as to what they had got there, yet no one felt anything but kindly towards the old vicar. His simple, happy life led amongst them for forty years, and open to all men in its daily course; his sweet-tempered, cordial ways; his practical kindness, made him beloved by all; and neither he nor they thought much or cared much for admiration of his talents. Respect for his office was all the respect he thought of; and that was conceded to him from old traditional and hereditary association. In looking back to the last century, it appears curious to see how little our ancestors had the power of putting two things together, and perceiving either the discord or harmony thus produced. Is it because we are farther off from those times, and have, consequently, a greater range of vision? Will our descendants have a wonder about us, such as we have about the inconsistency of our forefathers, or a surprise at our blindness that we do not perceive that, holding such and such opinions, our course of action must be so and so, or that the logical consequence of particular opinions must be convictions which at present we hold in abhorrence? It seems puzzling to look back on men such as our vicar, who almost held the doctrine that the King could do no wrong, yet were ever ready to talk of the glorious Revolution, and to abuse the Stuarts for having entertained the same doctrine, and tried to put it in practice. But such discrepancies ran through good men's lives in those days. It is well for us that we live at the present time, when everybody is logical and consistent. This little discussion must be taken in place of Dr. Wilson's sermon, of which no one could remember more than the text half an hour after it was delivered. Even the doctor himself had the recollection of the words he had uttered swept out of his mind, as, having doffed his gown and donned his surplice, he came out of the dusk of his vestry and went to the church door, looking into the broad light which came upon the plain of the churchyard on the cliffs; for the sun had not yet set, and the pale moon was slowly rising through the silvery mist that obscured the distant moors. There was a thick, dense crowd, all still and silent, looking away from the church and the vicar, who awaited the bringing of the dead. They were watching the slow black line winding up the long steps, resting their heavy burden here and there, standing in silent groups at each landing-place; now lost to sight as a piece of broken, overhanging ground intervened, now emerging suddenly nearer; and overhead the great church bell, with its medieval inscription, familiar to the vicar, if to no one else who heard it:

"I to the grave do summon all,"

kept on its heavy booming monotone, with which no other sound from land or sea, near or distant, intermingled, except the cackle of the geese on some far-away farm on the moors, as they were coming home to roost; and that one noise from so great a distance seemed only to deepen the stillness. Then there was a little movement in the crowd; a little pushing from side to side, to make a path for the corpse and its bearers—an aggregate of the fragments of room.

With bent heads and spent strength, those who carried the coffin moved on; behind came the poor old gardener, a brown-black funeral cloak thrown over his homely dress, and supporting his wife with steps scarcely less feeble than her own. He had come to church that afternoon with a promise to her that he would return to lead her to the funeral of her firstborn; for he felt, in his sore, perplexed heart, full of indignation and dumb anger, as if he must go and hear something which should exorcise the unwonted longing for revenge that disturbed his grief and made him conscious of that great blank of consolation which faithlessness produces. And for the time he was faithless. How came God to permit such cruel injustice of man? Permitting it, He could not be good. Then what was life and what was death, but woe and despair? The beautiful solemn words of the ritual had done him good, and restored much of his faith. Though he could not understand why such sorrow had befallen him any more than before, he had come back to something of his childlike trust; he kept saying to himself in a whisper, as he mounted the weary steps, "It is the Lord's doing"; and the repetition soothed him unspeakably. Behind this old couple followed their children, grown men and women, come from distant place or farmhouse service: the servants at the vicarage, and many a neighbour, anxious to show their sympathy, and most of the sailors from the crews of the vessels in port, joined in procession, and followed the dead body into the church.

There was too great a crowd immediately within the door for Sylvia and Molly to go in again, and they accordingly betook themselves to the place where the deep grave was waiting, wide and hungry, to receive its dead. There, leaning against the headstones all around, were many standing—looking over the broad and placid sea, and turned to the soft salt air which blew on their hot eyes and rigid faces; for no one spoke of all that number. They were thinking of the violent death of him over whom the solemn words were now being said in the gray old church, scarcely out of their hearing, had not the sound been broken by the measured lapping of the tide far beneath.

Suddenly every one looked round towards the path from the churchyard steps. Two sailors were supporting a ghastly figure that, with feeble motions, was drawing near the open grave.

"It's t' specksioneer as tried to save him! it's him as was left for dead!" the people murmured round.

"It's Charley Kinraid, as I'm a sinner!" said Molly, starting forward to greet her cousin.

But as he came on she saw that all his strength was needed for the mere action of walking. The sailors, in their strong sympathy, had yielded to his earnest entreaty, and carried him up the steps, in order that he might see the last of his messmate. They placed him near the grave, resting against a stone; and he was hardly there before the vicar came forth, and the great crowd poured out of the church, following the body to the grave.

Sylvia was so much wrapped up in the solemnity of the occasion that she had no thought to spare at the first moment for the pale and haggard figure opposite; much less was she aware of her cousin Philip, who now, singling her out for the first time from among the crowd, pressed to her side, with an intention of companionship and protection.

As the service went on, ill-checked sobs rose from behind the two girls, who were among the foremost in the crowd, and by and by the cry and the wail became general. Sylvia's tears rained down her face, and her distress became so evident that it attracted the attention of many in that inner circle. Among others who noticed it, the specksioneer's hollow eyes were caught by the sight of the innocent blooming child-like face opposite to him, and he wondered if she were a relation; yet, seeing that she bore no badge of mourning, he rather concluded that she must have been a sweetheart of the dead man's.

And now all was over: the rattle of the gravel on the coffin; the last long, lingering look of friends and lovers; the rosemary sprigs had been cast down by all who were fortunate enough to have brought them—and oh! how much Sylvia wished she had remembered this last act of respect—and slowly the outer rim of the crowd began to slacken and disappear.

A Press-gang Riot at Monkshaven (Whitby)

From *Sylvia's Lovers*, 1863

This riot, which Mrs. Gaskell describes so graphically, did actually take place on February 23rd, 1797, and the prototype of Daniel Robson was hanged at York, for encouraging the rioters. Mrs. Gaskell got copies of the documents relating to the trial and execution, and she interviewed several of the old residents of Whitby, when writing her story.

EVERYONE who was capable of understanding the state of feeling in Monkshaven at this time must have been aware that at any moment an explosion might take place; and probably there were those who had judgment enough to be surprised that it did not take place sooner than it did. For until February there were only occasional cries and growls of rage, as the press-gang made their captures first here, then there; often, apparently, tranquil for days, then heard of at some distance along the coast, then carrying off a seaman from the very heart of the town. They seemed afraid of provoking any general hostility, such as that which had driven them from Shields, and would have conciliated the inhabitants if they could; the officers on the service and on board the three men-of-war coming often into the town, spending largely, talking to all with cheery friendliness, and making themselves very popular in such society as they could obtain access to at the houses of the neighbouring magistrates or at the rectory. But this, however agreeable, did not forward the object the impress service had in view; and, accordingly, a more decided step was taken at a time when, although there was no apparent evidence as to the fact, the town was full of the Greenland mariners coming quietly in to renew their yearly engagements, which, when done, would legally entitle them to protection from impressment. One night—it was on a Saturday, February 23rd, when there was a bitter black frost, with a north-east wind sweeping through the streets, and men and women were close shut in their houses—all were startled in their household content and warmth by the sound of the fire-bell busily swinging, and pealing out for help. The fire-bell was kept in the market-house where High Street and Bridge Street met: everyone knew what it meant. Some dwelling, or maybe a boiling-house, was on fire, and neighbourly assistance was summoned with all speed, in a town where no water was laid on, nor fire-engines kept in readiness. Men snatched up their hats, and rushed out, wives following, some with the readiest wraps they could lay hands on, with which to clothe the over-hasty husbands, others from that mixture of dread and curiosity which draws people to the scene of any disaster. Those of the market people who were making the best of their way homewards, having waited in the town till the early darkness concealed their path, turned back at the sound of the ever-clanging fire-bell, ringing out faster and faster as if the danger became every instant more pressing.

As men ran against or alongside of each other, their breathless question was ever, "Where is it?" and no one could tell; so they pressed onwards into the market-place, sure of obtaining the information desired there, where the fire-bell kept calling out with its furious metal tongue.

The dull oil lamps in the adjoining streets only made darkness visible in the thronged market-place, where the buzz of many men's unanswered questions was rising louder and louder. A strange feeling of dread crept over those nearest to the closed market-house. Above them in the air the bell was still clanging; but before them was a door fast shut and locked; no one to speak and tell them why they were summoned—where they ought to be. They were at the heart of the mystery, and it was a silent blank! Their unformed dread took shape at the cry from the outside of the crowd, from where men were still coming down the eastern side of Bridge Street. "The gang! the gang!" shrieked out someone. "The gang are upon us! Help! help!" Then the fire-bell had been a decoy; a sort of seething the kid in its mother's milk, leading men into a snare through their kindliest feelings. Some dull sense of this added to utter dismay, and made all struggle and strain to get to all the outlets save that in which a fight was now going on; the swish of heavy whips, the thud of bludgeons, the groans, the growls of wounded or infuriated men, coming with terrible distinctness through the darkness to the quickened ear of fear.

A breathless group rushed up the blackness of a narrow entry to stand still awhile, and recover strength for fresh running. For a time nothing but heavy pants and gasps were heard amongst them. No one knew his neighbour, and their good feeling, so lately abused and preyed upon, made them full of suspicion. The first who spoke was recognized by his voice.

"Is it thee, Daniel Robson?" asked his neighbour, in a low tone.

"Ay! Who else should it be."

"A dunno."

"If a am to be anyone else, I'd like to be a chap of nobbut eight stun. A'm welly done for!"

"It were as bloody a shame as ever I heered on. Who's to go t' t' next fire, a'd like to know!"

"A tell yo' what, lads," said Daniel, recovering his breath, but speaking in gasps. "We were a pack o' cowards to let 'em carry off yon chaps as easy as they did, a'm reckoning!"

"A think so, indeed," said another voice.

Daniel went on:

"We was two hunder, if we was a man; an t' gang has niver numbered above twelve."

"But they was armed. A seen t' glitter on their cutlasses," spoke out a fresh voice.

"What then!" replied he who had latest come, and who stood at the mouth of the entry. "A had my whaling-knife wi' me i' my pea-jacket as my missus threw at me, and a'd ha' ripped 'em up as soon as winking, if a could ha' thought what was best to do wi' that — bell making such a din right above us. A man can but die onest, and we was ready to go int' t' fire for t' save folks' lives, and yet we'd none on us t' wit to see as we might ha' saved yon poor chaps as screeched out for help."

"They'll ha' getten 'em to t' Randyvow by now," said someone.

"They cannot tak' 'em aboard till morning; t' tide won't serve," said the last speaker but one.

Daniel Robson spoke out the thought that was surging up into the brain of everyone there.

"There's a chance for us a'. How many be we?" By dint of touching each other the numbers were counted. Seven. "Seven. But if us seven turns out and rouses t' town, there'll be many a score ready to gang t' t' Mariners' Arms, and it'll be easy work reskying them chaps as is pressed. Us seven, each man-jack on us, go and seek up his friends, and get him as well as he can to t' church steps; then, mebbe, there'll be some there as'll not be so soft as we was, letting them poor chaps be carried off from under our noses, just because our ears was busy listening to yon confounded bell, whose clip-clapping tongue a'll tear out afore this week is out."

Before Daniel had finished speaking, those nearest to the entrance muttered their assent to his project, and had stolen off, keeping to the darkest side of the streets and lanes, which they threaded in different directions; most of them going straight as sleuth-hounds to the haunts of the wildest and most desperate portion of the seafaring population of Monkshaven. For, in the breasts of many, revenge for the misery and alarm of the past winter took a deeper and more ferocious form than Daniel had thought of when he made his proposal of a rescue. To him it was an adventure like many he had been engaged in in his younger days; indeed, the liquor he had drunk had given him a fictitious youth for the time; and it was more in the light of a rough frolic of which he was to be the leader that he limped along (always lame from old attacks of rheumatism), chuckling to himself at the apparent stillness of the town, which gave no warning to the press-gang at the Rendezvous of anything in the wind. Daniel, too, had his friends to summon; old hands like himself, but "deep uns," also, like himself, as he imagined.

It was nine o'clock when all who were summoned met at the church steps; and by nine o'clock, Monkshaven, in those days, was more quiet and asleep than many a town at present is at midnight. The church and churchyard above them were flooded with silver light, for the moon was high in the heavens: the irregular steps were here and there in pure white clearness, here and there in blackest shadow. But more than half-way up to the top men clustered like bees; all pressing so as to be near enough to question those who stood nearest to the planning of the attack. Here and there a woman, with wild gestures and shrill voice that no entreaty would hush down to the whispered pitch of the men, pushed her way through the crowd—this one imploring immediate action, that adjuring those around her to smite and spare not those who had carried off her "man"—the father, the breadwinner. Low down in the darkened, silent town were many whose hearts went with the angry and excited crowd, and who would bless them and caress them for that night's deeds. Daniel soon found himself a laggard in planning, compared to some of those around him. But when, with the rushing sound of many steps and but few words, they had arrived at the blank, dark, shut-up Mariners' Arms, they paused in surprise at the uninhabited look of the whole house: it was Daniel once more who took the lead.

"Speak 'em fair," said he; "try good words first. Hobbs 'll mebbe let 'em out quiet, if we can catch a word wi' him. A say, Hobbs," said he, raising his voice, "is a' shut up for t' night; for a'd be glad of a glass. A'm Daniel Robson, thou knows."

Not one word in reply, any more than from the tomb; but his speech had been heard nevertheless. The crowd behind him began to jeer and to threaten; there was no longer any keeping down their voices, their rage, their terrible oaths. If doors and windows had not of late been strengthened with bars of iron in anticipation of some such occasion, they would have been broken in with the onset of the fierce and now yelling crowd who rushed against them with the force of a battering-ram, to recoil in baffled rage from the vain assault. No sign, no sound from within, in that breathless pause.

"Come away round here! a've found a way to t' back o' behint, where belike it's not so well fenced," said Daniel, who had made way for younger and more powerful men to conduct the assault, and had employed his time meanwhile in examining the back premises. The men rushed after him, almost knocking him down, as he made his way into the lane into which the doors of the outbuildings belonging to the inn opened. Daniel had already broken the fastening of that which opened into a damp, mouldy-smelling shippon, in one corner of which a poor lean cow shifted herself on her legs, in an uneasy, restless manner, as her sleeping-place was invaded by as many men as could cram themselves into the dark hold. Daniel, at the end farthest from the door, was almost smothered before he could break down the rotten wooden shutter, that, when opened, displayed the weedy yard of the old inn, the full clear light defining the outline of each blade of grass by the delicate black shadow behind.

This hole, used to give air and light to what had once been a stable, in the days when horse travellers were in the habit of coming to the Mariners' Arms, was large enough to admit the passage of a man; and Daniel, in virtue of its discovery, was the first to get through. But he was larger and heavier than he had been; his lameness made him less agile, and the impatient crowd behind him gave him a helping push that sent him down on the round stones with which the yard was paved, and for the time disabled him so much that he could only just crawl out of the way of leaping feet and heavy nailed boots, which came through the opening till the yard was filled with men, who now set up a fierce, derisive shout, which, to their delight, was answered from within. No more silence, no more dead opposition: a living struggle, a glowing, raging fight! and Daniel thought he should be obliged to sit there still, leaning against the wall, inactive, while the strife and the action were going on in which he had once been foremost.

He saw the stones torn up; he saw them used with good effect on the unguarded back-door; he cried out in useless warning as he saw the upper windows open, and aim taken among the crowd; but just then the door gave way, and there was an involuntary forward motion in the throng, so that no one was disabled by the shots as to prevent their forcing their way in with the rest. And now the sounds came veiled by the walls as of some raging ravening beast growling over his prey; the noise came and went—once utterly ceased; and Daniel raised himself with difficulty to ascertain the cause, when again the roar came clear and fresh, and men poured into the yard again, shouting and rejoicing over the rescued victims of the press-gang. Daniel hobbled up, and shouted, and rejoiced, and shook hands with the rest, hardly caring to understand that the lieutenant and his gang had quitted the house by a front window, and that all had poured out in search of them; the greater part, however, returning to liberate the prisoners, and then glut their vengeance on the house and its contents.

From all the windows, upper and lower, furniture was now being thrown into the yard. The smash of glass, the heavier crash of wood, the cries, the laughter, the oaths, all excited Daniel to the utmost; and, forgetting his bruises, he pressed forwards to lend a helping hand. The wild, rough success of his scheme almost turned his head. He hurraed at every flagrant piece of destruction; he shook hands with everyone around him, and, at last, when the destroyers inside paused to take breath, he cried out:

"If a was as young as onest a was, a'd have t' Randyvow down, and mak' a bonfire on it. We'd ring t' fire-bell t' some purpose."

No sooner said than done. Their excitement was ready to take the slightest hint of mischief; old chairs, broken tables, odd drawers, smashed chests were rapidly and skilfully heaped into a pyramid, and one, who at the first broaching of the idea had gone for live coals the speedier to light up the fire, came now through the crowd with a large shovelful of red-hot cinders. The rioters stopped to take breath and look on like children at the uncertain flickering blaze, which sprang high one moment and dropped down the next only to creep along the base of the heap of wreck, and make secure of its future work. Then the lurid blaze darted up wild, high, and irrepressible; and the men around gave a cry of fierce exultation, and in rough mirth began to try and push each other in. In one of the pauses of the rushing, roaring noise of the flames, the moaning low and groan of the poor alarmed cow fastened up in the shippon caught Daniel's ear, and he understood her groans as well as if they had been words. He limped out of the yard through the now deserted house, where men were busy at the mad work of destruction, and found his way back to the lane into which the shippon opened. The cow was dancing about at the roar and dazzle and heat of the fire; but Daniel knew how to soothe her, and in a few minutes he had a rope round her neck, and led her gently out from the scene of her alarm. He was still in the lane when Simpson, the man-of-all-work at the Mariners' Arms, crept out of some hiding-place in the deserted out-building, and stood suddenly face to face with Robson.

The man was white with rage and fear.

"Here, tak' thy beast, and lead her where she'll noan hear yon cries and shouts. She's fairly moidered wi' heat an' noise."

"They're brenning every rag I have i' t' world," gasped out Simpson; "I niver had much, and now I'm a beggar."

"Well! thou shouldn't ha' turned again' thine own townfolks, and harboured t' gang. Sarves thee reet. A'd noan be here leading beasts if a were as young as a were; a'd be in t' thick on it."

"It was thee set 'em on—a heerd thee—a see'd thee a helping on 'em t' break in; they'd ne'r ha' thought on attacking t' house, and setting fire to yon things if thou hadn't spoken on it." Simpson was now fairly crying. But Daniel did not realise what the loss of all the small property he had in the world was to the poor fellow (rapscallion though he was, broken-down, unprosperous ne'er-do-weel!) in his pride at the good work he believed he had set on foot.

"Ay," said he; "it's a great thing for folk to have a chap for t' lead 'em wi' a head on his shoulders. A misdoubt me if there were a felly there as would ha' thought o' routling out yon wasps' nest; it taks a deal o' mother-wit to be up to things. But t' gang'll niver harbour there again, one while. A only wish we'd cotched 'em. An' a should like t' ha' given Hobbs a bit o' my mind."

"He's had his sauce," said Simpson dolefully. "He and me is ruined."

"Tut, tut, thou's got thy brother, he's rich enough. And Hobbs 'll do a deal better; he's had his lesson now, and he'll stick to his own side time to come. Here, tak' thy beast an' look after her, for my bones is aching. An' mak' thysel' scarce, for some o' them fellys has getten their blood up, an' won't be for treating thee o'er well if they fall in wi' thee."

"Hobbs ought to be served out; it were he as made t' bargain wi' lieutenant; and he's off safe wi' his wife and his money-bag, and a'm left a beggar this night in Monkshaven street. My brother and me has had words, and he'll do nought for me but curse me. A had three crown-pieces, and a good pair o' breeches, and a shirt, and a dare say better nor two pair o' stockings. A wish t' gang, and thee, and Hobbs, and them mad folk up yonder were a' down i' hell. A do."

"Coom, lad," said Daniel, noways offended at his companion's wish on his behalf. "A'm noan flush mysel', but here's half a crown, and tuppence, it's a' a've gotten wi' me; but it'll keep thee and t' beast i' food and shelter this neet, and get thee a glass o' comfort, too. A had thought o' taking one mysel', but a shannot ha' a penny left, so a'll just toddle whoam to my missus."

Daniel was not in the habit of feeling any emotion at actions not directly affecting himself; or else he might have despised the poor wretch who immediately clutched at the money and overwhelmed that man with slobbery thanks whom he had not a minute before been cursing. But all Simpson's stronger passions had been long ago used up; now he only faintly liked and disliked, where once he loved and hated; his only vehement feeling was for himself; that cared for, other men might wither or flourish as best suited them.

Many of the doors which had been close shut when the crowd went down the High Street were partially open as Daniel slowly returned; and light streamed from them on the otherwise dark road. The news of the successful attempt at rescue had reached those who had sate in mourning and in desolation an hour or two ago, and several of these pressed forwards as from their watching corner they recognised Daniel's approach; they pressed forward into the street to shake him by the hand, to thank him (for his name had been bruited abroad as one of those who had planned the affair), and at several places he was urged to have a dram—urgency that he was loath for many reasons to refuse, but his increasing uneasiness and pain made him for once abstinent, and only anxious to get home and rest. But he could not help being both touched and flattered at the way in which those who formed his "world" looked upon him as a hero; and was not insensible to the words of blessing which a wife, whose husband had been impressed and rescued this night, poured down upon him as he passed.

"There, there—dunnot crack thy throat wi' blessing. Thy man would ha' done as much for me, though mebbe he mightn't ha' shown so much gumption and capability; but them's gifts, and not to be proud on."

When Daniel reached the top of the hill on the road home, he turned to look round; but he was lame and bruised. He had gone along slowly, the fire had pretty nearly died out; only a red hue in the air about the houses at the end of the long High Street, and a hot lurid mist against the hill-side beyond where the Mariners' Arms had stood, were still left as signs and token of the deed of violence.

Daniel looked and chuckled. "That comes o' ringing fire-bell," said he to himself; "it were shame for it to be telling a lie, poor oud story-teller."

A Game of Blind-man's-buff

From *Sylvia's Lovers*, 1863

Moss Brow, Molly Corney's old home, is still in existence, and the room in which the game was played can be seen.

SYLVIA was by all acknowledged and treated as the belle. When they played at blind-man's-buff, go where she would, she was always caught; she was called out repeatedly to do what was required in any game, as if all had a pleasure in seeing her light figure and deft ways. She was sufficiently pleased with all this to have got over her shyness with all except Charley. When others paid her their rustic compliments she tossed her head, and made her little saucy repartees; but when he said something low and flattering, it was too honey-sweet to her heart to be thrown off thus. And, somehow, the more she yielded to this fascination the more she avoided Philip. He did not speak flatteringly—he did not pay compliments—he watched her with discontented, longing eyes, and grew more inclined every moment, as he remembered his anticipation of a happy evening, to cry out in his heart *vanitas vanitatum*.

And now came crying the forfeits. Molly Brunton knelt down, her face buried in her mother's lap; the latter took out the forfeits one by one, and as she held them up she said the accustomed formula:

"A fine thing, and a very fine thing, what must he (or she) do who owns this thing?"

One or two had been told to kneel to the prettiest, bow to the wittiest, and kiss those they loved best; others had had to bite an inch off the poker, or such plays upon words. And now came Sylvia's pretty new ribbon that Philip had given her (he almost longed to snatch it out of Mrs. Corney's hands and burn it before all their faces, so annoyed was he with the whole affair).

"A fine thing and a very fine thing—a most particular fine thing—choose how she came by it. What must she do as owns this thing?"

"She must blow out t' candle and kiss t' candlestick."

In one instant Kinraid had hold of the only candle within reach; all the others had been put up high on inaccessible shelves and other places. Sylvia went up and blew out the candle, and before the sudden partial darkness was over he had taken the candle into his fingers and, according to the traditional meaning of the words, was in the place of the candlestick, and as such was to be kissed. Everyone laughed at innocent Sylvia's face as the meaning of her penance came into it, everyone but Philip, who almost choked.

"I'm candlestick," said Kinraid, with less of triumph in his voice than he would have had with any other girl in the room.

"Yo' mun kiss t' candlestick," cried the Corneys, "or you'll niver get your ribbon back."

"And she sets a deal o' store by that ribbon," said Molly Brunton maliciously.

"I'll none kiss t' candlestick, nor him either," said Sylvia, in a low voice of determination, turning away, full of confusion.

"Yo'll not get yo'r ribbon if yo' dunnot," cried one and all.

"I don't care for t' ribbon," said she, flashing up with a look at her tormentors, now her back was turned to Kinraid. "An' I won't play any more at such-like games," she added, with fresh indignation rising in her heart as she took her old place in the corner of the room a little away from the rest.

Philip's spirits rose, and he yearned to go to her and tell her how he approved of her conduct. Alas, Philip! Sylvia, though as modest a girl as ever lived, was no prude, and had been brought up in simple, straightforward country ways; and with any other young man, excepting, perhaps, Philip's self, she would have thought no more of making a rapid pretence of kissing the hand or cheek of the temporary "candlestick" than our ancestresses did in a much higher rank on similar occasions. Kinraid, though mortified by his public rejection, was more conscious of this than the inexperienced Philip; he resolved not to be balked, and watched his opportunity. For the time he went on playing as if Sylvia's conduct had not affected him in the least, and as if he was hardly aware of her defection from the game. As she saw others submitting, quite as a matter of course, to similar penances, she began to be angry with herself for having thought twice about it, and almost to dislike herself for the strange consciousness which had made it at the time seem impossible to do what she was told. Her eyes kept filling with tears as her isolated position in the gay party, the thought of what a fool she had made of herself, kept recurring to her mind; but no one saw her, she thought, thus crying; and, ashamed to be discovered when the party should pause in their game, she stole round behind them into the great chamber in which she had helped to lay out the supper, with the intention of bathing her eyes, and taking a drink of water. One instant Charley Kinraid was missing from the circle of which he was the life and soul; and then back he came with an air of satisfaction on his face, intelligible enough to those who had seen his game; but unnoticed by Philip, who, amidst the perpetual noise and movements around him, had not perceived Sylvia's leaving the room, until she came back at the end of about a quarter of an hour, looking lovelier than ever, her complexion brilliant, her eyes drooping, her hair neatly and freshly arranged, tied with a brown ribbon instead of that she was supposed to have forfeited. She looked as if she did not wish her return to be noticed, stealing softly behind the romping lads and lasses with noiseless motions, and altogether such a contrast to them in her cool freshness and modest neatness that both Kinraid and Philip found it difficult to keep their eyes off her. But the former had a secret triumph in his heart which enabled him to go on with his merry-making as if it absorbed him; while Philip dropped out of the crowd and came up to where she was standing silently by Mrs. Corney, who, arms akimbo, was laughing at the frolic and fun around her. Sylvia started a little when Philip spoke, and kept her soft eyes averted from him after the first glance; she answered him shortly, but with unaccustomed gentleness. He had only asked her when she would like him to take her home; and she, a little surprised at the idea of going home when to her the evening seemed only beginning, had answered:

"Go home? I don't know! It's New Year's eve!"

Philip Hepburn Leaves the New Year's Party

From *Sylvia's Lovers*, 1863

SHUTTING the door behind him, he went out into the dreary night, and began his lonesome walk back to Monkshaven. The cold sleet almost blinded him as the sea wind drove it straight in his face; it cut against him as it was blown with drifting force. The roar of the wintry sea came borne on the breeze; there was more light from the whitened ground than from the dark laden sky above. The field-paths would have been a matter of perplexity had it not been for the well-known gaps in the dyke-side, which showed the whitened land beyond, between the two dark stone walls. Yet he went clear and straight along his way, having unconsciously left all guidance to the animal instinct which co-exists with the human soul, and sometimes takes strange charge of the human body, when all the nobler powers of the individual are absorbed in acute suffering. At length he was in the lane, toiling up the hill, from which, by day, Monkshaven might be seen. Now all features of the landscape before him were lost in the darkness of night, against which the white flakes came closer and nearer, thicker and faster. On a sudden, the bells of Monkshaven church rang out a welcome to the new year, 1796. From the direction of the wind, it seemed as if the sound was flung with strength and power right into Philip's face. He walked down the hill to its merry sound—its merry sound, his heavy heart. As he entered the long High Street of Monkshaven, he could see the watching lights put out in parlour, chamber, or kitchen. The new year had come, and expectation was ended. Reality had begun.

He turned to the right, into the court where he lodged with Alice Rose. There was a light still burning there, and cheerful voices were heard. He opened the door; Alice, her daughter, and Coulson stood as if awaiting him. Hester's wet cloak hung on a chair before the fire; she had her hood on, for she and Coulson had been to the watch-night.

The solemn excitement of the services had left its traces upon her countenance and in her mind. There was a spiritual light in her usually shadowed eyes, and a slight flush on her pale cheek. Merely personal and self-conscious feelings were merged in a loving good-will to all her fellow-creatures. Under the influence of this large charity, she forgot her habitual reserve, and came forward as Philip entered to meet him with her New Year's wishes—wishes that she had previously interchanged with the other two.

"A happy New Year to you, Philip, and may God have you in His keeping all the days thereof!"

He took her hand, and shook it warmly in reply. The flush on her cheek deepened as she withdrew it. Alice Rose said something curtly about the lateness of the hour and her being much tired; and then she and her daughter went upstairs to the front chamber and Philip and Coulson to that which they shared at the back of the house.

Kinraid's Return to Monkshaven

From *Sylvia's Lovers*, 1863

This description of the meeting of Sylvia's two lovers after her marriage to Philip Hepburn is the most dramatic scene in the story.

SOMEONE stood in the lane just on the other side of the gap; his back was to the morning sun; all she saw at first was the uniform of a naval officer, so well known in Monkshaven in those days.

Sylvia went hurrying past him, not looking again, although her clothes almost brushed his as he stood there still. She had not gone a yard—no, not half a yard—when her heart leaped up and fell again dead within her, as if she had been shot.

"Sylvia!" he said, in a voice tremulous with joy and passionate love. "Sylvia!"

She looked round; he had turned a little, so that the light fell straight on his face. It was bronzed, and the lines were strengthened; but it was the same face she had last seen in Haytersbank Gully three long years ago and had never thought to see in life again.

He was close to her, and held out his fond arms; she went fluttering towards their embrace, as if drawn by the old fascination; but when she felt them close round her, she started away, and cried out with a great pitiful shriek, and put her hands up to her forehead as if trying to clear away some bewildering mist.

Then she looked at him once more, a terrible story in her eyes, if he could but have read it.

Twice she opened her stiff lips to speak, and twice the words were overwhelmed by the surges of her misery, which bore them back into the depths of her heart.

He thought that he had come upon her too suddenly, and he attempted to soothe her with soft murmurs of love, and to woo her to his outstretched hungry arms once more. But when she saw this motion of his, she made a gesture as though pushing him away; and with an inarticulate moan of agony she put her hands to her head once more, and turning away, began to run blindly towards the town for protection.

For a minute or so he was stunned with surprise at her behaviour; and then he thought it accounted for by the shock of his accost, and that she needed time to understand the unexpected joy. So he followed her swiftly, ever keeping her in view, but not trying to overtake her too speedily.

"I have frightened my poor love," he kept thinking. And by this thought he tried to repress his impatience and check the speed he longed to use; yet he was always so near behind that her quickened sense heard his well-known footsteps following, and a mad notion flashed across her brain that she would go to the wide full river, and end the hopeless misery she felt enshrouding her. There was a sure hiding-place from all human reproach and heavy mortal woe beneath the rushing waters borne landwards by the morning tide.

No one can tell what changed her course; perhaps the thought of her sucking child; perhaps her mother; perhaps an angel of God; no one on earth knows, but as she ran along the quay-side she all at once turned up an entry, and through an open door.

He, following all the time, came into a quiet, dark parlour, with a cloth and tea things on the table ready for breakfast; the change from the bright sunny air out of doors to the deep shadow of this room made him think for the first moment that she had passed on, and that no one was there, and he stood for an instant baffled, and hearing no sound but the beating of his own heart; but an irrepressible sobbing gasp made him look round, and there he saw her cowered behind the door, her face covered tight up, and sharp shudders going through her whole frame.

"My love, my darling!" said he, going up to her, and trying to raise her, and to loosen her hands away from her face. "I have been too sudden for thee; it was thoughtless in me; but I have so looked forward to this time, and seeing thee come along the field, and go past me; but I should ha' been more tender and careful of thee. Nay! let me have another look of thy sweet face."

All this he whispered in the old tones of manœuvring love, in that voice she had yearned and hungered to hear in life, and had not heard, for all her longing, save in her dreams.

She tried to crouch more and more into the corner, into the hidden shadow—to sink into the ground out of sight.

Once more he spoke, beseeching her to lift up her face, to let him hear her speak.

But she only moaned.

"Sylvia," said he, thinking he could change his tactics, and pique her into speaking, that he would make a pretence of suspicion and offence.

"Sylvia! one would think you were not glad to see me back again at length. I only came in late last night, and my first thought on wakening was of you; it has been ever since I left you."

Sylvia took her hands away from her face; it was grey as the face of death; her awful eyes were passionless in her despair.

"Where have yo' been?" she asked, in slow, hoarse tones, as if her voice were half strangled within her.

"Been!" said he, a red light coming into his eyes, as he bent his looks upon her; now, indeed, a true and not an assumed suspicion entering his mind.

"Been!" he repeated; then, coming a step nearer to her, and taking her hand, not tenderly this time, but with a resolution to be satisfied.

"Did not your cousin—Hepburn, I mean—did not he tell you?—he saw the press-gang seize me—I gave him a message to you—I bade you keep true to me as I would be to you."

Between every clause of this speech he paused and gasped for an answer; but none came. Her eyes dilated and held his steady gaze prisoner as with a magical charm—neither could look away from the other's wild, searching gaze. When he had ended, she was silent for a moment, then she cried out, shrill and fierce:

"Philip!" No answer.

Wilder and shriller still, "Philip!" she cried.

He was in the distant ware-room completing the last night's work before the regular shop hours began; before breakfast, also, that his wife might not find him waiting and impatient.

He heard her cry; it cut through doors, and still air, and great bales of woollen stuff; he thought that she had hurt herself, that her mother was worse, that her baby was ill, and he hastened to the spot whence the cry proceeded.

On opening the door that separated the shop from the sitting-room, he saw the back of a naval officer, and his wife on the ground, huddled up in a heap; when she perceived him come in, she dragged herself up by means of a chair, groping like a blind person, and came and stood facing him.

The officer turned fiercely round, and would have come towards Philip, who was so bewildered by the scene that even yet he did not understand who the stranger was, did not perceive for an instant that he saw the realisation of his greatest dread.

But Sylvia laid her hand on Kinraid's arm, and assumed to herself the right of speech. Philip did not know her voice, it was so changed.

"Philip," she said, "this is Kinraid come back again to wed me. He is alive; he has niver been dead, only taken by t' press-gang. And he says yo' saw it, and knew it all t' time. Speak, was it so?"

Philip knew not what to say, whither to turn, under what refuge of words or acts to shelter.

Sylvia's influence was keeping Kinraid silent, but he was rapidly passing beyond it.

"Speak!" he cried, loosening himself from Sylvia's light grasp, and coming towards Philip, with a threatening gesture. "Did I not bid you tell her how it was? did I not bid you say how I would be faithful to her, and she was to be faithful to me? Oh! you damned scoundrel! have you kept it from her all that time, and let her think me dead, or false? Take that!"

His closed fist was up to strike the man, who hung his head with bitterest shame and miserable self-reproach; but Sylvia came swift between the blow and its victim.

"Charley, thou shan't strike him," she said. "He is a damned scoundrel" (this was said in the hardest, quietest tone), "but he is my husband."

"Oh! thou false heart!" exclaimed Kinraid, turning sharp on her. "If ever I trusted woman, I trusted you, Sylvia Robson."

He made as though throwing her from him, with a gesture of contempt that stung her to life.

"Oh, Charley!" she cried, springing to him, "dunnot cut me to the quick; have pity on me, though he had none. I did so love thee; it was my very heart-strings as gave way when they told me thou was drowned—father, and the Corneys, and all, iverybody. Thy hat and the bit of ribbon I gave thee were found drenched and dripping wi' sea-water; and I went mourning for thee all the day long—dunnot turn away from me; only hearken this once, and then kill me dead, and I'll bless you—and have niver been mysel' since; niver ceased to feel the sun grow dark and the air chill and dreary when I thought on the time when thou was alive. I did, my Charley, my own love! And I thought that thou was dead for iver, and I wished I were lying beside thee. Oh, Charley! Philip, there where he stands, could tell you this was true. Philip, wasn't it so?"

"Would God I were dead!" moaned forth the unhappy, guilty man. But she had turned to Kinraid, and was speaking again to him, and neither of them heard or heeded him—they were drawing closer and closer together—she, with her cheeks and eyes aflame, talking eagerly.

"And father was taken up, and all for setting some free as t' press-gang had taken by a foul trick; and he were put in York prison, and tried, and hung! hung! Charley!—good kind father was hung on a gallows; and mother lost her sense and grew silly in grief, and we were like to be turned out on t' wide world, and poor mother dateless—and I thought yo' were dead—oh! I thought yo' were dead, I did—oh, Charley, Charley!"

By this time they were in each other's arms, she with her head on his shoulder, crying as if her heart would break.

Philip came forwards and took hold of her to pull her away; but Charley held her tight, mutely defying Philip. Unconsciously, she was Philip's protection, in that hour of danger, from a blow which might have been his death if strong will could have aided it to kill.

"Sylvia!" said he, grasping her tight. "Listen to me. He did not love you as I did. He had loved other women. I, you—you alone. He had loved other girls before you, and had left off loving them. I—I wish God would free my heart from the pang; but it will go on till I die, whether you love me or not. And then—where was I? Oh! that very night that he was taken, I was a-thinking on you and on him; and I might ha' given you his message, but I heard those speaking of him who knew him well; they talked of his false, fickle ways. How was I to know he would keep true to thee? It might be a sin in me, I cannot say; my heart and my sense are gone dead within me. I know this, I have loved you as no man but me ever loved before. Have some pity and forgiveness on me, if it's only because I have been so tormented with my love."

He looked at her with feverish eager wistfulness; it faded away into despair as she made no sign of having even heard his words. He let go his hold of her, and his arm fell loosely by his side.

"I may die," he said, "for my life is ended!"

"Sylvia!" spoke out Kinraid, bold and fervent, "your marriage is no marriage. You were tricked into it. You are my wife, not his. I am your husband; we plighted each other our troth. See! here is my half of the sixpence."

He pulled it out from his bosom, tied by a black ribbon round his neck.

"When they stripped me and searched me in the French prison, I managed to keep this. No lies can break the oath we swore to each other. I can get your pretence of a marriage set aside. I am in favour with my admiral, and he will do a deal for me, and will back me out. Come with me; your marriage shall be set aside, and we'll be married again, all square and above-board. Come away. Leave that damned fellow to repent of the trick he played an honest sailor; we'll be true, whatever has come and gone. Come, Sylvia."

His arm was round her waist, and he was drawing her towards the door, his face all crimson with eagerness and hope. Just then the baby cried.

"Hark!" said she, starting away from Kinraid, "baby is crying for me. His child—yes, it is his child—I had forgotten that—forgotten all. I'll make my vow now, lest I lose mysel' again. I'll niver forgive yon man, nor live with him as his wife again. All that's done and ended. He's spoilt my life—he's spoilt it for as long as iver I live on this earth; but neither you nor him shall spoil my soul. It goes hard wi' me, Charley, it does indeed. I'll just give you one kiss—one little kiss—and then, so help me God, I'll niver see nor hear till—no, not that, not that is needed—I'll niver see—sure that's enough—I'll niver see yo' again on this side heaven, so help me God! I'm bound and tied, but I have sworn my oath to him as well as yo': there's things I will do, and there's things I won't. Kiss me once more. God help me, he is gone!"

Roger Hamley's Farewell

From *Wives and Daughters*, 1866

The house mentioned in this incident is Church House, Knutsford, where Mrs. Gaskell's uncle, Dr. Holland, resided. It is now known as Hollingford House.

THE day of Roger's departure came. Molly tried hard to forget it in the working away at a cushion she was preparing as a present to Cynthia; people did worsted-work in those days. One, two, three. One, two, three, four, five, six, seven; all wrong; she was thinking of something else, and had to unpick it. It was a rainy day, too; and Mrs. Gibson, who had planned to go out and pay some calls, had to stay indoors. This made her restless and fidgety. She kept going backwards and forwards to different windows in the drawing-room to look at the weather, as if she imagined that while it rained at one window, it might be fine weather at another. "Molly—come here! who is that man wrapped up in a cloak,—there—near the Park wall, under the beech-tree—he has been there this half-hour and more, never stirring, and looking at this house all the time! I think it's very suspicious."

Molly looked, and in an instant recognised Roger under all his wraps. Her first instinct was to draw back. The next to come forwards, and say, "Why, mamma, it's Roger Hamley! Look now—he's kissing his hand; he's wishing us good-bye in the only way he can!" And she responded to his sign; but she was not sure if he perceived her modest, quiet movement, for Mrs. Gibson became immediately so demonstrative that Molly fancied that her eager, foolish pantomimic motions must absorb all his attention.

"I call this so attentive of him," said Mrs. Gibson, in the midst of a volley of kisses of her hand. "Really it is quite romantic. It reminds me of former days—but he will be too late! I must send him away; it is half-past twelve!" And she took out her watch and held it up, tapping it with her forefinger, and occupying the very centre of the window. Molly could only peep here and there, dodging now up, now down, now on this side, now on that of the perpetually moving arms. She fancied she saw something of a corresponding movement on Roger's part. At length he went away slowly, slowly, and often looking back, in spite of the tapped watch. Mrs. Gibson at last retreated, and Molly quietly moved into her place to see his figure once more before the turn of the road hid it from her view. He, too, knew where the last glimpse of Mr. Gibson's house was to be obtained, and once more he turned, and his white handkerchief floated in the air. Molly waved hers high up, with eager longing that it should be seen. And then, he was gone! and Molly returned to her worsted-work, happy, glowing, sad, content, and thinking to herself how sweet is friendship!

When she came to a sense of the present, Mrs. Gibson was saying:

"Upon my word, though Roger Hamley has never been a great favourite of mine, this little attention of his has reminded me very forcibly of a very charming young man—a *soupirant*, as the French would call him—Lieutenant Harper—you must have heard me speak of him, Molly?"

"I think I have!" said Molly absently.

"Well, you remember how devoted he was to me when I was at Mrs. Duncombe's, my first situation, and I only seventeen. And when the recruiting party was ordered to another town, poor Mr. Harper came and stood opposite the schoolroom window for nearly an hour, and I know it was his doing that the band played 'The girl I left behind me,' when they marched out the next day. Poor Mr. Harper! It was before I knew dear Mr.

Kirkpatrick! Dear me. How often my poor heart has had to bleed in this life of mine! not but what dear papa is a very worthy man, and makes me very happy. He would spoil me, indeed, if I would let him. Still, he is not as rich as Mr. Henderson."

That last sentence contained the germ of Mrs. Gibson's present grievance. Having married Cynthia, as her mother put it—taking credit to herself as if she had had the principal part in the achievement—she now became a little envious of her daughter's good fortune in being the wife of a young, handsome, rich, and moderately fashionable man, who lived in London. She naïvely expressed her feelings on this subject to her husband one day when she was really not feeling quite well, and when consequently her annoyances were much more present to her mind than her sources of happiness.

"It is such a pity!" said she, "that I was born when I was. I should so have liked to belong to this generation."

"That's sometimes my own feeling," said he. "So many new views seem to be opened in science, that I should like, if it were possible, to live till their reality was ascertained, and one saw what they led to. But I don't suppose that's your reason, my dear, for wishing to be twenty or thirty years younger."

"No, indeed. And I did not put it in that hard, unpleasant way; I only said I should like to belong to this generation. To tell the truth, I was thinking of Cynthia. Without vanity, I believe I was as pretty as she is—when I was a girl, I mean; I had not her dark eyelashes, but then my nose was straighter. And now look at the difference! I have to live in a little country town with three servants, and no carriage; and she with her inferior good looks will live in Sussex Place, and keep a man and a brougham, and I don't know what. But the fact is, in this generation there are so many more rich young men than there were when I was a girl."

"Oh, oh! so that's your reason, is it, my dear? If you had been young now you might have married somebody as well off as Walter?"

"Yes!" said she. "I think that was my idea. Of course, I should have liked him to be you. I always think if you had gone to the Bar you might have succeeded better, and lived in London, too. I don't think Cynthia cares much where she lives, yet you see it has come to her."

"What has—London?"

"Oh, you dear, facetious man. Now that's just the thing to have captivated a jury. I don't believe Walter will ever be so clever as you are. Yet he can take Cynthia to Paris, and abroad, and everywhere. I only hope all this indulgence won't develop the faults in Cynthia's character. It's a week since we heard from her, and I did write so particularly to ask her for the autumn fashions before I bought my new bonnet. But riches are a great snare."

"Be thankful you are spared temptation, my dear."

"No, I'm not. Everybody likes to be tempted. And, after all, it's very easy to resist temptation, if one wishes."

"I don't find it so easy," said her husband.

"Here's medicine for you, mamma," said Molly, entering with a letter held up in her hand. "A letter from Cynthia."

"Oh, you dear little messenger of good news! There was one of the heathen deities in Mangnall's Questions whose office it was to bring news. The letter is dated from Calais. They're coming home! She's bought me a shawl and a bonnet! The dear creature! Always thinking of others before herself: good fortune cannot spoil her. They've a fortnight left of their holiday! Their house is not quite ready; they're coming here. Oh, now, Mr. Gibson, we must have the new dinner-service at Watt's I've set my heart on so long! 'Home' Cynthia calls this house. I'm sure it has been a home to her, poor darling! I doubt if there is another man in the world who would have treated his step-daughter like dear papa! And, Molly, you must have a new gown."

"Come, come! Remember I belong to the last generation," said Mr. Gibson.

"And Cynthia won't mind what I wear," said Molly, bright with pleasure at the thought of seeing her again.

"No! but Walter will. He has such a quick eye for dress, and I think I rival papa; if he is a good stepfather, I'm a good stepmother, and I could not bear to see my Molly shabby, and not looking her best. I must have a new gown too. It won't do to look as if we had nothing but the dresses which we wore at the wedding!"

But Molly stood out against the new gown for herself, and urged that if Cynthia and Walter were to come to visit them often, they had better see them as they really were, in dress, habits, and appointments. When Mr. Gibson had left the room, Mrs. Gibson softly reproached Molly for her obstinacy.

"You might have allowed me to beg for a new gown for you, Molly, when you knew how much I admired that figured silk at Brown's the other day. And now, of course, I can't be so selfish as to get it for myself, and you to have nothing. You should learn to understand the wishes of other people. Still, on the whole, you are a dear, sweet girl, and I only wish—well, I know what I wish; only dear papa does not like it to be talked about. And now cover me up close, and let me go to sleep, and dream about my dear Cynthia and my new shawl!"

Cousin Phillis

From *Cousin Phillis*, first published as a serial in the *Cornhill Magazine* from November, 1863, to February, 1864, and afterwards issued in book form in 1865. This exquisite prose idyll represents Mrs. Gaskell's best work, and has been described as "a gem without a flaw"; as a short story it is certainly a model. The breath of the open country is ever around it. The places so graphically described are associated with Mrs. Gaskell's maternal grandfather's farm at Sandlebridge, near Knutsford.

A VISIT TO HOPE FARM

"MAKE up your mind, and go off and see what this farmer-minister is like, and come back and tell me—I should like to hear."...

I went along the lane, I recollect, switching at all the taller roadside weeds, till, after a turn or two, I found myself close in front of the Hope Farm. There was a garden between the house and the shady, grassy lane; I afterwards found that this garden was called the court; perhaps because there was a low wall round it, with an iron railing on the top of the wall, and two great gates between pillars crowned with stone balls for a state entrance to the flagged path leading up to the front door. It was not the habit of the place to go in either by these great gates or by the front door; the gates, indeed, were locked, as I found, though the door stood wide open. I had to go round by a side-path lightly worn on a broad grassy way, which led past the court-wall, past a horse-mount, half covered with stonecrop and a little wild yellow fumitory, to another door—"the curate," as I found it was termed by the master of the house, while the front door, "handsome and all for show," was termed the "rector." I knocked with my hand upon the "curate" door; a tall girl, about my own age, as I thought, came and opened it, and stood there silent, waiting to know my errand. I see her now—Cousin Phillis. The westering sun shone full upon her, and made a slanting stream of light into the room within. She was dressed in dark blue cotton of some kind; up to her throat, down to her wrists, with a little frill of the same wherever it touched her white skin. And such a white skin as it was! I have never seen the like. She had light hair, nearer yellow than any other colour. She looked me steadily in the face with large, quiet eyes, wondering, but untroubled by the sight of a stranger. I thought it odd, that so old, so full-grown as she was, she should wear a pinafore over her gown.

Before I had quite made up my mind what to say in reply to her mute inquiry of what I wanted there, a woman's voice called out, "Who is it, Phillis? If it is anyone for butter-milk send them round to the back door."

I thought I could rather speak to the owner of that voice than to the girl before me; so I passed her, and stood at the entrance of a room, hat in hand, for this side-door opened straight into the hall or house-place where the family sate when work was done. There was a brisk little woman of forty or so ironing some huge muslin cravats under the light of a long vine-shaded casement window. She looked at me distrustfully till I began to speak. "My name is Paul Manning," said I; but I saw she did not know the name. "My mother's name was Moneypenny," said I—"Margaret Moneypenny."

"And she married one John Manning, of Birmingham," said Mrs. Holman eagerly. "And you'll be her son. Sit down! I am right glad to see you. To think of your being Margaret's son! Why, she was almost a child not so long ago. Well, to be sure, it is five-and-twenty years ago. And what brings you into these parts?"

She sate herself down, as if oppressed by her curiosity as to all the five-and-twenty years that had passed since she had seen my mother. Her daughter Phillis took up her knitting—a man's long grey worsted stocking, I remember—and knitted away without looking at her work. I felt that the steady gaze of those deep grey eyes was upon me, though once, when I stealthily raised mine to hers, she was examining something on the wall above my head.

When I had answered all my cousin Holman's questions, she heaved a long breath, and said, "To think of Margaret Moneypenny's boy being in our house! I wish the minister was here. Phillis, in what field is thy father to-day?"

"In the five-acre; they are beginning to cut the corn."

"He'll not like being sent for then, else I should have liked you to have seen the minister. But the five-acre is a good step off. You shall have a glass of wine and a bit of cake before you stir from this house, though. You're bound to go, you say, or else the minister comes in mostly when the men have their four o'clock."

"I must go—I ought to have been off before now."

"Here, then, Phillis, take the keys." She gave her daughter some whispered directions, and Phillis left the room.

"She is my cousin, is she not?" I asked. I knew she was, but somehow I wanted to talk of her, and did not know how to begin.

"Yes—Phillis Holman. She is our only child—now."

Either from that "now," or from a strange momentary wistfulness in her eyes, I knew that there had been more children, who were now dead.

"How old is Cousin Phillis?" said I, scarcely venturing on the new name, it seemed too prettily familiar for me to call her by it; but Cousin Holman took no notice of it, answering straight to the purpose.

"Seventeen last May-Day; but the minister does not like to hear me calling it May-Day," said she, checking herself with a little awe. "Phillis was seventeen on the first day of May last," she repeated in an emended edition.

"And I am nineteen in another month," thought I to myself; I don't know why.

Then Phillis came in, carrying a tray with wine and cake upon it.

"We keep a house-servant," said Cousin Holman, "but it is churning day, and she is busy." It was meant as a little proud apology for her daughter's being the handmaiden.

"I like doing it, mother," said Phillis, in her grave, full voice.

I felt as if I were somebody in the Old Testament—who, I could not recollect—being served and waited upon by the daughter of the host. Was I like Abraham's steward, when Rebekah gave him to drink at the well? I thought Isaac had not gone the pleasantest way to work in winning him a wife. But Phillis never thought about such things. She was a stately, gracious young woman, in the dress and with the simplicity of a child.

As I had been taught, I drank to the health of my new-found cousin and her husband; and then I ventured to name my Cousin Phillis with a little bow of my head towards her; but I was too awkward to look and see how she took my compliment. "I must go now," said I, rising.

The Dawn of Love

From *Cousin Phillis*, 1865

"HE had never spoken much about you before, but the sudden going away unlocked his heart, and he told me how he loved you, and how he hoped on his return that you might be his wife."

"Don't," said she, almost gasping out the word, which she had tried once or twice before to speak; but her voice had been choked. Now she put her hand backwards; she had quite turned away from me, and felt for mine. She gave it a soft lingering pressure; and then she put her arms down on the wooden division, and laid her head on it, and cried quiet tears. I did not understand her at once, and feared lest I had mistaken the whole case, and only annoyed her. I went up to her. "Oh, Phillis, I am so sorry—I thought you would, perhaps, have cared to hear it; he did talk so feelingly, as if he did love you so much, and somehow I thought it would give you pleasure."

She lifted up her head and looked at me. Such a look! Her eyes, glittering with tears as they were, expressed an almost heavenly happiness; her tender mouth was curved with rapture—her colour vivid and blushing; but as if she was afraid her face expressed too much, more than the thankfulness to me she was essaying to speak, she hid it again almost immediately. So it was all right then, and my conjecture was well-founded. I tried to remember something more to tell her of what he had said, but again she stopped me.

"Don't," she said. She still kept her face covered and hidden. In half a minute she added, in a very low voice, "Please, Paul, I think I would rather not hear any more—I don't mean but what I have—but what I am very much obliged—only—only, I think I would rather hear the rest from himself when he comes back."

And then she cried a little more, in quite a different way. I did not say any more, I waited for her. By-and-by she turned towards me—not meeting my eyes, however; and putting her hand in mine just as if we were two children, she said, "We had best go back now—I don't look as if I had been crying, do I?"

"You look as if you had a bad cold," was all the answer I made.

"Oh! but I am—I am quite well, only cold; and a good run will warm me. Come along, Paul."

So we ran, hand in hand, till, just as we were on the threshold of the house, she stopped:

"Paul, please, we won't speak about *that* again."

I never saw her so lovely, or so happy. I think she hardly knew why she was so happy all the time. I can see her now, standing under the budding branches of the grey trees, over which a tinge of green seemed to be deepening day after day, her sunbonnet fallen back on her neck, her hands full of delicate wood-flowers, quite unconscious of my gaze, but intent on sweet mockery of some bird in neighbouring bush or tree. She had the art of warbling, and replying to the notes of different birds, and knew their song, their habits and ways, more accurately than anyone else I ever knew. She had often done it at my request the spring before; but this year she really gurgled, and whistled, and warbled just as they did, out of the very fulness and joy of her heart. She was more than ever the very apple of her father's eye; her mother gave her both her own share of love and that of the dead child, who had died in infancy. I have heard Cousin Holman murmur, after a long dreamy look at Phillis, and tell herself how like she was growing to Johnnie, and soothe herself with plaintive, inarticulate sounds, and many gentle shakes of the head, for the aching sense of loss she would never get over in this world. The old servants about the place had the dumb loyal attachment to the child of the land common to most agricultural labourers; not often stirred into activity or expression. My Cousin Phillis was like a rose that had come to full bloom on the sunny side of a lonely house, sheltered from storms. I have read in some book of poetry:

"A maid whom there were none to praise,

And very few to love."

And somehow those lines always remind me of Phillis; yet they were not true of her either. I never heard her praised; and out of her own household there were very few to love her; but though no one spoke out their appreciation, she always did right in her parents' eyes, out of her natural simple goodness and wisdom.

III
Stories

The only biography which Mrs. Gaskell wrote was *The Life of Charlotte Brontë*, which is one of the best biographies ever written. It has now become a classic. At the time of her death, in 1865, Mrs. Gaskell was collecting material for a Life of Madame Sévigné.

Mrs. Gaskell has written very little that is autobiographical. She always studied to keep herself in the background, though her stories contain much that is based on her own life.

Autobiographical

Mary Barton

Preface to the Original Edition of 1848

THREE years ago I became anxious (from circumstances that need not be more fully alluded to) to employ myself in writing a work of fiction. Living in Manchester, but with a deep relish and fond admiration for the country, my first thought was to find a framework for my story in some rural scene; and I had already made a little progress in a tale, the period of which was more than a century ago, and the place on the borders of Yorkshire, when I bethought me how deep might be the romance in the lives of some of those who elbowed me daily in the busy streets of the town in which I resided. I had always felt a deep sympathy with the care-worn men, who looked as if doomed to struggle through their lives in strange alternations between work and want; tossed to and fro by circumstances, apparently in even a greater degree than other men. A little manifestation of this sympathy, and a little attention to the expression of feelings on the part of some of the workpeople with whom I was acquainted had laid open to me the hearts of one or two of the more thoughtful among them; I saw that they were sore and irritable against the rich, the even tenor of whose seemingly happy lives appeared to increase the anguish caused by the lottery-like nature of their own. Whether the bitter complaints made by them of the neglect which they experienced from the prosperous—especially from the masters, whose fortunes they had helped to build up—were well-founded or no, it is not for me to judge. It is enough to say, that this belief of the injustice and unkindness which they endure from their fellow-creatures taints what might be resignation to God's will, and turns it to revenge in many of the poor uneducated factory-workers of Manchester.

The more I reflected on this unhappy state of things between those so bound to each other by common interests, as the employers and employed must ever be, the more anxious I became to give some utterance to the agony which, from time to time, convulses this dumb people; the agony of suffering without the sympathy of the happy, or of erroneously believing that such is the case. If it be an error that the woes, which come with ever-returning tide-like flood to overwhelm the workmen in our manufacturing towns, pass unregarded by all but the sufferers, it is at any rate an error so bitter in its consequences to all parties, that whatever public effort can do in the way of merciful deeds, or helpless love in the way of "widow's mites" could do, should be done, and that speedily, to disabuse the work-people of so miserable a misapprehension. At present they seem to me to be left in a state, wherein lamentations and tears are thrown aside as useless, but in which the lips are compressed for curses, and the hands clenched and ready to smite.

I know nothing of Political Economy, or the theories of trade. I have tried to write truthfully; and if my accounts agree or clash with any system, the agreement or disagreement is unintentional.

To myself the idea which I have formed of the state of feeling among too many of the factory-people in Manchester, and which I endeavoured to represent in this tale (completed above a year ago), has received some confirmation from the events which have so recently occurred among a similar class on the Continent.

October, 1848.

Edinburgh Society in 1830

From *Round the Sofa*, 1859

Mrs. Gaskell spent a winter in Edinburgh in 1830-31, and she has woven some of her recollections in *Round the Sofa*. The Mr. Sperano mentioned was probably Agostino Ruffini, a friend of Mazzini's, though he went as an exile to Edinburgh at a later period.

AFTER we had been about a fortnight in Edinburgh Mr. Dawson said, in a sort of half-doubtful manner to Miss Duncan:

"My sister bids me say, that every Monday evening a few friends come in to sit round her sofa for an hour or so—some before going to gayer parties—and that if you and Miss Greatorex would like a little change, she would only be too glad to see you. Any time from seven to eight to-night; and I must add my injunctions, both for her sake and for that of my little patient's, here, that you leave at nine o'clock. After all, I do not know if you will care to come; but Margaret bade me ask you," and he glanced up suspiciously and sharply at us. If either of us had felt the slightest reluctance, however well disguised by manner, to accept this invitation, I am sure he would have at once detected our feelings, and withdrawn it, so jealous and chary was he of anything pertaining to the appreciation of this beloved sister.

But, if it had been to spend an evening at the dentist's, I believe I should have welcomed the invitation, so weary was I of the monotony of the nights in our lodgings; and as for Miss Duncan, an invitation to tea was of itself a pure and unmixed honour, and one to be accepted with all becoming form and gratitude; so Mr. Dawson's sharp glances over his spectacles failed to detect anything but the truest pleasure, and he went on:

"You'll find it very dull, I dare say. Only a few old fogies like myself, and one or two good, sweet young women; I never know who'll come. Margaret is obliged to lie in a darkened room—only half lighted, I mean—because her eyes are weak—oh, it will be very stupid, I dare say; don't thank me till you've been once and tried it, and then if you like it, your best thanks will be, to come again every Monday, from half-past seven to nine, you know. Good-bye, good-bye."

Hitherto I had never been out to a party of grown-up people; and no court-ball to a London young lady could seem more redolent of honour and pleasure than this Monday evening to me.

Dressed out in new stiff book-muslin, made up to my throat—a frock which had seemed to me and my sisters the height of earthly grandeur and finery— Alice, our old nurse, had been making it at home, in contemplation of the possibility of such an event during my stay in Edinburgh, but which had then appeared to me a robe too lovely and angelic to be ever worn short of heaven—I went with Miss Duncan to Mr. Dawson's at the appointed time. We entered through one small lofty room—perhaps I ought to call it an ante-chamber, for the house was old-fashioned, and stately and grand—the large square drawing-room, into the centre of which Mrs. Dawson's sofa was drawn. Behind her a little was placed a table with a great cluster candlestick upon it, bearing seven or eight wax-lights; and that was all the light in the room, which looked to me very vast and indistinct after our pinched-up apartment at the Mackenzies'. Mrs. Dawson must have been sixty; and yet her face looked very soft and smooth and childlike. Her hair was quite grey; it would have looked white but for the snowiness of her cap, and satin ribbon. She was wrapped in a kind of dressing-gown of French grey merino. The furniture of the room was deep rose-colour, and white and gold; the paper which covered the walls was Indian, beginning low down with a profusion of tropical leaves and birds and insects, and gradually diminishing in richness of detail, till at the top it ended in the most delicate tendrils and most filmy insects.

Mr. Dawson had acquired much riches in his profession, and his house gave one this impression. In the corners of the rooms were great jars of Eastern china, filled with flower leaves and spices; and in the middle of all this was placed the sofa, on which poor Margaret Dawson passed whole days, and months, and years, without the power of moving by herself. By-and-by Mrs. Dawson's maid brought in tea and macaroons for us, and a little cup of milk and water and a biscuit for her. Then the door opened. We had come very early, and in came Edinburgh professors, Edinburgh beauties, and celebrities, all on their way to some other gayer and later party, but coming first to see Mrs. Dawson, and tell her their *bons-mots*, or their interests, or their plans. By each learned man, by each lovely girl, she was treated as a dear friend, who knew something more about their own individual selves, independent of their reputation and general society-character, than anyone else.

It was very brilliant and very dazzling, and gave enough to think about and wonder about for many days.

Monday after Monday we went, stationary, silent; what could we find to say to anyone but Mrs. Margaret herself? Winter passed, summer was coming.

People began to drop off from Edinburgh, only a few were left, and I am not sure if our Monday evenings were not all the pleasanter.

There was Mr. Sperano, the Italian exile, banished even from France, where he had long resided, and now teaching Italian with meek diligence in the northern city; there was Mr. Preston, the Westmorland squire, or, as he preferred to be called, statesman, whose wife had come to Edinburgh for the education of their numerous family, and who, whenever her husband had come over on one of his occasional visits, was only too glad to accompany him to Mrs. Dawson's Monday evenings, he and the invalid lady having been friends from long ago. These and ourselves kept steady visitors, and enjoyed ourselves all the more from having the more of Mrs. Dawson's society.

Cumberland Sheep-shearers

From *Household Words*, 1853

A graphic account of a visit which Mr. and Mrs. Gaskell and their daughters made to the sheep-shearing at a Westmorland farm near Keswick. The article aroused much interest among the readers of *Household Words*. John Forster, writing to Dickens, asked "who the deuce had written the delightful article on sheep-shearing?"

THREE or four years ago we spent part of a summer in one of the dales in the neighbourhood of Keswick. We lodged at the house of a small Statesman, who added to his occupation of a sheep-farmer that of a woollen manufacturer. His own flock was not large, but he bought up other people's fleeces, either on commission, or for his own purposes; and his life seemed to unite many pleasant and various modes of employment, and the great jolly, burly man throve upon all, both in body and mind.

One day his handsome wife proposed to us that we should accompany her to a distant sheep-shearing, to be held at the house of one of her husband's customers, where she was sure we should be heartily welcome, and where we should see an old-fashioned shearing, such as was not often met with now in the Dales. I don't know why it was, but we were lazy, and declined her invitation. It might be that the day was a broiling one, even for July, or it might be a fit of shyness; but, whichever was the reason, it very unaccountably vanished soon after she was gone, and the opportunity seemed to have slipped through our fingers. The day was hotter than ever; and we should have twice as much reason to be shy and self-conscious, now that we should not have our hostess to introduce and chaperone us. However, so great was our wish to go that we blew these obstacles to the winds, if there were any that day; and, obtaining the requisite directions from the farm-servant, we set out on our five-mile walk, about one o'clock on a cloudless day in the first half of July.

Our party consisted of two grown-up persons and four children, the youngest almost a baby, who had to be carried the greater part of that weary length of way. We passed through Keswick, and saw the groups of sketching, boating tourists, on whom we, as residents for a month in the neighbourhood, looked down with some contempt as mere strangers, who were sure to go about blundering, or losing their way, or being imposed upon by guides, or admiring the wrong things, and never seeing the right things. After we had dragged ourselves through the long straggling town, we came to a part of the highway where it wound between copses sufficiently high to make a "green thought in a green shade"; the branches touched and interlaced overhead, while the road was so straight that all the quarter of an hour that we were walking we could see the opening of blue light at the other end, and note the quivering of the heated, luminous air beyond the dense shade in which we moved. Every now and then, we caught glimpses of the silver lake that shimmered through the trees; and, now and then, in the dead noontide stillness, we could hear the gentle lapping of the water on the pebbled shore—the only sound we heard, except the low, deep hum of myriads of insects revelling out their summer lives. We had all agreed that talking made us hotter, so we and the birds were very silent. Out again into the hot, bright, sunny, dazzling road, the fierce sun above our heads made us long to be at home; but we had passed the half-way, and to go on was shorter than to return. Now we left the highway, and began to mount. The ascent looked disheartening, but at almost every step we gained increased freshness of air; and the crisp, short mountain-grass was soft and cool in comparison with the high-road. The little wandering breezes, that came every now and then athwart us, were laden with fragrant scents—now of wild thyme—now of the little scrambling, creeping white rose, which ran along the ground and pricked our feet with its sharp thorns; and now we came to a trickling streamlet, on whose spongy banks grew great bushes of the bog-myrtle, giving a spicy odour to the air. When our breath failed us during that steep ascent, we had one invariable dodge by which we hoped to escape the "fat and scant of breath" quotation; we turned round and admired the lovely views, which from each succeeding elevation became more and more beautiful.

At last, perched on a level which seemed nothing more than a mere shelf of rock, we saw our destined haven—a grey stone farm-house, high over our heads, high above the lake as we were—with out-buildings enough around it to justify the Scotch name of a "town"; and near it one of those great bossy sycamores, so common in similar situations all through Cumberland and Westmorland. One more long tug, and then we should be there. So, cheering the poor tired little ones, we set off bravely for that last piece of steep rocky path; and we never looked behind till we stood in the coolness of the deep porch, looking down from our natural terrace on the glassy Derwentwater, far, far below, reflecting each tint of the blue sky, only in darker, fuller colours every one. We seemed on a level with the top of Catbells; and the tops of great trees lay deep down—so deep that we felt as if they were close enough together and solid enough to bear our feet if we chose to spring down and walk upon them. Right in front of where we stood there was a ledge of the rocky field that surrounded the house. We had knocked at the door, but it was evident that we were unheard in the din and merry clatter of voices within, and our old original shyness returned. By-and-by someone found us out, and a hearty burst of hospitable welcome ensued. Our coming was all right; it was understood in a minute who we were; our real hostess was hardly less urgent in her civilities than our temporary hostess, and both together bustled out of the room upon which the outer door entered, into a large bedroom which opened out of it—the state apartment, in all such houses in Cumberland—where the children make their first appearance and where the heads of the household lie down to die if the Great Conqueror gives them sufficient warning for such decent and composed submission as is best in accordance with the simple dignity of their lives.

Into this chamber we were ushered, and the immediate relief from its dark coolness to our over-heated bodies and dazzled eyes was inexpressibly refreshing. The walls were so thick that there was room for a very comfortable window-seat in them, without there being any projection into the room; and the long, low shape prevented the skyline from being unusually depressed, even at that height; and so the light was subdued, and the general tint through the room deepened into darkness, where the eye fell on that stupendous bed, with its posts, and its head-piece, and its footboard, and its trappings of all kinds of the deepest brown; and the frame itself looked large enough for six or seven people to lie comfortably therein, without even touching each other. In the hearth-place stood a great pitcher filled with branches of odorous mountain flowers; and little bits of rosemary and lavender were strewed about the room, partly, as I afterwards learnt, to prevent incautious feet from slipping about on the polished oak floor. When we had noticed everything, and rested, and cooled (as much as we could do before the equinox), we returned to the company assembled in the house-place.

This house-place was almost a hall of grandeur. Along one side ran an oaken dresser, all decked with the same sweet evergreens, fragments of which strewed the bedroom floor. Over this dresser were shelves, bright with most exquisitely polished pewter. Opposite to the bedroom door was the great hospitable fireplace, ensconced within its proper chimney corners, and having the "master's cupboard" on its right-hand side. Do you know what a "master's cupboard" is? Mr. Wordsworth could have told you; ay, and have shown you one at Rydal Mount, too. It is a cupboard about a foot in width, and a foot and a half in breadth, expressly reserved for the use of the master of the household. Here he may keep pipe and tankard, almanac and what not; and although no door bars the access of any hand, in this open cupboard his peculiar properties rest secure, for is it not "the master's cupboard"? There was a fire in the house-place, even on this hot day; it gave a grace and a vividness to the room, and being kept within proper limits, it seemed no more than was requisite to boil the kettle. For, I should say, that the very minute of our arrival our hostess (so I shall designate the wife of the farmer at whose house the sheep-shearing was to be held) proposed tea; and although we had not dined, for it was but little past three, yet, on the principle of "Do at Rome as the Romans do," we assented with a good grace, thankful to have any refreshment offered us, short of water-gruel, after our long and tiring walk, and rather afraid of our children "cooling too quickly."

While the tea was preparing, and it took six comely matrons to do it justice, we proposed to Mrs. C. (our real hostess) that we should go and see the sheep-shearing. She accordingly led us away into a back yard, where the process was going on. By a back yard I mean a far different place from what a Londoner would so designate; our back yard, high up on the mountainside, was a space about forty yards by twenty, overshadowed by the noble sycamore, which might have been the very one that suggested to Coleridge:

"This sycamore (oft musical with bees—
Such tents the Patriarchs loved)," etc., etc.

At the gate by which this field was entered from the yard stood a group of eager-eyed boys, panting like the sheep, but not like them from fear, but from excitement and joyous exertion. Their faces were flushed with brown-crimson, their scarlet lips were parted into smiles, and their eyes had that peculiar blue lustre in them, which is only gained by a free life in the pure and blithesome air. As soon as these lads saw that a sheep was wanted by the shearers within, they sprang towards one in the field—the more boisterous and stubborn an old ram the better—and tugging and pulling and pushing and shouting—sometimes mounted astride of the poor obstreperous brute, and holding his horns like a bridle—they gained their point, and dragged their captive up to the shearer, like little victors as they were, all glowing and ruddy with conquest. The shearers sat each astride on a long bench, grave and important—the heroes of the day. The flock of sheep to be shorn on this occasion consisted of more than a thousand, and eleven famous shearers had come, walking in from many miles' distance to try their skill, one against the other; for sheep-shearings are a sort of rural Olympics. They were all young men in their prime, strong, and well made; without coat or waistcoat, and with upturned shirt-sleeves. They sat each across a long bench or narrow table, and caught up the sheep from the attendant boys who had dragged it in; they lifted it on to the bench, and placing it by a dexterous knack on its back, they began to shear the wool off the tail and under parts; then they tied the two hind-legs and the two fore-legs together, and laid it first on one side and then on the other, till the fleece came off in one whole piece; the art was to shear all the wool off, and yet not to injure the sheep by any awkward cut; if any such an accident did occur, a mixture of tar and butter was immediately applied; but every wound was a blemish on the shearer's fame. To shear well and completely, and yet do it quickly, shows the perfection of the clippers. Some can finish off as many as six score sheep in a summer's day; and if you consider the weight and uncouthness of the animal, and the general heat of the weather, you will see that, with justice, clipping or shearing is regarded as harder work than mowing. But most shearers are content with despatching four or five score; it is only on unusual occasions, or when Greek meets Greek, that six score are attempted or accomplished.

When the sheep is divided into its fleece and itself, it becomes the property of two persons. The women seize the fleece, and, standing by the side of a temporary dresser (in this case made of planks laid across barrels, beneath which sharp scant shadow could be obtained from the eaves of the house), they fold it up. This, again, is an art, simple as it may seem; and the farmers' wives and daughters about Langdale Head are famous for it. They begin with folding up the legs, and then roll the whole fleece up, tying it with the neck; and the skill consists, not merely in doing this quickly and firmly, but in certain artistic pulls of the wool so as to display the finer parts, and not, by crushing up the fibre, to make it appear coarse to the buyer. Six comely women were thus employed; they laughed, and talked, and sent shafts of merry satire at the grave and busy shearers, who were too earnest in their work to reply, although an occasional deepening of colour, or twinkle of the eye, would tell that the remark had hit. But they reserved their retorts, if they had any, until the evening, when the day's labour would be over, and when, in the licence of country humour, I imagine, some of the saucy speakers would meet with their match. As yet, the applause came from their own party of women; though now and then one of the old men, sitting under the shade of a sycamore, would take his pipe out of his mouth to spit, and, before beginning again to send up the softly curling white wreaths of smoke, he would condescend on a short, deep laugh and a "Well done, Maggie!" "Give it him, lass!" for, with the not unkindly jealousy of age towards youth, the old grandfathers invariably took part with the women against the young men. These sheared on, throwing the fleeces to the folders, and casting the sheep down on the ground with gentle strength, ready for another troop of boys to haul it to the right-hand side of the farmyard, where the great outbuildings were placed; where all sorts of country vehicles were crammed and piled, and seemed to throw up their scarlet shafts into the air, as if imploring relief from the crowd of shandries and market carts that pressed upon them. Out of the sun, in the dark shadow of a cart-house, a pan of red-hot coals glowed in a trivet; and upon them was placed an iron basin holding tar and raddle, or ruddle. Hither the right-hand troop of boys dragged the poor naked sheep to be "smitten"—that is to say, marked with the initials or cypher of the owner. In this case the sign of the possessor was a circle or spot on one side, and a straight line on the other; and, after the sheep were thus marked, they were turned out to the moor, amid the crowd of bleating lambs that sent up an incessant moan for their lost mothers; each found out the ewe to which it belonged the moment she was turned out of the yard, and the placid contentment of the sheep that wandered away up the hill-side, with their little lambs trotting by them, gave just the necessary touch of peace and repose to the scene. There were all the classical elements for the representation of life: there were the "old men and maidens, young men and children" of the Psalmist; there were all the stages and conditions of being that sing forth their farewell to the departing crusaders in the "Saint's Tragedy."

We were very glad indeed that we had seen the sheep-shearing, though the road had been hot, and long, and dusty, and we were as yet unrefreshed and hungry.

My French Master

From *Household Words*, 1853

WE seemed to have our French lessons more frequently in the garden than in the house; for there was a sort of arbour on the lawn near the drawing-room window, to which we always found it easy to carry a table and chairs, and all the rest of the lesson paraphernalia, if my mother did not prohibit a lesson *al-fresco*.

M. de Chalabre wore, as a sort of morning costume, a coat, waistcoat, and breeches, all made of the same kind of coarse grey cloth, which he had bought in the neighbourhood. His three-cornered hat was brushed to a nicety, his wig sat as no one else's did. (My father's was always awry.) And the only thing wanted to his costume when he came was a flower. Sometimes I fancied he purposely omitted gathering one of the roses that clustered up the farm-house in which he lodged, in order to afford my mother the pleasure of culling her choicest carnations and roses to make him up his nosegay, or "posy," as he liked to call it. He had picked up that pretty country word, and adopted it as an especial favourite, dwelling on the first syllable with all the languid softness of an Italian accent. Many a time have Mary and I tried to say it like him, we did so admire his way of speaking.

Once seated round the table, whether in the house or out of it, we were bound to attend to our lessons; and somehow he made us perceive that it was a part of the same chivalrous code that made him so helpful to the helpless, to enforce the slightest claim of duty to the full. No half-prepared lessons for him! The patience and the resource with which he illustrated and enforced every precept; the untiring gentleness with which he made our stubborn English tongues pronounce, and mis-pronounce, and re-pronounce certain words; above all, the sweetness of temper which never varied, were such as I have never seen equalled. If we wondered at these qualities when we were children, how much greater has been our surprise at their existence since we have been grown up, and have learnt that, until his emigration, he was a man of rapid and impulsive action, with the imperfect education implied in the circumstance that at fifteen he was a sous-lieutenant in the Queen's regiment, and must, consequently, have had to apply himself hard and conscientiously to master the language which he had in after life to teach.

Twice we had holidays to suit his sad convenience. Holidays with us were not at Christmas, and Midsummer, Easter, and Michaelmas. If my mother was unusually busy, we had what we called a holiday, though in reality it involved harder work than our regular lessons; but we fetched, and carried, and ran errands, and became rosy, and dusty, and sang merry songs in the gaiety of our hearts. If the day was remarkably fine, my dear father—whose spirits were rather apt to vary with the weather—would come bursting in with his bright, kind, bronzed face, and carry the day by storm with my mother. "It was a shame to coop such young things up in a house," he would say, "when every other young animal was frolicking in the air and sunshine. Grammar!—what was that but the art of arranging words?—and he never knew a woman but could do that fast enough. Geography!—he would undertake to teach us more geography in one winter evening, telling us of the countries where he had been, with just a map before him, than we could learn in ten years with that stupid book, all full of hard words. As for the French—why, that must be learnt; for he should not like M. de Chalabre to think we slighted the lessons he took so much pains to give us; but surely we could get up the earlier to learn our French." We promised by acclamation; and my mother—sometimes smilingly, sometimes reluctantly—was always compelled to yield. And these were the usual occasions for our holidays.

It was the fashion in those days to keep children much less informed than they are now on the subjects which interest their parents. A sort of hieroglyphic or cipher talk was used in order to conceal the meaning of much that was said if children were present. My mother was proficient in this way of talking, and took, we fancied, a certain pleasure in perplexing my father by inventing a new cipher, as it were, every day. For instance, for some time I was called Martia, because I was very tall of my age; and, just as my father began to understand the name—and, it must be owned, a good while after I had learned to prick up my ears whenever Martia was named—my mother suddenly changed me into "the buttress," from the habit I had acquired of leaning my languid length against a wall. I saw my father's perplexity about this "buttress" for some days, and could have helped him out of it, but I durst not. And so, when the unfortunate Louis the Sixteenth was executed, the news was too terrible to be put into plain English, and too terrible also to be known to us children, nor could we at once find the clue to the cipher in which it was spoken about. We heard about "the Iris being blown down," and saw my father's honest, loyal excitement about it, and the quiet reserve which always betokened some secret grief on my mother's part.

We had no French lessons; and somehow the poor, battered, storm-torn Iris was to blame for this. It was many weeks after this before we knew the full reason of M. de Chalabre's deep depression when he again came amongst us; why he shook his head when my mother timidly offered him some snowdrops on that first morning on which he began lessons again; why he wore the deep mourning of that day, when all of the dress that could be black was black, and the white muslin frills and ruffles were unstarched and limp, as if to bespeak the very abandonment of grief. We knew well enough the meaning of the next hieroglyphic announcement, "The wicked, cruel boys had broken off the White Lily's head!" That beautiful queen, whose portrait once had been shown to us, with her blue eyes and her fair, resolute look, her profusion of lightly powdered hair, her white neck adorned with strings of pearls! We could have cried, if we had dared, when we heard the transparent, mysterious words. We did cry at night, sitting up in bed, with our arms round each other's necks, and vowing, in our weak, passionate, childish way, that if we lived long enough, that lady's death avenged should be. No one who cannot remember that time can tell the shudder of horror that thrilled through the country at hearing of this last execution. At the moment there was no time for any consideration of the silent horrors endured for centuries by the people, who at length rose in their madness against their rulers. This last blow changed our dear M. de Chalabre. I never saw him again in quite the same gaiety of heart as before this time. There seemed to be tears very close behind his smiles for ever after. My father went to see him when he had been about a week absent from us—no reason given, for did not we, did not everyone know the horror the sun had looked upon? As soon as my father had gone, my mother gave it in charge to us to make the dressing-room belonging to our guest-chamber as much like a sitting-room as possible. My father hoped to bring back M. de Chalabre for a visit to us; but he would probably like to be a good deal alone; and we might move any article of furniture we liked, if we only thought it would make him comfortable.

The Interchange of Novels between English and American Authors

From Introduction to Mabel Vaughan, 1857

IF it were not an Irish way of expressing myself, I should call prefaces in general, the author's supplement to his work; either explaining his reasons for writing it, or giving some additional matter, which could not be included, or else was forgotten in the book itself.

Now as I am not the author of the following story, I cannot give her reasons for writing it, nor add to what she has already said; nor can I even give my opinion of it, as by so doing I should have to reveal much of the plot in order to justify praise, or explain criticism.

Such alterations as might be required to render certain expressions clear to English readers the authoress has permitted me to make in the body of the work; some foot-notes I have appended explanatory of what were formerly to me mysterious customs and phrases; and, here and there, I have been tempted to make additions, always with the kindly granted permission of the authoress.

In conclusion, I may say a few words on the pleasant intercourse we English are having with our American relations, in the interchange of novels, which seems to be going on pretty constantly between the two countries. Our cousinly connection with the Americans dates from common ancestors, of whom we are both proud. To a certain period, every great name which England boasts is a direct subject of pride to the American; since the time when the race diverged into two different channels, we catch a reflex lustre from each other's great men. When we are stirred to our inmost depths by some passage or other in *Uncle Tom*, we say from all our hearts, "And I also am of the same race as this woman." When we hear of noble deeds—or generous actions; when Lady Franklin is helped in her woeful, faithful search by sympathising Americans; when the *Resolute* is brought home to our shores by the gallant American sailors, we hail the brave old Anglo-Saxon blood, and understand how they came to do it, as we instinctively comprehend a brother's motives for his actions, though he should speak never a word.

It is Anglo-Saxon descent which makes us both so undemonstrative, or perhaps I should rather say, so ready to express our little dissatisfaction with each other, while the deeper feelings (such as our love and confidence in each other) are unspoken. Though we do not talk much about these feelings we value every tie between us that can strengthen them; and not least amongst those come the links of a common literature. I may be thought too like the tanner in the old fable, who recommended leather as the best means of defence for a besieged city, but I am inclined to rank the exchange of novels between England and America as of more value, as conducive to a pleasant acquaintanceship with each other, than the exchange of works of a far higher intrinsic value. Through the means of works of fiction, we obtain glimpses into American home-life; of their modes of thought, their traditional observances, and their social temptations, quite beyond and apart from the observations of a traveller, who after all, only sees the family in the street, or on the festival days, not in the quiet domestic circle, into which the stranger is rarely admitted.

These American novels unconsciously reveal all the little household secrets; we see the meals as they are put upon the table, we learn the dresses which those who sit down in them wear (and what a temptress "Fashion" seems to be in certain cities to all manner of vulgar extravagance!); we hear their kindly family discourse, we enter into their home struggles, and we rejoice when they gain the victory. Now all this knowledge of what the Americans really are is good for us, as tending to strengthen our power of understanding them, and consequently to increase our sympathy with them. Let us trust that they learn something of the same truth from reading fiction written on this side of the Atlantic; the truth that, however different may be national manifestations of the fact, still, below accents, manners, dress, and language, we have

"All of us one human heart."

E. C. G.

Biographical
Description of Charlotte Brontë

From the Life of Charlotte Brontë

THIS is perhaps a fitting time to give some personal description of Miss Brontë. In 1831, she was a quiet, thoughtful girl, of nearly fifteen years of age, very small in figure—"stunted" was the word she applied to herself— but as her limbs and head were in just proportion to the slight, fragile body, no word in ever so slight a degree suggestive of deformity could properly be applied to her; with soft, thick, brown hair, and peculiar eyes, of which I find it difficult to give a description, as they appeared to me in her later life. They were large, and well-shaped; their colour a reddish brown; but if the iris was closely examined, it appeared to be composed of a great variety of tints. The usual expression was of quiet, listening intelligence; but now and then, on some just occasion for vivid interest or wholesome indignation, a light would shine out, as if some spiritual lamp had been kindled, which glowed behind those expressive orbs. I never saw the like in any other human creature. As for the rest of her features, they were plain, large, and ill set; but, unless you began to catalogue them, you were hardly aware of the fact, for the eyes and power of the countenance overbalanced every physical defect; the crooked mouth and the large nose were forgotten, and the whole face arrested the attention, and presently attracted all those whom she herself would have cared to attract. Her hands and feet were the smallest I ever saw; when one of the former was placed in mine, it was like the soft touch of a bird in the middle of my palm. The delicate long fingers had a peculiar fineness of sensation, which was one reason why all her handiwork, of whatever kind— writing, sewing, knitting—was so clear in its minuteness. She was remarkably neat in her whole personal attire; but she was dainty as to the fit of her shoes and gloves.

I can well imagine that the grave serious composure, which, when I knew her, gave her face the dignity of an old Venetian portrait, was no acquisition of later years, but dated from that early age when she found herself in the position of an elder sister to motherless children. But in a girl only just entered on her teens, such an expression would be called (to use a country phrase) "old-fashioned"; and in 1831, the period of which I now write, we must think of her as a little, set, antiquated girl, very quiet in manners, and very quaint in dress; for, besides the influence exerted by her father's ideas concerning the simplicity of attire befitting the wife and daughters of a country clergyman, her aunt, on whom the duty of dressing her nieces principally devolved, had never been in society since she left Penzance, eight or nine years before, and the Penzance fashions of that day were still dear to her heart.

Patrick Brontë's Views on the Management of his Children

From the *Life of Charlotte Brontë*

THE ideas of Rousseau and Mr. Day on education had filtered down through many classes, and spread themselves widely out. I imagine Mr. Brontë must have formed some of his opinions on the management of children from these two theorists. His practice was not half so wild or extraordinary as that to which an aunt of mine was subjected by a disciple of Mr. Day's. She had been taken by this gentleman and his wife to live with them as their adopted child, perhaps about five-and-twenty years before the time of which I am writing. They were wealthy people and kind-hearted, but her food and clothing were of the very simplest and rudest description, on Spartan principles. A healthy merry child, she did not much care for dress or eating; but the treatment which she felt as a real cruelty was this. They had a carriage, in which she and the favourite dog were taken an airing on alternate days; the creature whose turn it was to be left at home being tossed in a blanket—an operation which my aunt especially dreaded. Her affright at the tossing was probably the reason why it was persevered in. Dressed-up ghosts had become common, and she did not care for them, so the blanket exercise was to be the next mode of hardening her nerves. It is well known that Mr. Day broke off his intention of marrying Sabrina, the girl whom he had educated for this purpose, because, within a few weeks of the time fixed for the wedding, she was guilty of the frivolity, while on a visit from home, of wearing thin sleeves. Yet Mr. Day and my aunt's relations were benevolent people, only strongly imbued with the crotchet that by a system of training might be educed the hardihood and simplicity of the ideal savage, forgetting the terrible isolation of feelings and habits, which their pupils would experience, in the future life which they must pass among the corruptions and refinements of civilisation.

Mr. Brontë wished to make his children hardy, and indifferent to the pleasures of eating and dress. In the latter he succeeded, as far as regarded his daughters; but he went at his object with unsparing earnestness of purpose. Mrs. Brontë's nurse told me that one day when the children had been out on the moors, and rain had come on, she thought their feet would be wet, and accordingly she rummaged out some coloured boots which had been given to them by a friend—the Mr. Morgan, who married "Cousin Jane," she believes. These little pairs she ranged round the kitchen fire to warm; but, when the children came back, the boots were nowhere to be found; only a very strong odour of burnt leather was perceived. Mr. Brontë had come in and seen them; they were too gay and luxurious for his children, and would foster a love of dress; so he had put them into the fire. He spared nothing that offended his antique simplicity.

Visit to Charlotte Brontë at Haworth Vicarage

From the *Life of Charlotte Brontë*

HAWORTH is a long, straggling village: one steep narrow street—so steep that the flagstones with which it is paved are placed end-ways, that the horses' feet may have something to cling to, and not slip down backwards; which if they did, they would soon reach Keighley. But if the horses had cats' feet and claws, they would do all the better. Well, we (the man, horse, car, and I) clambered up this street, and reached the church dedicated to St. Autest (who was he?); then we turned off into a lane on the left, past the curate's lodging at the Sexton's, past the school-house, up to the Parsonage yard-door. I went round the house to the front door, looking to the church;—moors everywhere beyond and above. The crowded grave-yard surrounds the house and small grass enclosure for drying clothes.

I don't know that I ever saw a spot more exquisitely clean; the most dainty place for that I ever saw. To be sure, the life is like clock-work. No one comes to the house; nothing disturbs the deep repose; hardly a voice is heard; you catch the ticking of the clock in the kitchen, or the buzzing of a fly in the parlour, all over the house. Miss Brontë sits alone in her parlour; breakfasting with her father in his study at nine o'clock. She helps in the housework; for one of their servants, Tabby, is nearly ninety, and the other only a girl. Then I accompanied her in her walks on the sweeping moors: the heather-bloom had been blighted by a thunderstorm a day or two before, and was all of a livid brown colour, instead of the blaze of purple glory it ought to have been. Oh! those high, wild, desolate moors, up above the whole world, and the very realms of silence! Home to dinner at two. Mr. Brontë has his dinner sent in to him. All the small table arrangements had the same dainty simplicity about them. Then we rested, and talked over the clear, bright fire; it is a cold country, and the fires were a pretty warm dancing light all over the house. The parlour had been evidently furnished within the last few years, since Miss Brontë's success had enabled her to have a little more money to spend. Everything fits into, and is in harmony with, the idea of a country parsonage, possessed by people of very moderate means. The prevailing colour of the room is crimson, to make a warm setting for the cold grey landscape without. There is her likeness by Richmond, and an engraving from Lawrence's picture of Thackeray; and two recesses, on each side of the high, narrow, old-fashioned mantel-piece, filled with books—books given to her, books she has bought, and which tell of her individual pursuits and tastes; *not* standard books.

She cannot see well, and does little beside knitting. The way she weakened her eyesight was this: When she was sixteen or seventeen, she wanted much to draw; and she copied niminipimini copper-plate engravings out of annuals ("stippling," don't the artists call it?), every little point put in, till at the end of six months she had produced an exquisitely faithful copy of the engraving. She wanted to learn to express her ideas by drawing. After she had tried to *draw* stories, and not succeeded, she took the better mode of writing; but in so small a hand, that it is almost impossible to decipher what she wrote at this time.

But now to return to our quiet hour of rest after dinner. I soon observed that her habits of order were such that she could not go on with the conversation, if a chair was out of its place; everything was arranged with delicate regularity. We talked over the old times of her childhood; of her elder sister's (Maria's) death—just like that of Helen Burns in *Jane Eyre*; of those strange, starved days at school, of the desire (almost amounting to illness) of expressing herself in some way—writing or drawing; of her weakened eyesight, which prevented her doing anything for two years, from the age of seventeen to nineteen; of her being a governess; of her going to Brussels; whereupon I said I disliked Lucy Snowe, and we discussed M. Paul Emanuel; and I told her of —'s admiration of *Shirley*, which pleased her, for the character of Shirley was meant for her sister Emily, about whom she is never tired of talking, nor I of listening. Emily must have been a remnant of the Titans—great-granddaughter of the giants who used to inhabit earth. One day, Miss Brontë brought down a rough, common-looking oil-painting, done by her brother, of herself—a little rather prim-looking girl of eighteen—and the two other sisters, girls of sixteen and fourteen, with cropped hair, and sad, dreamy-looking eyes.... Emily had a great dog—half mastiff, half bull-dog—so savage, etc.... This dog went to her funeral, walking side by side with her father; and then, to the day of its death, it slept at her room door, snuffing under it, and whining every morning.

We have generally had another walk before tea, which is at six; at half-past eight, prayers; and by nine, all the household are in bed, except ourselves. We sit up together till ten, or past; and after I go, I hear Miss Brontë come down and walk up and down the room for an hour or so.

We went, not purposely, but accidentally, to see various poor people in our distant walks. From one we had borrowed an umbrella; in the house of another we had taken shelter from a rough September storm. In all these cottages, her quiet presence was known. At three miles from her home, the chair was dusted for her, with a kindly "Sit ye down, Miss Brontë"; and she knew what absent or ailing members of the family to inquire after. Her quiet, gentle words, few though they might be, were evidently grateful to those Yorkshire ears. Their welcome to her, though rough and curt, was sincere and hearty.

We talked about the different courses through which life ran. She said, in her own composed manner, as if she had accepted the theory as a fact, that she believed some were appointed beforehand to sorrow and much disappointment; that it did not fall to the lot of all—as Scripture told us—to have their lives fall in pleasant places; that it was well for those who had rougher paths, to perceive that such was God's will concerning them, and try to moderate their expectations, leaving hope to those of a different doom, and seeking patience and resignation as the virtues they were to cultivate. I took a different view: I thought that human lots were more equal than she imagined; that to some happiness and sorrow came in strong patches of light and shadow (so to speak), while in the lives of others they were pretty equally blended throughout. She smiled, and shook her head, and said she was trying to school herself against ever anticipating any pleasure; that it was better to be brave and submit faithfully; there was some good reason, which we should know in time, why sorrow and disappointment were to be the lot of some on earth. It was better to acknowledge this, and face out the truth in a religious faith.

On Reviewers

From the *Life of Charlotte Brontë*

AN author may bring himself to believe that he can bear blame with equanimity, from whatever quarter it comes; but its force is derived altogether from the character of this. To the public, one reviewer may be the same impersonal being as another; but an author has frequently a far deeper significance to attach to opinions. They are the verdicts of those whom he respects and admires, or the mere words of those for whose judgment he cares not a jot. It is this knowledge of the individual worth of the reviewer's opinion which makes the censures of some sink so deep, and prey so heavily upon an author's heart. And thus, in proportion to her true, firm regard for Miss Martineau, did Miss Brontë suffer under what she considered her misjudgment not merely of writing, but of character.

She had long before asked Miss Martineau to tell her whether she considered that any want of womanly delicacy or propriety was betrayed in *Jane Eyre*.

And on receiving Miss Martineau's assurance that she did not, Miss Brontë entreated her to declare it frankly if she thought there was any failure of this description in any future work of "Currer Bell's." The promise then given of faithful truth-speaking, Miss Martineau fulfilled when *Villette* appeared. Miss Brontë writhed under what she felt to be injustice.

This seems a fitting place to state how utterly unconscious she was of what was, by some, esteemed coarse in her writings. One day, during that visit at the Briery when I first met her, the conversation turned upon the subject of women's writing fiction; and someone remarked on the fact that, in certain instances, authoresses had much outstepped the line which men felt to be proper in works of this kind. Miss Brontë said she wondered how far this was a natural consequence of allowing the imagination to work too constantly; Sir James and Lady Kay Shuttleworth and I expressed our belief that such violations of propriety were altogether unconscious on the part of those to whom reference had been made. I remember her grave, earnest way of saying, "I trust God will take from me whatever power of invention or expression I may have, before He lets me become blind to the sense of what is fitting or unfitting to be said!"

Again, she was invariably shocked and distressed when she heard of any disapproval of *Jane Eyre* on the ground above-mentioned. Someone said to her in London, "You know, you and I, Miss Brontë, have both written naughty books!" She dwelt much on this; and, as if it weighed on her mind, took an opportunity to ask Mrs. Smith, as she would have asked a mother— if she had not been motherless from earliest childhood—whether, indeed, there was anything so wrong in *Jane Eyre*.

I do not deny for myself the existence of coarseness here and there in her works, otherwise so entirely noble. I only ask those who read them to consider her life—which has been openly laid bare before them—and to say how it could be otherwise. She saw few men; and among these few were one or two with whom she had been acquainted since early girlhood—who had shown her much friendliness and kindness—through whose family she had received many pleasures—for whose intellect she had a great respect—but who talked before her, if not to her, with as little reticence as Rochester talked to Jane Eyre. Take this in connection with her poor brother's sad life, and the outspoken people among whom she lived—remember her strong feeling of the duty of representing life as it really is, not as it ought to be—and then do her justice for all that she was, and all that she would have been (had God spared her), rather than censure her because her circumstances forced her to touch pitch, as it were, and by it her hand was for a moment defiled. It was but skin-deep. Every change in her life was purifying her; it hardly could raise her. Again I cry, "If she had but lived!"

A Proposal of Marriage

From the *Life of Charlotte Brontë*

THE difficulty that presented itself most strongly to me, when I first had the honour of being requested to write this biography, was how I could show what a noble, true, and tender woman Charlotte Brontë really was, without mingling up with her life too much of the personal history of her nearest and most intimate friends. After much consideration of this point, I came to the resolution of writing truly, if I wrote at all; of withholding nothing, though some things, from their very nature, could not be spoken of so fully as others.

One of the deepest interests of her life centres naturally round her marriage, and the preceding circumstances; but more than all other events (because of more recent date, and concerning another as intimately as herself), it requires delicate handling on my part, lest I intrude too roughly on what is most sacred to memory. Yet I have two reasons, which seem to me good and valid ones, for giving some particulars of the course of events which led to her few months of wedded life—that short spell of exceeding happiness. The first is my desire to call attention to the fact that Mr. Nicholls was one who had seen her almost daily for years; seen her as a daughter, a sister, a mistress and a friend. He was not a man to be attracted by any kind of literary fame. I imagine that this, by itself, would rather repel him when he saw it in the possession of a woman. He was a grave, reserved, conscientious man, with a deep sense of religion, and of his duties as one of its ministers.

In silence he had watched her, and loved her long. The love of such a man— a daily spectator of her manner of life for years—is a great testimony to her character as a woman.

How deep his affection was I scarcely dare to tell, even if I could in words. She did not know—she had hardly begun to suspect—that she was the object of any peculiar regard on his part, when, in this very December, he came one evening to tea. After tea she returned from the study to her own sitting-room, as was her custom, leaving her father and his curate together. Presently she heard the study door open, and expected to hear the succeeding clash of the front door. Instead, came a tap; and, "like lightning, it flashed upon me what was coming. He entered. He stood before me. What his words were you can imagine; his manner you can hardly realise, nor can I forget it. He made me, for the first time, feel what it costs a man to declare affection when he doubts response.... The spectacle of one, ordinarily so statue-like, thus trembling, stirred, and overcome, gave me a strange shock. I could only entreat him to leave me then, and promise a reply on the morrow. I asked if he had spoken to Papa. He said he dared not. I think I half led, half put him out of the room."

So deep, so fervent, and so enduring was the affection Miss Brontë had inspired in the heart of this good man! It is an honour to her; and, as such, I have thought it my duty to speak thus much, and quote thus fully from her letter about it. And now I pass to my second reason for dwelling on a subject which may possibly be considered by some, at first sight, of too private a nature for publication. When Mr. Nicholls had left her, Charlotte went immediately to her father and told him all. He always disapproved of marriages, and constantly talked against them. But he more than disapproved at this time; he could not bear the idea of this attachment of Mr. Nicholls to his daughter. Fearing the consequences of agitation to one so recently an invalid, she made haste to give her father a promise that, on the morrow, Mr. Nicholls should have a distinct refusal. Thus quietly and modestly did she, on whom such hard judgments had been passed by ignorant reviewers, receive this vehement, passionate declaration of love—thus thoughtfully for her father and unselfishly for herself, put aside all consideration of how she should reply, excepting as he wished!

The immediate result of Mr. Nicholls' declaration of attachment was, that he sent in his resignation of the curacy of Haworth; and that Miss Brontë held herself simply passive, as far as words and actions went, while she suffered acute pain from the strong expressions which her father used in speaking of Mr. Nicholls, and from the too evident distress and failure of health on the part of the latter.

Charlotte Brontë's Funeral

From the Life of Charlotte Brontë

I HAVE always been much struck with a passage in Mr. Forster's *Life of Goldsmith*. Speaking of the scene after his death, the writer says:

"The staircase of Brick Court is said to have been filled with mourners, the reverse of domestic; women without a home, without domesticity of any kind, with no friend but him they had come to weep for; outcasts of that great, solitary, wicked city, to whom he had never forgotten to be kind and charitable."

This came into my mind when I heard of some of the circumstances attendant on Charlotte's funeral.

Few beyond that circle of hills knew that she, whom the nations praised far off, lay dead that Easter morning. Of kith and kin she had more in the grave to which she was soon to be borne than among the living. The two mourners, stunned with their great grief, desired not the sympathy of strangers. One member out of most of the families in the parish was bidden to the funeral;

and it became an act of self-denial in many a poor household to give up to another the privilege of paying their last homage to her; and those who were excluded from the formal train of mourners thronged the churchyard and church, to see carried forth, and laid beside her own people, her whom, not many months ago, they had looked at as a pale white bride, entering on a new life with trembling happy hope.

Among those humble friends who passionately grieved over the dead, was a village girl who had been betrayed some little time before, but who had found a holy sister in Charlotte. She had sheltered her with her help, her counsel, her strengthening words; had ministered to her needs in her time of trial. Bitter, bitter was the grief of this poor young woman, when she heard that her friend was sick unto death, and deep is her mourning until this day. A blind girl, living some four miles from Haworth, loved Mrs. Nicholls so dearly that, with many cries and entreaties, she implored those about her to lead her along the roads, and over the moor-paths, that she might hear the last solemn words, "Earth to earth, ashes to ashes, dust to dust; in sure and certain hope of the resurrection to eternal life, through our Lord Jesus Christ."

Such were the mourners over Charlotte Brontë's grave.

I have little more to say. If my readers find that I have not said enough, I have said too much. I cannot measure or judge of such a character as hers. I cannot map out vices, and virtues, and debatable land. One who knew her long and well—the "Mary" of this *Life*—writes thus of her dead friend:

"She thought much of her duty, and had loftier and clearer notions of it than most people, and held fast to them with more success. It was done, it seems to me, with much more difficulty than people have of stronger nerves, and better fortunes. All her life was but labour and pain; and she never threw down the burden for the sake of present pleasure. I don't know what use you can make of all I have said. I have written it with the strong desire to obtain appreciation for her. Yet, what does it matter? She herself appealed to the world's judgment for her use of some of the faculties she had—not the best—but still the only ones she could turn to strangers' benefit. They heartily, greedily enjoyed the fruits of her labours, and then found out she was much to be blamed for possessing such faculties. Why ask for a judgment on her from such a world?"

Shorter Extracts

Old Maids

From "Libbie Marsh's Three Eras," *Howitt's Journal.*

"NEVER say aught lightly of the wife's lot whose husband is given to drink!"

"Dear, what a preachment! I tell you what, Libbie, you're as born an old maid as ever I saw. You'll never be married to either drunken or sober."

Libbie's face went rather red, but without losing its meek expression.

"I know that as well as you can tell me; and more reason, therefore, as God has seen fit to keep me out of woman's natural work, I should try and find work for myself. I mean," seeing Annie Dixon's puzzled look, "that, as I know I'm never likely to have a home of my own, or a husband that would look to me to make all straight, or children to watch over and care for, all which I take to be woman's natural work, I must not lose time in fretting and fidgeting after marriage, but just look about me for somewhat else to do. I can see many a one misses it in this. They will hanker after what is ne'er likely to be theirs, instead of facing it out, and settling down to be old maids, and, as old maids, just looking round for the odd jobs God leaves in the world for such as old maids to do. There's plenty of such work, and there's the blessing of God on them as does it." Libbie was almost out of breath at this outpouring of what had long been her inner thoughts.

Mercy for the Erring

From *Ruth.*

Frederick Denison Maurice mentioned the story of *Ruth* in one of his lectures, speaking of Mrs. Gaskell as "a noble-hearted and pure-minded writer, who had given a story as true to human experience as it is to the divinest morality."

"NOW I wish God would give me power to speak out convincingly what I believe to be His truth, that not every woman who has fallen is depraved; that many—how many the Great Judgment Day will reveal to those who have shaken off the poor, sore, penitent hearts on earth—many, many crave and hunger after a chance for virtue—the help which no man gives to them—help—that gentle, tender help which Jesus gave once to Mary Magdalen." Mr. Benson was almost choked by his own feelings.

"Come, come, Mr. Benson, let us have no more of this morbid way of talking. The world has decided how such women are to be treated; and, you may depend upon it, there is so much practical wisdom in the world that its way of acting is right in the long run, and that no one can fly in its face with impunity, unless, indeed, they stoop to deceit and imposition."

"I take my stand with Christ against the world," said Mr. Benson solemnly, disregarding the covert allusion to himself. "What have the world's ways ended in? Can we be much worse than we are?"

"Speak for yourself, if you please."

"Is it not time to change some of our ways of thinking and acting? I declare before God, that if I believe in any one human truth, it is this—that to every woman, who, like Ruth, has sinned, should be given a chance of self-redemption—and that such a chance should be given in no supercilious or contemptuous manner, but in the spirit of the holy Christ."

"Such as getting her into a friend's house under false colours."

"I do not argue on Ruth's case. In that I have acknowledged my error. I do not argue on any case. I state my firm belief, that it is God's will that we should not dare to trample any of His creatures down to the hopeless dust; that it is God's will that the women who have fallen should be numbered among those who have broken hearts to be bound up, not cast aside as lost beyond recall. If this be God's will, as a thing of God it will stand; and He will open a way."

A Clergyman's Soliloquy

From *North and South*.

Mrs. Gaskell's own father gave up his appointment as a Unitarian minister from conscientious reasons, and the beautiful character of Mr. Hale surely owes something to Mr. Stevenson. Mr. Travers Madge, a Unitarian minister in Manchester, and a friend and fellow-worker of the Gaskells, also gave up his position as a minister because he objected to being a paid preacher.

"THIS is the soliloquy of one who was once a clergyman in a country parish, like me; it was written by a Mr. Oldfield, minister of Carsington, in Derbyshire, a hundred and sixty years ago, or more. His trials are over. He fought the good fight." These last two sentences he spoke low, as if to himself. Then he read aloud:

"When thou canst no longer continue in thy work without dishonour to God, discredit to religion, foregoing thy integrity, wounding conscience, spoiling thy peace, and hazarding the loss of thy salvation; in a word, when the conditions upon which thou must continue (if thou wilt continue) in thy employments are sinful, and unwarranted by the word of God, thou mayest, yea, thou must believe that God will turn thy very silence, suspension, deprivation, and laying aside, to His glory, and the advancement of the Gospel's interest. When God will not use thee in one kind, yet He will in another. A soul that desires to serve and honour Him shall never want opportunity to do it; nor must thou so limit the Holy One of Israel, as to think He hath but one way in which He can glorify Himself by thee. He can do it by thy silence as well as by thy preaching; thy laying aside as well as thy continuance in thy work. It is not pretence of doing God the greatest service, or performing the weightiest duty, that will excuse the least sin, though that sin capacitated or gave us the opportunity for doing that duty. Thou wilt have little thanks, O my soul! if, when thou art charged with corrupting God's worship, falsifying thy vows, thou pretendest a necessity for it in order to a continuance in the ministry."

As he read this, and glanced at much more which he did not read, he gained resolution for himself, and felt as if he too could be brave and firm in doing what be believed to be right; but as he ceased he heard Margaret's low convulsive sob; and his courage sank down under the keen sense of suffering.

"Margaret, dear!" said he, drawing her closer, "think of the early martyrs; think of the thousands who have suffered."

"But, father," said she, suddenly lifting up her flushed, tear-wet face, "the early martyrs suffered for the truth, while you—oh! dear, dear papa!"

"I suffer for conscience' sake, my child!" said he, with a dignity that was only tremulous from the acute sensitiveness of his character; "I must do what my conscience bids. I have borne long with self-reproach that would have roused any mind less torpid and cowardly than mine."

My Lady Ludlow's Tea-party

From My Lady Ludlow.

MRS. BROOKE is a rough diamond, to be sure. People have said that of me, I know. But, being a Galindo, I learnt manners in my youth and can take them up when I choose. But Mrs. Brooke never learnt manners, I'll be bound. When John Footman handed her the tray with the tea-cups, she looked up at him as if she were sorely puzzled by that way of going on. I was sitting next to her, so I pretended not to see her perplexity, and put her cream and sugar in for her, and was all ready to pop it into her hands—when who should come up but that impudent lad Tom Diggles (I call him lad, for all his hair is powdered, for you know that it is not naturally grey hair) with his tray full of cakes and what not, all as good as Mrs. Medlicott could make them. By this time, I should tell you, all the parsonesses were looking at Mrs. Brooke, for she had shown her want of breeding before; and the parsonesses, who were just a step above her in manners, were very much inclined to smile at her doings and sayings. Well! what does she do but pull out a clean Bandana pocket-handkerchief, all red and yellow silk; spread it over her best silk gown—it was, like enough, a new one, for I had it from Sally, who had it from her cousin Molly, who is dairy-woman "at the Brookes'," that the Brookes were mighty set-up with an invitation to drink tea at the Hall. There we were, Tom Diggles ever on the grin (I wonder how long it is since he was own brother to a scarecrow, only not so decently dressed), and Mrs. Parsoness of Headleigh—I forget her name, and it's no matter, for she's an ill-bred creature, I hope Bessy will behave herself better—was right-down bursting with laughter, and as near a hee-haw as ever a donkey was; when what does my lady do? Ay! there's my own dear Lady Ludlow, God bless her! She takes out her own pocket-handkerchief, all snowy cambric, and lays it softly down on her velvet lap, for all the world as if she did it every day of her life, just like Mrs. Brooke, the baker's wife; and when one got up to shake the crumbs into the fireplace, the other did just the same. But with such a grace! and such a look at us all! Tom Diggles went red all over; and Mrs. Parsoness of Headleigh scarce spoke for the rest of the evening; and the tears came into my old silly eyes; and Mr. Gray, who was before silent and awkward in a way which I tell Bessy she must cure him of, was made so happy by this pretty action of my lady's that he talked away all the rest of the evening, and was the life of the company.

The Foxglove

From *Ruth*, 1853

Writing of the old traditions of Cheshire, Mrs. Gaskell said, "I was once saying to an old blind country-woman how much I admired the foxglove. She looked mysteriously solemn as she told me they were not like other flowers; they had 'knowledge' in them!"

"I HAVE an annual holiday, which I generally spend in Wales; and often in this immediate neighbourhood."

"I do not wonder at your choice," replied Ruth. "It is a beautiful country."

"It is, indeed; and I have been inoculated by an old innkeeper at Conway with a love for its people, and history, and traditions. I have picked up enough of the language to understand many of their legends; and some are very fine and awe-inspiring, others very poetic and fanciful."

Ruth was too shy to keep up the conversation by any remark of her own, although his gentle, pensive manner was very winning.

"For instance," said he, touching a long bud-laden stem of foxglove in the hedge-side, at the bottom of which one or two crimson speckled flowers were bursting from their green sheaths, "I dare say, you don't know what makes this foxglove bend and sway so gracefully. You think it is blown by the wind, don't you?" He looked at her with a grave smile which did not enliven his thoughtful eyes, but gave an inexpressible sweetness to his face.

"I always thought it was the wind. What is it?" asked Ruth innocently.

"Oh, the Welsh tell you that this flower is sacred to the fairies, and that it has the power of recognising them, and all spiritual beings who pass by, and that it bows in deference to them as they waft along. Its Welsh name is Maneg Ellyllyn—the good people's glove; and hence, I imagine, our folk's-glove or foxglove."

"It's a very pretty fancy," said Ruth, much interested, and wishing that he would go on, without expecting her to reply.

A Tonic for Sorrow

From *Mary Barton*

OH! I do think that the necessity for exertion, for some kind of action (bodily or mental) in time of distress, is a most infinite blessing, although the first efforts at such seasons are painful. Something to be done implies that there is yet hope of some good thing to be accomplished, or some additional evil that may be avoided; and by degrees the hope absorbs much of the sorrow.

It is the woes that cannot in any earthly way be escaped that admit least earthly comforting. Of all trite, worn-out, hollow mockeries of comfort that were ever uttered by people who will not take the trouble of sympathising with others, the one I dislike the most is the exhortation not to grieve over an event, "for it cannot be helped." Do you think if I could help it, I would sit still with folded hands, content to mourn? Do you not believe that as long as hope remained I would be up and doing? I mourn because what has occurred cannot be helped. The reason you give me for not grieving is the very and sole reason of my grief. Give me nobler and higher reasons for enduring meekly what my Father sees fit to send, and I will try earnestly and faithfully to be patient; but mock me not, or any other mourner, with the speech: "Do not grieve, for it cannot be helped. It is past remedy."

A New Commandment

From *Mary Barton*

I SOMETIMES think there's two sides to the commandment; and that we may say, "Let others do unto you, as you would do unto them," for pride often prevents our giving others a great deal of pleasure, in not letting them be kind, when their hearts are longing to help; and when we ourselves should wish to do just the same, if we were in their place. Oh! how often I've been hurt, by being coldly told by persons not to trouble myself about their care, or sorrow, when I saw them in great grief, and wanted to be of comfort. Our Lord Jesus was not above letting folk minister to Him, for He knew how happy it makes one to do aught for another. It's the happiest work on earth.

Virtue has its own Reward

From *Ruth*

PEOPLE may talk as they will about the little respect that is paid to virtue, unaccompanied by the outward accidents of wealth or station; but I rather think it will be found that, in the long run, true and simple virtue always has its proportionate reward in the respect and reverence of everyone whose esteem is worth having. To be sure, it is not rewarded after the way of the world as mere worldly possessions are, with low obeisance and lip-service; but all the better and more noble qualities in the hearts of others make ready and go forth to meet it on its approach, provided only it be pure, simple, and unconscious of its own existence.

Thomas Wright the Prison Philanthropist of Manchester

From *Mary Barton*

THE month was over—the honeymoon to the newly married; the exquisite convalescence to the "living mother of a living child"; "the first dark days of nothingness" to the widow and the child bereaved; the term of penance, of hard labour, and of solitary confinement, to the shrinking, shivering, hopeless prisoner.

"Sick, and in prison, and ye visited me." Shall you, or I, receive such blessing? I know one who will. An overseer of a foundry, an aged man, with hoary hair, has spent his Sabbaths, for many years, in visiting the prisoners and the afflicted, in Manchester New Bailey; not merely advising and comforting, but putting means into their power of regaining the virtue and the peace they had lost; becoming himself their guarantee in obtaining employment, and never deserting those who have once asked help from him.[1]

[1] Vide *Manchester Guardian* of Wednesday, March 18th, 1846; and also the Reports of Captain Williams, prison inspector.

Do the Right whatever the Consequences

From *Ruth*

IT is better not to expect or calculate consequences. The longer I live, the more fully I see that. Let us try simply to do right actions, without thinking of the feelings they are to call out in others. We know that no holy or self-denying effort can fall to the ground vain and useless; but the sweep of eternity is large, and God alone knows when the effect is to be produced. We are trying to do right now, and to feel right; don't let us perplex ourselves with endeavouring to map out how she should feel, or how she should show her feelings.

Appreciations and Testimonia

Professor Minto

"Mrs Gaskell was indeed a born story-teller, charged through and through with the story-teller's peculiar element, a something which may be called suppressed gipsiness, a restless instinct which impelled her to be constantly making trial in imagination of various modes of life. Her imagination was perpetually busy with the vicissitudes which days and years brought round to others; she entered into their lives, laughed with them, wept with them, speculated on the cardinal incidents and circumstances, the good qualities and the 'vicious moles of nature,' which had made them what they were, schemed how they might have been different, and lived through the windings and turnings of their destinies, the excitement of looking forward to the unknown....

"'Sir,' she seems to say to the nature-worshipper, 'let us take a peep into some English household. Let us watch its inmates in comfort and in distress, I will tell you their history. You shall see how a Lancashire mechanic entertains his friends, how a country doctor gets on with his neighbours, how a coquettish farmer's daughter behaves to her lovers. I have no strange experiences to reveal to you, only the life that lies at your doors; but I will show you its tragedies and its comedies. I will describe the characters of your countrymen to you, and I will tell you things about them that will interest you, some things that will make you weep and many that will make you smile.'" (*Fortnightly Review*, 1878.)

Dr. A. W. Ward

"The 'century of praise' which it would not be difficult to compose from the tributes, public and private, paid to the genius of Mrs. Gaskell by eminent men and women of her own generation, need hardly be invoked by its successors, to whom her writings still speak. Such a list would include, among other eulogies, those of Carlyle and Ruskin, of Dickens, who called her his 'Scheherazade,' and of Thackeray, of Charles Kingsley and of Matthew Arnold, of whom his sister, the late Mrs. W. E. Forster, drew a picture in his own happy manner, 'stretched at full length on a sofa reading a Christmas tale of Mrs. Gaskell, which moves him to tears, and the tears to complacent admiration of his own sensibility.' Lord Houghton, John Forster, George Henry Lewes, Tom Taylor, were among her declared admirers; to whom should be added among statesmen, Cobden and the late Duke of Argyll. Among Mrs. Gaskell's female fellow-writers, Charlotte Brontë, and George Eliot, Harriet Martineau and Mrs. Beecher Stowe (*facies non omnibus una*) were at least alike to each other in their warm admiration of her. To these names should be added that of one whose praise came near home to Mrs. Gaskell's heart—Mrs. Stanley, the mother of Dean Stanley. Among French lovers of her genius Ampère has already been mentioned, and with him should be named Guizot and Jules Simon." (Introduction to *Mary Barton*, Knutsford Edition, 1906.)

Susanna Winkworth

"When we first knew Mrs. Gaskell she had not yet become celebrated, but from the earliest days of our intercourse with her we were struck with her genius, and used to say to each other that we were sure she could write books, or do anything else in the world that she liked. And the more we knew of her, the more we admired her. She was a noble-looking woman, with a queenly presence, and her high, broad, serene brow and finely-cut, mobile features, were lighted up by a constantly varying play of expression as she poured forth her wonderful talk. It was like the gleaming ripple and rush of a clear, deep stream in sunshine. Though one of the most brilliant persons I ever saw, she had none of the restlessness and eagerness that spoils so much of our conversation nowadays. There was no hurry or high pressure about her, but she seemed always surrounded by an atmosphere of ease, leisure, and playful geniality, that drew out the best side of everyone who was in her company.

"When you were with her, you felt as if you had twice the life in you that you had at ordinary times. All her great intellectual gifts—her quick, keen observation, her marvellous memory, her wealth of imaginative power, her rare felicity of instinct, her graceful and racy humour—were so warmed and brightened by sympathy and feeling, that while actually with her, you were less conscious of her power than of her charm.

"No one ever came near her in the gift of telling a story. In her hands the simplest incident—a meeting in the street, a talk with a factory-girl, a country walk, an old family history—became picturesque and vivid and interesting. Her fun, her pathos, her graphic touches, her sympathetic insight were inimitable." (*Memorials of two sisters: Susanna and Catherine Winkworth*, 1908.)

Thomas Seccombe

"Her novels are perenially fresh. They do not fatigue, or sear, or narcotise. We return to them with an unfading and constant delight. Her books engender a feeling of gratitude towards the writer along with a strong sentimental regret—regret that a life so happy, so sympathetic, so well balanced, and, in short so beautiful, could not have been prolonged, that her vivid mind and pen should not have irradiated our particular generation.

"Could you imagine England personified as a sentient and intelligent being, on the death of Elizabeth Gaskell, as on the death of Charles Lamb or Walter Scott, you would expect her to draw a long sigh as one feeling sensibly poorer for a loss that never could be repaired. You may think this to be a deliberate exaggeration, but it certainly is not. So far as artistic perfection is attainable in such a formless and chaotic thing as the modern novel, it is my deliberate belief that Mrs. Gaskell has no absolute rival in the measure of complete success which she was enabled to achieve....

"If you ask for the normal type of English novel in the highest degree of perfection to which it ever attained, I should certainly be inclined to say take *Mary Barton*, *North and South*, *Sylvia's Lovers*, and *Wives and Daughters*. Not one of them altogether or entirely attained to the perfection of which Mrs. Gaskell herself was capable. But they fully and adequately reveal her power and likewise her intention of subordinating herself in some degree to a form of the potentialities and limitations of which alike, it seems to me, she had an intuition surpassing the utmost efforts of any of her greater contemporaries." (Introduction to *Sylvia's Lovers*, 1910.)

Lady Ritchie

"Mrs. Gaskell put herself into her stories; her emotions, her amusements all poured out from a full heart, and she retold the experience of her own loyal work among the poor, of her playtime among the well-to-do. And as she knew more and more she told better and better what she had lived through. She told the story of those she had known, of those she had loved—so, at least, it seems to some readers, coming after long years and re-reading more critically, perhaps, with new admiration. Another fact about her is that she faced the many hard problems of her life's experience—faced them boldly, and set the example of writing to the point. It has been followed by how many with half her knowledge and insight, and without her generous purpose, taking grim subjects for art's sake rather than for humanity's sake, as she did." (*Blackstick Papers*, 1908.)

Frederick Greenwood

"The kindly spirit which thinks no ill looks out of her pages irradiate; and while we read them, we breathe the purer intelligence that prefers to deal with emotions and passions which have a living root in minds within the pale of salvation, and not with those that rot without it. This spirit is more especially declared in *Cousin Phillis* and *Wives and Daughters*—their author's latest works; they seem to show that for her the end of life was not descent among the clods of the valley, but ascent into the purer air of the heaven-aspiring hills.

"We are saying nothing of the merely intellectual qualities displayed in these later works. Twenty years to come, that may be thought the more important question of the two; in the presence of her grave we cannot think so; but it is true, all the same, that as mere works of art and observation, these later novels of Mrs. Gaskell's are among the finest of our time. There is a scene in *Cousin Phillis*—where Holman, making hay with his men, ends the day with a psalm—which is not excelled as a picture in all modern fiction; and the same may be said of that chapter of this last story in which Roger smokes a pipe with the Squire after the quarrel with Osborne. There is little in either of these scenes, or in a score of others which succeed each other like gems in a cabinet, which the ordinary novel-maker could 'seize.' There is no 'material' for *him* in half a dozen farming men singing hymns in a field, or a discontented old gentleman smoking tobacco with his son; still less could he avail himself of the miseries of a little girl sent to be happy in a fine house full of fine people; but it is just in such things as these that true genius appears brightest and most unapproachable." (*Cornhill Magazine*, 1865.)

Miss Catherine J. Hamilton

"For purity of tone, earnestness of spirit, depth of pathos, and lightness of touch, Mrs. Gaskell has not left her superior in fiction.

"One who knew her said: 'She was what her books show her to have been, a wise, good woman.'

"She was even more than wise or good, she had that true poetic feeling which exalts whatever it touches, and makes nothing common or unclean. She had that clear insight which sees all and believes in the best." (*Women Writers*, Second Series.)

Richard D. Graham

"Mrs. Gaskell through all the toils and excitements of authorship remained a true woman in the sweetest and worthiest meaning of the name. In all the ordinary relations of life she was admirable, neglecting no social or domestic duty, shrinking from every attempt to lionise her, and charming no less by her personal attractions and the grace of her manner, than by the sweetness of her disposition." (*The Masters of Victorian Literature.*)

Edna Lyall

"Of all the novelists of Queen Victoria's reign there is not one to whom the present writer turns with such a sense of love and gratitude as to Mrs. Gaskell. This feeling is undoubtedly shared by thousands of men and women, for about all the novels there is that wonderful sense of sympathy, that broad human interest which appeals to readers of every description."

G. Barnett Smith

"We were struck in reading her various volumes with this fact—that there is really less in them than there is in most other authors which she herself could wish to be altered. In fact, there is no purer author in modern times. And what has she lost by being pure? Has she failed to give a fair representation of any class of human beings whom she professes to depict? Not one; and her work stands now as an excellent model for those who would avoid the tendencies of the sensuous school, and would seek another basis upon which to acquire a reputation which should have some chances of durability. The author of *Wives and Daughters* will never cease to hold a high place in our regard. Could she do so we should despair for the future of fiction in England. Hers was one of those spirits which led the way to a purer day." (*Cornhill Magazine, February, 1874.*)

Clement K. Shorter

"Mrs. Gaskell as an artist has clearly used other experiences than those that Knutsford offered, and, transmuting all through her kindly and generous nature, has given us the delightful pure idyll (*Cranford*) that we know, the most tenderly humorous book that our literature has seen since Goldsmith wrote. One of the great distinctions of Mrs. Gaskell is in the kindliness of her humour; she is, strange to say, the only woman novelist who is entirely kindly, benevolently humorous.... This benevolent humour of Mrs. Gaskell is to be found in all her books, and it is to be found above all in *Cranford.*" (Introduction to *Cranford.* The World's Classics, 1906.)

Bibliography

Bibliography of Mrs. Gaskell's Works in Chronological Order

1837.   Sketches among the Poor. *Blackwood's Magazine.* January.

1840.   Clopton Hall. *Howitt's Visits to Remarkable Places.*

1847.   Libbie Marsh's Three Eras. *Howitt's Journal,* I.

Sexton's Hero. *Howitt's Journal,* II.

1848.   Christmas Storms and Sunshine. *Howitt's Journal,* III.

MARY BARTON. A tale of Manchester Life. 2 vols. London. Chapman & Hall. Fifth Edition 1854; German Edition 1849; French Translation 1856. Has been published by at least a dozen publishers since the copyright ran out.

1849.   Hand and Heart. *Sunday School Penny Magazine.*

1850.   Lizzie Leigh. *Household Words.* March 30.

Well of Pen Morfa. *Household Words.* November 16 and 23.

The Heart of John Middleton. *Household Words.* December 28.

THE MOORLAND COTTAGE. Chapman & Hall. Republished in 1892.

1851.   Mr. Harrison's Confessions. *Ladies' Companion.* February, March, April.

Disappearances. *Household Words.* June 7.

Cranford. *Household Words.* December 13, 1851, to May, 1853.

1852.   The Schah's English Gardener. *Household Words.* June 19.

The Old Nurse's Story. *Household Words.* Christmas Number.

Bessy's Troubles at Home. *Sunday School Penny Magazine.* January.

1853.   Cumberland Sheep-shearers. *Household Words.* January 22.

CRANFORD. Chapman & Hall. 1 vol.

Cheap editions 1853-5; French Translation 1856; German Translation 1857. Republished by more than twenty publishers in England and America since the copyright ran out.

Morton Hall. *Household Words*. November 19 and 26.

Traits and Stories of Huguenots. *Household Words*. December 10.

My French Master. *Household Words*. December 17 and 24.

The Squire's Story. *Household Words*. Christmas Number.

Introduction to The Scholar's Story. *Household Words*. Christmas Number.

RUTH, a novel. Chapman & Hall. 3 vols. Third Edition 1855; American Edition 1855; French Translation 1856. Published by three other publishers in 1857 1861, 1872. Reissued after the copyright ceased by three different publishers.

1854.   Modern Greek Songs. *Household Words*. February 25.

Company Manners. *Household Words*. May 20.

North and South. *Household Words*. September 2, 1854, to January 27, 1855.

LIZZIE LEIGH. Chapman and Hall. 1 vol. German Edition 1855.

1855.   An Accused Race. *Household Words*. August 25.

Half a Lifetime Ago. *Household Words*. October 6, 13, 20.

NORTH AND SOUTH. Chapman & Hall. 2 vols. Second Edition 1855; Fourth Edition 1859; American Edition 1864; French Edition 1859. Reissued by two publishers after the copyright ran out.

1856.   The Poor Chare. *Household Words*. December 13 and 27.

1857.   LIFE OF CHARLOTTE BRONTË. Smith, Elder & Co. 2 vols. Third Edition revised and corrected 1857; American Edition 1857; Cheap Edition 1860; French Edition 1877.

After the copyright ran out it was reissued in the Haworth Edition in 1900 with introduction and notes by Clement Shorter. Thornton Edition with introduction by B. W. Willett and notes by Temple Scott, 1901. Republished by three other publishers.

Edited MABEL VAUGHAN by Miss Cummins and wrote Preface. Sampson Low & Co.

1858.   Doom of the Griffiths. *Harper's Magazine*. January.

My Lady Ludlow. *Household Words*. June 19 to September 25.

Right at Last (under title of Sin of a Father). *Household Words*. November 27.

The Half Brothers. *Dublin University Magazine*. November.

Manchester Marriage. *Household Words*. Christmas Number.

1859.   Lois the Witch. *All the Year Round*. October 8 and 22.

The Ghost in the Garden Room. *All the Year Round*. Christmas Number. (Reprinted under title of The Crooked Branch.)

ROUND THE SOFA. London: Sampson Low & Co. 2 vols. French Translation 1860; Second French Edition 1865.

1860.   RIGHT AT LAST AND OTHER TALES. Sampson Low & Co. American Edition Harper & Brothers.

Curious if True. *Cornhill Magazine*. February.

1861.   The Grey Woman. *All the Year Round*. January 5, 12, 19.

MY LADY LUDLOW AND OTHER TALES. London: Sampson Low & Co. New Edition 1866; American Edition 1867.

1862.   Six Weeks at Heppenheim. *Cornhill Magazine*. May.

Preface to GARIBALDI AT CAPRERA. Macmillan & Co.

1863.   A Dark Night's Work. *All the Year Round*. January 24 to March 21.

A DARK NIGHT'S WORK. German Translation 1865; English Editions published 1863 and 1871. Smith, Elder & Co.

An Italian Institution. *All the Year Round.* March 21.

The Cage at Cranford. *All the Year Round.* November 28.

Cousin Phillis. *Cornhill Magazine.* November, 1863, to February, 1864.

Crowley Castle. *All the Year Round.* Christmas Number.

SYLVIA'S LOVERS. London: Smith, Elder & Co. 3 vols. German Translation 1864; French Translation 1865. Since the copyright ran out it has been republished in a cheap edition.

Robert Gould Shaw. *Macmillan's Magazine.* December.

1864. French Life. *Fraser's Magazine.* April, May, June.

Wives and Daughters. *Cornhill Magazine.* August, 1864, to January, 1866.

1865. COUSIN PHILLIS AND OTHER TALES. London: Smith, Elder & Co. French Translation 1866; German Edition 1867.

THE GREEN WOMAN AND OTHER TALES. London: Smith, Elder & Co.

1866. WIVES AND DAUGHTERS. London: Smith, Elder & Co. 3 vols. American Edition 1866; German Translation 1867; French Translation 1868.

1906. Two Fragments of Ghost Stories printed for the first time in COUSIN PHILLIS, Knutsford Edition.

Short poem "On Visiting the Grave of my Stillborn Little Girl," written in 1836 and published for the first time in the biographical introduction to MARY BARTON, Knutsford Edition.

Milton Keynes UK
Ingram Content Group UK Ltd.
UKHW011139220424
441551UK00006B/666